Hemmed in by the peaks, the lake lost the sun early. As the yellow rays faded, its surface changed from blue to green and pink—the colors of the still sunlit rocks and trees. . . . The trees themselves seemed rapt as if their stillness was more than vegetative, concealing some sympathetic vibration of the inner bark.

—David Rains Wallace,
The Dark Range

The HIKER'S hip pocket GUIDE to the Mendocino Highlands

by
Bob Lorentzen

BORED FEET PUBLICATIONS
MENDOCINO, CALIFORNIA
1992

©1992 by Robert S. Lorentzen
First printing, July 1992
Printed in the United States of America on 50% recycled paper

Illustrations by Joshua Edelman
Symbols by Jann Patterson-Watters and Taylor Cranney
Maps by Bob Lorentzen, Elizabeth Petersen, U.S. Forest Service,
    California Department of Parks and Recreation and USGS
Design by Judy Detrick and Elizabeth Petersen
Yolla Bolly map printed by Black Bear Press, Caspar, California
Sierra Club Books has generously given permission to use the
quotation on page 2 from *The Dark Range: A Naturalist's Night
Notebook*, by David Rains Wallace, ©1978.

Published by
Bored Feet Publications
Post Office Box 1832
Mendocino, California 95460
(707) 964-6629

Library of Congress Cataloging-in-Publication Data
Lorentzen, Bob, 1949-
    The hiker's hip pocket guide to the Mendocino highlands / by Bob Lorentzen.
    240 pp.
    Includes bibliographical references and index.
    ISBN 0-939431-05-X : $13.95
    1. Hiking—California, Northern—Guidebooks. 2. California, Northern—
Guidebooks. I. Title.
GV199.42.C22N674 1992   92-23637
917.94'1—dc20   CIP

ISBN 0-939431-05-X

10 9 8 7 6 5 4 3 2 1

Dedicated to my parents, each of them:

Carolyn Harman Lorentzen, passionate believer in life, who carried me across the Pacific, bore me and showed me my first visions of nature.

Karl Lorentzen, backroads explorer and bookman, whose passion to know and understand instilled in me a sense of truth and a (mostly) objective eye.

Patricia Downey Lorentzen, fountain of joy and balance, who first asked me to question war and has stood by me in both bright and dark times.

Jane Macdonald Lorentzen, whose calm acceptance and joyful laughter has brought new happiness, strength and security to the family.

With a special thanks to Bertha Lorentzen Bulow for sharing so much love and care.

ACKNOWLEDGMENTS

I wish to express my thanks to everyone who helped select, filter, groom and polish the contents of this book. In particular I thank Liz Petersen for her passionate, caring support, hundreds of hours of meticulous plant identification, and incisive design and photography; Joshua Edelman for his sensitive illustrations and durable humor; David Springer for levelheadedness and help sorting out the complex geology of the highlands; my editors: Jim Tarbell for plowing through a wilderness of trail mileages, ascents, descents and traverses; and Lucie Marshall for precision tuning and adjustments.

Thanks to my dedicated and proficient proofreaders Amanda Avery, Celeste Bautista, Donna Bettencourt, Marcia Bonham, Ross Bonham, Lenora Shepard and Katy Tahja; and to Alan Benesi, Carol Goodwin Blick, Owen Edwards, Anthony Miksak, Maureen Oliva, Linda Pack and Judy Tarbell for moral and logistical support.

For guidance and feedback on specific trails I thank Vaughn Hutchins and Mike Van Dame of Covelo Ranger District, Anne Fiorella of Corning Ranger District, Jeff Applegate and Pat Likens of Stonyford Ranger District, Ken Graves of Yolla Bolly Ranger District, Gene Graber of Mad River Ranger District, Tom Keter and Betty Strickland of Six Rivers National Forest, Peter Steel and Mary Power for help with the Northern California Coast Range Preserve, Michael Phelan of Brooktrails, Scott Adams and Catherine Robertson of BLM, Jeff Laird of Lake Mendocino, George Rose of Fetzer Vineyards, Tim Henke of Fairfield Osborn Preserve and Tom Nixon of Anderson Marsh State Park.

Thanks to Tom Mon Pere and the Outings Committee of the Mendocino-Lake Group of the Redwood Chapter, Sierra Club, Janet Butcher of Just Your Type, Ann Kilkenny and Joanne Schneiter of Mendocino Book Company, Marc Komer of Leaves of Grass, Shar Evans of HSU Bookstore, and Nicholas Lapkass of the Ukiah Library for his assistance in finding invaluable reference materials.

With special thanks to the readers of my first three books for providing encouragement, criticism and ideas, all important and powerful fuel for new explorations.

CONTENTS

Come on in. The earth, like the sun, like the air,
belongs to everyone — and to no one.
—Edward Abbey, *The Journey Home*

INTRODUCTION
WHICH WAY TO THE MENDOCINO HIGHLANDS?

One and a half million people settled in California in the last half of the nineteenth century, seeking their own pot of gold at the end of an undiscovered rainbow. For the immigrants who came north from San Francisco into the wild country beyond Sonoma County, the question was "Are you headed for the Coast or the Highlands?" Around 1860 the rugged, unmapped mountains beyond the Russian River were called the Mendocino Highlands or Mendocino Range.

While most newcomers settled along the Coast where seagoing ships offered the most reliable transportation, increasing numbers sought arable land tucked among the steep mountains of the Coast Range. The first settlements grew in the fertile valleys along the Russian River and around Clear Lake. Then people settled farther north around Little Lake, Long and Round Valleys. A few hardy individuals homesteaded in remote corners of the Highlands. But the mountains offered a hard life of marginal subsistence. Isolation and economic pressures forced many of the highlanders out. So today the Highlands are again sparsely populated.

The Mendocino Highlands offer magnificent natural lands of rich botanical diversity. Hundreds of miles of winding back roads, many not found on most maps, deliver surprises around each bend, and more than a million acres of public lands entice exploration on foot. Once the home of grizzly bears, still roamed by black bears, mountain lions and bountiful wildlife, the Mendocino Highlands encompass diverse landscapes.

This book will guide you to over 400 miles of scenic trails through wondrous country. The trails range from easy walks to difficult backpacks, with great places for mountain bikers and equestrians, and choices to fit the taste of every nature lover. These excursions will lead you to diverse habitats: forests, grasslands, stream canyons, waterfalls, lakes, marshes, ridges and mountain tops. You may also hike in two Nature Conservancy Preserves, an organic vineyard and garden, a wildlife refuge and places rich with Native American heritage. In short, there is something for everyone. So get out of your car and use your feet, bicycle, horse or wheelchair to explore the Mendocino Highlands.

HOW TO USE THIS BOOK

This book has two sections: accessible day hikes not far from towns and accommodations, and wilderness trails that take longer to reach and a little more planning to enjoy. Most trails are between 100 and 200 miles north of San Francisco. The northernmost trails are closer to Redding, Eureka and Oregon than to the Bay Area.

From Ukiah and Lakeport, some day hikes are as close as ten minutes drive, a few are more than an hour away. The wilderness trails are clustered in and around Yolla Bolly-Middle Eel and Snow Mountain Wilderness Areas, mostly within Mendocino National Forest. In the right season and with proper preparation, these spectacular hikes through secluded pristine country are well worth the effort. Most are suitable for any moderately fit person, while a few are especially rugged.

You do not have to start at the beginning of the book, although the introductions provide valuable information. Simply turn to the trail nearest your location and you will be on your way. Neighboring trails will be on the adjacent pages. The day hikes are organized north to south along Highway 101, then into Lake County and Mendocino National Forest. The wilderness trails are arranged clockwise for each of the two wilderness areas.

In the directions to most trails, you will find milepost numbers listed like this: M.36.7. These numbers refer to white highway mileposts placed frequently but at irregular intervals along highways by CalTrans, the State Department of Transportation. You can quickly determine the location of a trail by referring to its milepost number and its position in the book.

For each described trail, you will find a map, specific directions to the trailhead, the best time to go, appropriate warnings, elevation information and a detailed description with some history and/or natural history. More than 100 miles of additional trails are highlighted in the OTHER SUGGESTION listings in the access boxes.

You will find a group of symbols below the access information for each trail. They tell you at a glance the level of difficulty, type of trail, available facilities, whether there is a fee, and whether dogs are allowed. The list of symbols follows. Graphs show the elevation variations for each wilderness trail.

At the end of the book are appendices listing the trails suitable for a particular type of recreation: mountain biking, equestrian, backpacking and handicap accessible. You can locate them in the text by referring to the trail number.

THE SYMBOLS

WALK:
Less than 2 miles
Easy terrain

EASY HIKE:
2 to 10 miles
Easy terrain

MODERATE HIKE:
2 or more miles
Rougher terrain
Backpacking possible

DIFFICULT HIKE:
Strenuous terrain
Backpacking possible

**MOUNTAIN BIKE
TRAIL**

**TRAIL FOR
EQUESTRIANS**

HANDICAP ACCESS

**DOGS ALLOWED
ON LEASH**

CAR CAMPING

**WALK-IN OR
BIKE-IN CAMPING**

MOUNTAIN TO CLIMB
Bag a peak!

**INTERPRETIVE
NATURE TRAIL**

PICNIC SPOT:
May be tables or just
a good blanket spot

**RECOMMENDED
FOR FAMILIES**

WATER AVAILABLE
(May not be piped!)

**RESTROOM
AVAILABLE**

FISHING ACCESS

FEE AREA

THE DANGERS

When on the trail, always keep your senses wide open so that you can best appreciate nature's pleasures as well as her dangers. Don't let nature lull you into complacency. Here are ten rules to keep you out of danger and enhance your journey so that you may safely enjoy nature's beauty.

1. DON'T LITTER. Most of these places are unspoiled. Do your part to keep them that way. Show your appreciation for Mother Nature by hiking with a trash bag which you can fill with any trash you find in otherwise pristine places, even cigarette butts, matches and bottle caps.

2. NO TRESPASSING. Property owners have a right to privacy. Stay off private property. There are enough public places without walking through someone's front or back yard.

3. FIRE. Be extremely careful with it. Do not smoke on trails. Always extinguish campfires until cold to the touch. You generally need a campfire permit (free) to have a fire outside a developed campground. Fires may be banned altogether during the dry season.

4. CLIFFS AND FORDS. Nature provides plenty of inherent dangers. These are two of the worst. CLIFFS: Coast Range soils are often unstable. Don't get close to the cliff's edge, and never climb on cliffs unless there is a safe trail. FORDS: Surging waters can overcome even the most experienced hiker. Never cross a ford that seems unsafe. Always use a hiking stick and proceed carefully to cross moving streams. Even small creeks can become dangerous after winter rains or during spring run-off.

5. WILD THINGS: ANIMAL. Bears are wild animals. Never tempt a bear with food or try to fight one that is raiding your camp or pack. Most pests are much smaller. Watch out for ticks (some carry Lyme Disease—check yourself after a hike), wasps, mosquitoes, biting spiders, scorpions and rattlesnakes. Human animals can be the most dangerous, particularly during hunting seasons. Always listen for gunfire and wear bright clothing.

6. WILD THINGS: PLANT. These mean business too, especially poison oak and stinging nettles which can get you with the slightest touch. Many other plants are poisonous. It is best not to touch any plants unless you know by positive identification that they are safe. This is most important with mushrooms. Please do not pick the wildflowers.

7. TRAIL COURTESY. Never cut switchbacks. Equestrians always have the right of way on trails, because you can move aside for a horse much more easily than its rider can yield to you. Mountain bikers must yield to hikers and horses and slow to walking speed on blind corners. As wonderful as bikes are,

these metal machines, especially when moving fast, can cause serious injury when other trail users do not know one is coming. **Mountain bikes are not allowed in wilderness areas.**

8. TRAFFIC. Country roads are difficult and sometimes crowded. Drive carefully and courteously. Please turn out for faster traffic. You will enjoy the journey more if you do. If you stop, pull safely off the road.

9. CRIME. Be sure to lock your car when you park it at the trailhead. Leave valuables out of sight, or better yet, back at your lodging.

10. **ALWAYS TAKE RESPONSIBILITY FOR YOURSELF AND YOUR PARTY.** This is a trail guide, not a nursery school. The author cannot and will not be responsible for you in the wilds. Information contained in this book is correct to the best of the author's knowledge. Author and publisher assume no liability for damages arising from errors or omissions. **You must take the responsibility for your safety and health while on these trails.** These are wild places. Safety conditions of trails vary with seasons. Be cautious, heed the above warnings, and always check on local conditions. It is safer to hike with a friend. Know where you can get help in case of emergency.

THE HISTORY

Around 200 million years ago, the Pacific Ocean lapped against the base of the recently formed Sierra Nevada Range, the immense granitic uplift that defined 400 miles of the western rim of the North American continent. Dinosaurs were the dominant, most highly evolved creatures on earth.

From the Sierra Crest, the edge of the North American continental plate extended about 200 miles west. The Pacific oceanic plate collided with this edge of the North American plate, forcing the ocean floor upward, folding it and lifting it high above the sea. This collision formed the inner (or eastern) Coast Range. The South Yolla Bolly Range and Snow Mountain were uplifted around 150 million years ago, trapping an inland sea where the great Central Valley is today.

The Pacific and North American plates continued colliding, uplifting more ocean floor to form the outer (or western) Coast Range around thirty million years ago. Folding and minor faulting occurred in this uplift, creating fault-bounded basins like Ukiah, Round and Little Lake Valleys.

The inland sea slowly drained as the continental edge lifted. The Central Valley emerged, filled by sediments from erosion of the new mountains and drained by rivers that found a path to the Pacific through the Golden Gate. The Valley's rich soils supported vast perennial grasslands interspersed with abundant wetlands.

In relatively recent geologic times, about two million years ago, the Clear Lake volcanic region formed, building the hills and mountains that now surround Clear Lake. The Pleistocene ice age (the most recent, from two million to 10,000 years ago) formed glaciers in the upper elevations of the Coast Range and over much of the world.

The enormous amount of water held by these glaciers and the enlarged polar ice caps dropped the sea level 300 feet, creating a land bridge across the Bering Sea connecting Asia to Alaska. At least two major migrations of Mongolian peoples walked this bridge into North America, the first about 14,000 B.C., the second around 10,000 B.C.

The earliest evidence of human habitation around Clear Lake dates back to 8000 B.C. These ancestors of the Pomo found a land of abundance unpopulated by humans and chose to stay. They developed a sophisticated and intricate culture centered around village and extended family. The Pomo territory grew to cover 60 miles from Clear Lake to the coast and 80 miles from Sherwood Valley in the north to Sebastopol and the Russian River in the south. Many other tribes settled adjacent to Pomo territory: Huchnom, Yuki and Coast Yuki to the north; Wintun to the east; Wappo, Lake Miwok and Coast Miwok to the south. The Kato, Wailaki and Lassik lived north of the Yuki and Huchnom. Other than the coastal groups, all these tribes inhabited the area covered by this book.

In the last thousand years Pomo and surrounding peoples attained their most complex development anthropologists call the "California Culture." In northwestern California the California Culture became most sophisticated among the Pomo and Wintun, but all tribes were affected. They produced refined and diverse baskets, participated in intertribal ceremonies called "big time" and the spirit impersonation of the elaborate Kuksu religion, and developed creation myths centered around a world creator. All tribes of this California Culture engaged in extensive trade and cultural exchange with neighboring tribes near and far, traveling on foot over an extensive network of trails. (Some carried pack baskets with up to 100 pounds of goods, suspended from their foreheads by tump lines—imagine carrying a backpack with your head!) Clam shell and magnesite beads, a sort of money, facilitated this trade. An estimated 250,000 Native Americans lived in California at the height of the culture. While feuds and wars were not unknown, most tribes lived in peace with little organization for war.

The trade network must have buzzed with the news of the Russian settlement at Fort Ross in 1812. The Russians traded extensively with Coast Miwok and Southwestern (Kashaya) Pomo. They hired the natives for fair wages and paid to use

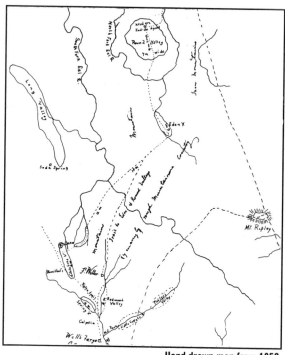

Hand drawn map from 1859

their land.

Then in 1821, 67 Spanish soldiers, armed with swords and muskets, rode horses into Lake Miwok and Southeastern Pomo territory, the first Spanish exploration into northwestern California. They scorned the natives and forced them to serve as guides. Over the next 15 years, thousands of Pomo and Lake Miwok and many from other tribes were baptized as Catholics, separated from their families and culture and forced to labor at Mission farms and cattle ranches.

The United States conquered California just in time for the Gold Rush. When other European settlers came looking for gold from 1849 on, many brought malignant attitudes toward all native peoples. Some had fought truly hostile plains tribes, while others simply feared any non-white people.

The once abundant native resources were stretched to the breaking point by this influx of settlers. Livestock brought by settlers ate the acorns and perennial plants. White hunters slaughtered the game, getting rich off the needs of miners.

When starving natives killed livestock for survival, vigilante settlers used the incidents to rationalize massacres, precipitating the Mendocino Indian War. Whole villages were either killed or captured by the regular army or the deputized vigilante groups that replaced the soldiers as they left to fight the Civil War. Captives were often forced into involuntary servitude (a polite term for slavery) as permitted under the

California Indenture Act of 1850. Many native people who were not murdered died of diseases brought by the invaders.

While racist and genocidal attitudes were sadly prevalent during the settlement period, not all the immigrants held them. Some courageous people even spoke out for the rights of the native people.

Today a small but hardy population of Native Americans survive. They finally won the vote in 1907, and other civil rights were acknowledged in the next 60 years. After decades of neglecting its native cultures, American society is showing new interest and respect for tribal traditions.

During the last third of the nineteenth century, immigrants to California settled every corner of the Mendocino Highlands (see Trails #1, 21 and 47 for examples) working hard to survive in a wild land. By the Great Depression of the 1930s, the number of people in the remote corners of the region had dwindled to very few, with a corresponding concentration of population in the more accessible valleys. Timber, orchards and vineyards replaced livestock as the primary industries. They still dominate the local economy today, though tourism becomes a bigger slice of the pie each year.

THE CLIMATE

Always check the weather forecast before starting a trip. This is especially important in the Mendocino Highlands, since weather can change dramatically from one day to the next and from one season to another. The importance of having current weather information increases exponentially for every 1000 feet higher your excursion will take you.

Climate differs considerably from one part of the Mendocino Highlands to another. (Refer to specific trail reports for further seasonal information.) Let's consider the climate generally from the lowest to the highest elevations, then look at the different seasons.

The valleys and areas below 1500 feet are most pleasant from autumn through spring, but are particularly hot in summer. They may be mild enough for year-round hiking if you are prepared for varying conditions.

Weather in mountain areas differs greatly according to elevation. Trails between 1500 and 4000 feet may be open to year-round hiking, although they can be chilly in winter and unpleasantly hot in summer. Trails above 4000 feet are generally closed by snow from autumn to spring; the higher the trail the shorter the season. Trails between 4000 and 5000 feet are at their prime in May and June, while trails above 5000 feet excel one or two months later. Even the high country can become hot and dry from mid-July into September.

The high mountains are also prone to summer thunderstorms. These range from minor inconveniences to violent, life-threatening fronts with heavy precipitation and severe lightning strikes. See page 97 for more about thunderstorms. When you stop to get your campfire permit, ask the ranger for the latest weather forecast for the specific area you will visit.

In planning your excursions, keep in mind the following about seasons in the Mendocino Highlands:

April and May offer sunny days interspersed with occasional storms. The wind may be gentle or howling. The landscape turns lush and beautiful in the low country, then at middle elevations. Bring layered clothing.

June and July bring summer to the low country first, then to the mountains. The low country can be too hot for comfortable hiking except perhaps in the early morning. People then head for the high country, seeking to escape the heat or at least catch a pleasant breeze. August is the hottest, also the most crowded month, when lakes and rivers beckon. Bring hats, cool clothes and swimsuits, but pack warm clothing for overnight trips.

September and October are beautiful, bringing calm, warm Indian summer days and cool nights. The land is dry and golden, the sunsets often spectacular. Bring rain gear, since storms may move in. In October, travelers in the high country must be prepared for sudden wintry storms.

November to March are the stormy months when it is essential to bring rain gear, wool clothing and waterproof boots. Still, fine sunny days often come between storms. While trails above 5000 feet are generally inaccessible during this period, spring comes early to trails below 1500 feet. Weather for middle elevation trails is harder to predict and prone to sudden changes. In winter storms can approach quickly at any time.

GET READY, GET SET, HIKE!

You must be chomping at the bit to get out on the trail by now. Here are a few suggestions of what you need to take on your hike: layered clothing—sweater, sweatshirt, hat, windbreaker or rain coat; insect repellent; sunscreen; sunglasses; and small first aid kit including moleskin for blisters. Highly recommended for all but the shortest walks: water container, water filter or purification tablets, extra food, pocket knife, flashlight or headlamp and extra batteries, matches and fire starter, map, compass (helps if you know how to use it), and of course your *Hiker's hip pocket Guide*!

Additional suggestions: spare socks, toilet paper and plastic trowel, binoculars, camera, field guides to birds, wildflowers and/or trees. If you are backpacking, you should read the introduction to the wilderness portion of the book and consult a backpacking equipment list.

When you are out on the trails, remember to slow down, open your senses and enjoy. Most people hike at a rate of 2 to 3 miles per hour. But steep terrain may slow all but the most hardy to as little as one mile per hour. Leave ample time to do the hike you plan at a pleasant pace. Hike not to count the miles, but to enjoy and appreciate nature. Happy trails to you!

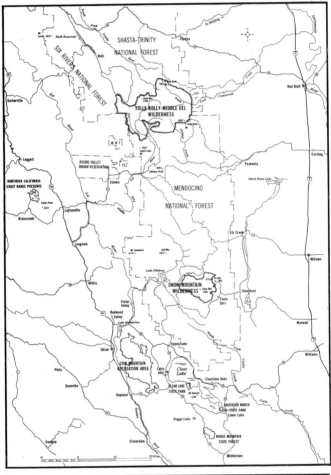

LEGEND

◉	County Seat	─(5)─	Interstate highway
○	City, town or village	─(101)─	U.S. highway
☐	Park or recreation area	─(128)─	State highway
▦	Wilderness area	───	Other principal roads
⌐¬	Forest boundary	─ ─ ─	Seasonal road
⌐¬	Indian reservation		

1.

NORTHERN CALIFORNIA
COAST RANGE PRESERVE
BIOLOGICAL DIVERSITY IN OLD GROWTH SANCTUARY

The Northern California Coast Range Preserve straddles the South Fork Eel River near its headwaters, protecting one of California's larger remaining virgin forests. The Kato people, the southernmost Athabascan-speaking tribe in California, roamed these hills for centuries, inhabiting the meadows and harvesting abundant food found in diverse habitats: pure and mixed forest, grassland, chaparral and riparian. The Kato inhabited a triangular area roughly defined by the contemporary towns of Branscomb, Laytonville and Cummings. They were relatives of the Sinkyone and Wailaki to the north. The Kato creation story views:

> *our earth as a vast horned animal that wallowed
> southward through the primeval waters with Nagaicho
> (the great traveler) standing on its head, until the
> beast came to rest lying down in its present position.*

Most of the Kato had already been forced onto reservations when the first white settlers reached Branscomb in 1885. Over the next 20 years, eight families homesteaded land now in the Preserve. Like the Kato, they lived in the meadows and relied on the land's natural resources for survival.

The settlers' lives were never easy, but twentieth century economics added additional pressures. When the depression hit in 1929, many settlers had moved on. Heath and Marjorie Angelo bought the boarded-up Elder homestead in 1931, later acquiring adjacent lands. The Angelos loved the area's wilderness nature and acted to preserve it. In 1959 they sold to the tiny Nature Conservancy, the organization's first venture in the western states. The Bureau of Land Management added adjoining virgin forests, completing today's 7520-acre sanctuary.

This richly layered biome, catching 85 inches of rain in an average year, supports a vast botanical diversity: 450 species of vascular plants, 93 mosses and 78 lichens. Over 60 mammal species reside or visit. Flying squirrels, ringtails, ermines and endangered spotted owls inhabit the forests. Pristine riparian corridors bring steelhead and salmon runs, which in turn sustain river otter, mink, bear and mountain lion. Chaparral on south slopes shelters brush rabbits, wood rats, chipmunks and bobcats. Northern California Coast Range Preserve is now managed by the University of California Natural Reserve System. Please watch for and do not disturb ongoing research projects, efforts to better understand, protect and preserve this pristine complex of interweaving habitats.

NORTHERN CALIFORNIA COAST RANGE PRESERVE:

DISTANCE: **7¼ miles round trip, or 7¾-mile semi-loop.**
TIME: Half day to full day.
TERRAIN: Follows dirt road through virgin forest along
   headwaters of wild river; descends to homestead beside
   meadow, climbs to brushy ridge and descends.
ELEVATION: TH (trailhead): 1440 feet. Gain/loss: to White
   House: 400 feet+/560 feet-, with loop: 900 feet+/960 feet-.
BEST TIME: Spring or summer.
WARNINGS: Watch for poison oak. Do not disturb any plants,
   animals or historical artifacts. Watch for rattlesnakes, ticks
   and scorpions. No mountain bikes, pets, radios, smoking or
   camping allowed.
DIRECTIONS TO TRAILHEAD: FROM HIGHWAY 101: Turn west
   in Laytonville onto Branscomb Road (M.70.). Go 16 miles to
   Wilderness Lodge Road, which forks right just beyond Eel
   River bridge. Go 3.5 miles to headquarters. Register, pick up
   a map and perhaps make a donation. Then drive 500 feet to
   parking.
   FROM HIGHWAY 1: Turn east north of Westport at M.79.1
   onto steep, winding, mostly unpaved Branscomb Road. Go 9.8
   miles, then left 3.5 miles on Wilderness Lodge Road.
FURTHER INFO: Northern California Coast Range Preserve
   (707) 984-6653.
OTHER SUGGESTION: CONGER TRAIL (5½ miles one way),
   WALKER MEADOW LOOP (May to October only, 2⅞ miles one
   way to South Meadow) and BLACK OAK MOUNTAIN TRAIL
   (2¾ miles one way) are mentioned in text where they leave
   main trail. Inquire about other trails.

From the parking lot 500 feet beyond headquarters, walk
northeast on narrow Wilderness Lodge Road paralleling the
South Fork Eel River. Climb gradually through mixed forest to
¼ mile. Perennials in the lush understory include creeping
snowberry, wood strawberry, wood rose, evergreen huckleberry, evergreen violet, inside-out flower, saxifrage, hairy honeysuckle and poison oak, all common along most of this hike. In
spring look for redwood sorrel, milkmaid, trillium, starflower,
wood anemone, fat solomon's seal, Indian warrior, vanilla leaf
and rattlesnake plantain.
   Pass sedum and leather fern on a rocky cutbank, then descend
east to wind along the river, where large virgin redwoods and

Douglas firs mix with tanoaks, madrones, bigleaf maples and bay laurels in mature forest.

Cross a bridge over Skunk Creek, lined with woodwardia and sword ferns, at ⅝ mile. A cross-section of a Douglas fir on your right shows the tree lived 400 years (firs may live 1200 years!). Soon a beautiful grove of redwoods stands between road and river. As you continue down the canyon, you may spot leopard lilies in May. Sinuously shaped madrones stretch for sunlight.

The Conger Trail forks right at one mile. (It climbs 1500 feet in 5½ miles to the Conger homestead.) Your road crosses a bridge over beautiful Elder Creek, then bends right, leaving the river to follow the creek. Walker Meadow Loop soon forks left to cross the river, rejoining the road near Wilderness Lodge (summer bridges at crossings, fords required rest of year).

As you continue on the road above Elder Creek, look for red larkspur on the left and serviceberry, miners lettuce and soap plant on the right. Pass the old Angelo place at 1¼ miles. Homesteaded by the Elder family in 1892, it is now the caretaker's residence. Two outhouses stand on the left, beside the beautiful clearing and orchard.

Your road starts climbing, offering fine views down to Elder Creek's pristine canyon. You soon pass a hydrologic bench

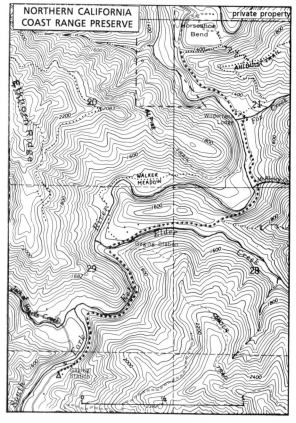

mark station where the creek, one of the rare undamaged and protected watersheds in the country, is monitored for flow and quality. Fill your canteen at a water faucet just beyond. Ascend along the lovely canyon, passing cream bush beneath mixed forest.

Climb east through oak woodlands at 1⅝ miles. After a rolling glade on the right, your route turns north to meet Black Oak Mountain Trail at a ridge. (It forks right to ascend the 3708-foot peak on the Preserve's eastern boundary.)

The road descends northeast, leaving Elder Creek drainage and returning to mature conifer forest. Look for slink pod, hazel, giant trillium and Oregon grape on a long steady descent, soon overlooking the Eel in its canyon far below. Pass a large redwood at 2⅛ miles and return to the riverside, lined with red alders. Your trail contours north. Climb above a grassy flat beside the river at 2¼ miles. You meet the north end of Walker Meadow Loop on your left in 250 feet.

Your road threads between the Eel River and big South Meadow. The Preserve's broad, flat clearings like this are former river terraces, shaped before the river cut its deeper canyon. The Kato people enlarged and managed these clearings by burning them, encouraging food plants like the white and canyon live oaks and manzanitas growing here. Baby blue eyes, poppies, irises, lupines, buttercups and popcorn flowers color the lush green clearing in spring. The road soon bends right, wrapping around the meadow's north end.

Cross a bridge over Fox Creek at 2⅝ miles and meet a junction. Ahlquist Trail forks right past old farm equipment rusting beneath fruit trees. The loop at the end of the described hike returns by that trail. The main road bends left past Wilderness Lodge, now used by researchers and educational groups. The original Wilderness Lodge, which burned in 1937, was a resort for city dwellers during the first quarter of the twentieth century.

The road heads northwest along the edge of the meadow, passing shooting star, woodland star and yarrow. A spur forks left at 2¾ miles, descending to a big emerald pool on the river. Your road climbs gradually above the winding Eel, becoming a narrow, less-traveled track lined with yerba de selva as it returns to the forest. The climb steepens as the terrain gets rockier. Bare slopes around 3⅛ miles sprout exquisite, petite rose-purple blooms of Kellogg's monkeyflower.

At 3¼ miles a hand-painted trail sign points right. (The road leaves the Preserve in ¼ mile, encountering private property.) From the junction you look west to Elkhorn Ridge and the rugged northwest corner of the Preserve. Take the narrow trail on the right, signed "WHITEHOUSE, TEN-MILE CREEK, WILDERNESS LODGE LOOP," heading east through mature forest. Watch for poison oak, Pacific dogwood and calypso

orchids as you traverse the steep slope. Descend to a fork at 3½ miles. Turn left, descending through a berry patch and apple orchard into a very large meadow and quickly come to the White House.

The stately, two-story Lovejoy homestead sits on the edge of the big meadow at Horseshoe Bend. Built in 1895, the White House still has many of its furnishings, including paintings and mirrors on the walls, old wood-burning stoves and the hand pump at the kitchen sink. It looks as if the family might have left last month for a trip to visit relatives. The home's isolation amidst such splendid natural beauty speaks eloquently of the adventure and hardships faced by the settlers who came here to carve a living from the wilderness.

You are welcome to look around, contemplating what it might have been like to live in such a place. Remains of a blacksmith shop (where two-eyed violets now grow), barn, outhouse and other outbuildings surround the house, along with old roses, daffodils, narcissus and foxgloves. But please disturb nothing and stay off adjacent private property to the north. In keeping with the Preserve spirit, take only memories or photographs, leave only footprints.

If you want the easiest hike, return on the same trail, for a 7¼-mile round trip. Our description continues on Wilderness Lodge Loop, which adds 500 feet elevation gain/loss and ½ mile to the total distance.

Return to the junction south of the house. Bear left, climbing steeply southeast through the forest. An old cross-cut saw blade leans incongruously against a six-foot-diameter Douglas fir giant. Before 3¾ miles you switchback right as your steep climb eases slightly. Ten more switchbacks bring you to the top of the slope and a junction on the brushy ridge at 4 miles. Ahlquist Trail goes left, climbing east along the ridge.

Turn right and descend west on the ridge through chaparral of manzanita, canyon live oak, chamise, coyote bush, coffeeberry and various kinds of ceanothus. Veer left around 4¼ miles, coming to a rest bench with a fine view of the wilderness. Sit and enjoy the view, unless the sun is too hot on this south-facing slope. On your left, Black Oak Mountain towers southeast. The ridge south of it forms the Preserve's southern boundary. South Meadow and Wilderness Lodge lie below in Eel River Canyon. You can hear the river but cannot see it from here. Elkhorn Ridge is due west.

Your trail descends east, then bends right. The trail levels in shady hardwood forest at 4⅜ miles. Resume your descent through forest of madrone, live oak and bay laurel. Your descent steepens as conifers mix with the hardwoods. The path levels briefly at 4⅝ miles, high above the rushing waters of Fox Creek. Wind right, then left, and descend steeply to the meadow and your junction opposite Wilderness Lodge.

From here it is about 2¾ miles back along the road to your starting point. If you want to explore more of this rugged country, take one of the side trails on your return.

2.
WILLITS CREEK/GOOSEBERRY LOOP
HEADWATERS AND RIDGES OF BROOKTRAILS REDWOOD PARK

Have you ever hiked in a hyleopolis? If you have walked at Brooktrails northwest of Willits, you probably explored the hyleopolitan community without hearing the term. A planner coined the word in the 1960s, upon the birth of Brooktrails subdivision. A hyleopolis is a residential community built in a forest. In Brooktrails the forest is held in trust, conserved for the community. Brooktrails Township Board formalized this hyleopolity in 1988 when they created the 2500-acre Brooktrails Redwood Park, where you can explore a dozen trails in pleasant second-growth forest.

The Northern Pomo had a small village, Tsaká (meaning "smoke village"), on the ridge near the present Brooktrails entrance. This community of about 12 buildings was allied with the principal village, Tsamómda, to the southwest. A Pomo trail connected these communities with Bakau, east on Outlet Creek, and Buldam on the coast near Big River. Pressure from white settlers forced the Pomo to abandon Tsaká before 1850.

Settlers first logged the Brooktrails area in the 1860s. A huge sawmill was built at Brooktrails in 1903. Soon Willits virtually revolved around the fortunes of that mill. The completion of Northwestern Pacific Railroad in 1902 expanded market opportunities. When the mill closed in 1924, Willits suffered a major economic downturn. The Diamond D Dude Ranch opened on upper Willits Creek, luring city slickers to ride some of the

25

WILLITS CREEK/GOOSEBERRY LOOP:

DISTANCE: **5½-mile loop**; 2¼ miles along Willits Creek on Huckleberry and Last Chance Trails, 1⅝ miles on Ridge Road, 1⅝ miles on Gooseberry Trail and back to trailhead.

TIME: Three or more hours.

TERRAIN: Climbs gently along creek, moderately to road; undulates along road, then descends through forest and down creek.

ELEVATION: TH (trailhead): 1600 feet. Gain/loss: first 2¼ miles: 680 feet+/40 feet-, loop: 1000 feet+/1000 feet-.

BEST TIME: April and May for wildflowers, but nice anytime.

WARNINGS: Do not park blocking fire road at trailhead. Stay off adjacent private property. Watch for poison oak and rattlesnakes. Watch for traffic on road.

DIRECTIONS TO TRAILHEAD: Turn west off Highway 101 onto Sherwood Road (stoplight, north end of Willits, M.47.2). Go 2.3 miles, then left on Primrose Road for .7 mile, then right on Poppy Lane for .7 mile to trailhead, on left beyond bridge.

FURTHER INFO: Brooktrails, weekdays (707) 459-2494.

OTHER SUGGESTION: FAWN LILY TRAIL on Primrose Drive .4 mile from Sherwood Road, starts as a broad fire road north along Lake Emily's east shore. Beyond the lake, take first left to follow Dutch Henry Creek. You can take FAWN LILY TRAIL, POPPY DRIVE AND SHERWOOD ROAD 9.3 paved miles to join 44-mile MENDOCINO HIKING & EQUESTRIAN TRAIL which ends at Mendocino. For overnight trips, park at main Brooktrails lot near fire station—inform someone at Brooktrails about your return date. (See *The Hiker's hip pocket Guide to the Mendocino Coast* for description of 44-mile trail). Ask at the office for a map of OTHER TRAILS in Brooktrails.

trails that exist today. Brooktrails was conceived as a second-home resort community. Today most of the township's 3000 residents live here year round.

This description follows one of the prettiest trails at Brooktrails along upper Willits Creek to its headwaters, 4 ⅝ miles round trip. You can continue on paved Ridge Road and Gooseberry Trail for a loop especially nice for mountain bikers.

Head northwest on the broad fire road behind the green gate. You soon overlook shady Willits Creek on your left, lined with

red alders, willows, oaks, redwoods and Douglas firs. Follow the nearly level old logging road bordered by trail plant, twisted stalk, yerba de selva, honeysuckle and starflower.

Join another old road and continue up the creek past madrones and tanoaks. Huckleberry, wood rose, inside-out flower, evergreen violet and columbine mingle with other understory plants. Your road bends left and fords the creek where hazel and woodwardia fern grow. Resume a gentle incline past gooseberry, redwood sorrel, buttercup and sword fern.

Beyond ¼ mile you pass the dam site for a new reservoir that will eventually supply water for a growing Brooktrails. An old redwood stump beneath bigleaf maples has springboard cuts, indicating it was taken before the advent of chainsaws. Enjoy the pretty, rocky canyon's moss-draped cliffs. They will someday be underwater. The path narrows, winding gently up the creek. Vanilla leaf and saxifrage grow on steep cutbanks.

Pass through an area of marshes and springs where you may see clintonia, wild ginger, coltsfoot and five-finger fern. Soon a small meadow is across the creek. A steep skid trail ascends left at ½ mile. Cross a tributary of Willits Creek and reach a junction. (The roadbed swings left, ascending southwest. Our loop returns on this, the Gooseberry Trail.)

Turn right to head northwest, fording the main creek in 50 feet. You might smell azaleas before fording back to the west bank in 150 feet. The spotted leaves of slink pods cluster beneath hazel on a north slope at the crossing.

The road ascends moderately, winding away from the creek.

Climb gently as horsetail, rush and sedge grow in bogs along the creek. Climb moderately on a long, well graded, shady hill, rising above the creek.

The track levels heading west at ⅞ mile. Climb gradually past two large moss-draped, lichen-spotted rocks as the creek murmurs far below. Pass Oregon grape and wind left past a steep cutbank topped with inside-out flower at one mile. The uncommon rock fern called green spleenwort grows at the base of the cutbank.

Suddenly the creek whispers on the right. Cross it and meet a junction at 1⅛ miles. Huckleberry Trail climbs on the right. Go left on Last Chance Trail, climbing gradually west along the shady, green-banked creek. Woodwardia and huckleberry overhang its mossy banks, with iris and poison oak nearby.

You soon ascend moderately, briefly on rough tread. Pass an immense maple, then abundant redwood sorrel beneath redwoods and Douglas firs two and three feet wide. Climb steeply to level at 1½ miles. Then a moderate climb rises above the creek into drier habitat. Madrones, tanoaks and chinquapins

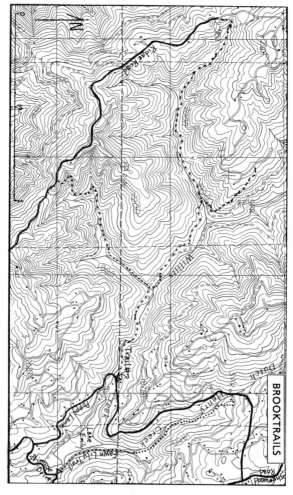

dominate the forest. At 1⅝ miles a dry bank supports tobacco brush, a very large-leaved ceanothus. Take a steeply slanting footpath around a washout at a gully.

The road resumes a moderate winding climb where you must step over several blowdowns. Climb gently to 1⅞ miles, approaching the creek bed where it trickles only in winter and spring. Step lightly as the path levels beneath redwoods, looking for calypso orchids in April and May.

Ascend gradually on eroded tread. Bear right at a fork, climbing moderately past prickly canyon gooseberry, with red blooms in spring and unpalatable fruit in early summer. Ascend gradually past fat solomon's seal, then moderately on deteriorating, overgrown tread. Beyond 2⅛ miles bear left on a tiny footpath around a large deadfall.

A tiny bridge across an eroded gully shows someone cares about the deteriorating trail. Ascend moderately on improving tread, winding left and right. The trail ends at paved Ridge Road beyond 2¼ miles.

You can retrace your route for a 4⅝-mile round trip. Or you can go left, following the road for 1⅝ miles to complete a 5½-mile loop. Watch for traffic if you do. The road undulates along the brushy ridgetop, climbing over knobs and dipping through saddles. Drop steeply to a saddle beyond 3⅞ miles, where you must watch carefully on the left for the easy-to-miss, unmarked Gooseberry Trail.

Go left, descending steeply south past lupine to a green gate. The old logging road makes an easy winding descent through forest with evergreen violets on steep slopes. The road makes a big bend to the right before 4⅛ miles for a moderate winding descent. Descend steeply to a gurgling creek around 4½ miles, then descend moderately, winding along the stream.

Your decline eases beyond 4¾ miles. Soon sedges line the small creek on your right. Gooseberry Trail ends before 5 miles. Turn right and retrace your route downstream to the trailhead at 5½ miles.

3.

LITTLE DARBY LOOP
FROM MOSSES AND FERNS TO CHAPARRAL

Rugged, brushy terrain limits access to this 1400-acre Bureau of Land Management holding on Little Darby Peak's south slope. The easy ¾-mile Forest Loop combines with the Brushland Loop for a 1¼-mile hike. BLM has an interpretive brochure for the nature trail, written with children in mind. You can also scramble along the intermittently steep and brushy firebreak to Little Darby Peak.

LITTLE DARBY LOOP:

DISTANCE: 1¼-mile loop, with 2¼-mile side trip to peak
(3½ miles total).
TIME: One or two hours for loop, half day to peak.
TERRAIN: Descends through forest to creek, then climbs
through forest, then chaparral before descending to picnic
area. Side trail follows steep firebreak to peak.
ELEVATION: TH (trailhead): 1800 feet. Gain/loss: loop: 340
feet+/340 feet-, with peak: 1210 feet+/1210 feet-.
BEST TIME: Spring for wildflowers. Nice anytime.
WARNINGS: Watch for poison oak.
DIRECTIONS TO TRAILHEAD: In downtown Willits, turn east
off Highway 101 at stoplight (M.47.0) onto Commercial
Street, which becomes Hearst Road at 0.7 mile. At 3.3 miles,
where Hearst Road turns left, go straight on Canyon Road to
signed parking on left, 6.75 miles from Highway 101.
FURTHER INFO: Bureau of Land Management (707) 462-3873.
OTHER SUGGESTION: TOMKI ROAD, .8 mile east of Little
Darby Trail is a lightly traveled county road. It climbs south
along creek canyons, then descends along headwaters of
Russian River to Redwood Valley in 11 miles. Impassable
during winter and spring run-off, it is a good mountain bike
ride or hike in late spring and autumn.

*This was the northeastern corner of Northern Pomo lands. The
village Kabeyo ("under rock village") was not far west on the
headwaters of Berry Creek. The Huchnom people lived on Tomki
Creek and Eel River to the east.*

Descend southwest from the parking area, passing through a
stile to the right of the locked gate. The broad track swings right
to cross a creek, then ascends north. As the path bends left at
⅛ mile, soap plants thrive on a bare cutbank.

The track levels in 100 feet at the picnic area, where a
restroom, two tables and grills sit beneath Douglas firs four feet
wide. The signed start of the Forest Loop is 100 feet ahead.
Descend gradually into the creek canyon, passing marker #1 for
the interpretive brochure, which warns of the extensive poison
oak found along this trail. Descend past the shiny leaves of
inside-out flower on the mossy forest floor.

As you approach the creek at ¼ mile, moss-draped live oaks

share the forest with Douglas firs, tanoaks and madrones. Descend to a bridge over a tributary, near its confluence with Big Canyon Creek. A rest area is across the bridge.

The main trail turns left, ascending west along the side stream. Bay laurel, hairy honeysuckle, sword and lady ferns thrive on this densely mossy north slope. In 250 feet your path switchbacks left, then right, climbing moderately. Continue upstream past the dark green leaves of saxifrage. Ascend short steep switchbacks, then climb gently past a six-foot-wide Douglas fir. At #7 on your left, a large fir marked "18" has two mosses and some lichens growing on its bark. These trees were numbered so forestry students could practice estimating lumber volume.

Your trail switchbacks left, climbing moderately away from the creek. As you pass #8, look to the right for a patch of uncommon rattlesnake plantain, attractive, dark green leaves with a white central vein. Its white flowers bloom on a single erect stalk in July.

Continue to a rest bench on the right. If you stop here, listen for the drilling sound or Woody Woodpecker-like laughter of pileated woodpeckers. The lichen called false Spanish moss drapes the limbs of live oaks. Ascend into drier habitat as the soil changes from the dark loam near the creeks to orange clay.

Reach a junction at ½ mile. The left fork returns to the picnic area in ¼ mile. Turn right on the Brushland Loop, ascending south through mixed forest with large Douglas firs. Since more sunlight penetrates the forest canopy here than down in the canyon, bracken ferns grow profusely. Contour west through a sunny clearing, then wind left and right on a gradual ascent. Switchback left and contour through tanoak-dominated forest.

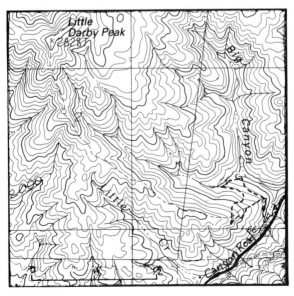

The path ascends moderately, switchbacking right and left, then climbs gradually.

Before ¾ mile you cross a firebreak that has become the boundary between the woodland behind you and the chaparral habitat ahead. (The side trail to Little Darby Peak takes off here; see climb box below.)

LITTLE DARBY PEAK

To extend this easy walk to a moderate hike, climb the firebreak to Little Darby Peak, a side trip of 2¼ miles. Ascend moderately west for the first ⅛ mile. Level briefly, then veer right, ascending gradually along the ridgetop. Dip, then climb to another knob. Look left to Big Darby Peak, only five feet higher than Little Darby Peak. Descend right, then climb moderately on soil of bright orange clay. The firebreak bends right, broadening as it contours on the brushy crest to ⅜ mile, Little Darby Peak rising steeply ahead.

Ascend moderately as brush crowds the trail, with knobcone pines on your right. After another knob, descend slightly. The track widens, rising gradually without hindrance from brush to a broad, level clearing around ⅝ mile. It offers a view west to Little Lake Valley and Willits. The path dips, then climbs moderately, winding with the ridgetop.

Your ascent along the firebreak steepens at ¾ mile, with views east to the high country beyond Eel River Canyon. Buck brush joins the chaparral. Make a short brushy descent, then climb moderately on a broad track. Fremont silktassel grows at ⅞ mile.

Climb steeply, with two small dips to one mile. Create your own switchbacks on the steepest ascent for the next ⅛ mile. One level respite offers a view south to the lake at Wente Scout Camp. Ascend steeply on the rocky firebreak, passing wind-blown Douglas firs, gnarled chamise and coyote bush.

Reach the broad 2828-foot-elevation summit just beyond 1⅛ miles, where a rock cairn is on the left. Mountain mahogany grows on the brushy north slope. You have fine views south and west, down Berry Creek to lush Little Lake Valley and the western flank of the Coast Range beyond. You can enjoy the views even more as you return along the steep fire line to the loop trail.

The loop trail reaches its summit 200 feet from the firebreak. As you begin descending, you look southwest to the Willits dump. Knobcone pines and chamise grow in the chaparral.

Switchback left for a grand view east toward the canyons of Tomki Creek and Eel River, the mountains of Mendocino National Forest beyond. Where your descending path switchbacks to the right, a wood rat has built his twig castle below the trail. Toyon shades the humble home. The path soon switches left and levels briefly. Make a short steep descent to ⅞ mile, where Indian warriors grow on a switchback to the right.

Descend south briefly, then switchback steeply left to descend moderately along the boundary between chaparral and forest. Cross the firebreak and make a winding descent past madrones. Owl hoots echo through the shadowy canyons in late afternoons.

Return to the main loop at one mile, where you turn right and wind down to the picnic area at 1⅛ miles. Walk the dirt road, returning to the parking lot at 1¼ miles.

4.

SHAKOTA

SHADY TRAIL ON LAKE MENDOCINO'S WEST SHORE

Shakota means rabbit in Pomo, a fitting name for this trail through chaparral and scrubby forest on Lake Mendocino's west shore. A Northern Pomo principal village, Chomchadila, was to the west, on the Russian River where Calpella is today. Kalpela was a chief there. Another major Pomo settlement, Shachamkau or Chamkawi, flourished here in Coyote Valley, its site now beneath the lake. The Pomo called the valley Shodakai. These settlements were in the heart of Northern Pomo territory, which reached from Fort Bragg to Longvale in the north, from Boonville to Clear Lake's west shore in the south.

The Army Corps of Engineers completed Coyote Dam, mostly for flood control, in 1958. Lake Mendocino had filled by 1959. The pleasant Visitor Center, styled after a Pomo dance house, has a fine exhibit of the world-renowned Pomo baskets.

Shakota Trail starts at the lower end of the Visitor Center parking lot (400 feet southwest of the restroom at the lower parking lot). Follow a paved service road 100 feet to the signed starting point of the dirt trail. Watch for poison oak as you head south beneath pine, cypress and mixed hardwoods.

Your trail soon climbs briefly. Look for soap plant, hound's tongue and Indian warrior in spring beneath manzanita bushes. A brief steep descent is lined with sticky monkeyflower. Contour south and cross a bridge over a gully, then ascend past milkmaids and shooting stars in spring to a view of Lake Mendocino.

Contour through chaparral with blue oak, California mountain mahogany and toyon. Cross another bridge at ¼ mile, then parallel a park road on your left. Madrones join the forest, with hedge nettle, bedstraw and checker lily in the understory. Pass through a brushy area where deer brush and blueblossom ceanothus grow with yerba santa. The path dips, then contours through an open area. Look for mule ears, sticky monkeyflower, California mountain mahogany, coyote bush, toyon and abundant potentilla, all plants that thrive in disturbed soil. Prolific poison oak vines also prosper in the altered habitat.

You soon pass the end of the adjacent public road. Your trail

DISTANCE: **3 miles one way** (6 miles round trip), plus
optional ⅜-mile side trip to overlook.

TIME: Three or more hours.

TERRAIN: Gentle ups and downs through woodlands and
chaparral on west shore of Lake Mendocino.

ELEVATION: TH: 800 feet. Gain/loss: 320 feet+/240 feet-.

BEST TIME: March and April for wildflowers. Nice year round.
Hot in summer, but you can swim in lake.

WARNINGS: Open 8 a.m. to sunset. Watch for poison oak and
rattlesnakes. Dogs not allowed in Pomo Picnic Area.

DIRECTIONS TO TRAILHEAD: Exit Highway 101 at Calpella
(M.30.4 from north, M.30.2 from south). Go right on Moore
Street. Before one mile go right, then left on Marina Drive.
Go one mile to Pomo Recreation Area. First right leads to
Visitor Center parking and trailhead. If that road is closed,
take second right to year-round parking. Or exit Highway 20
at M.35.5, go .9 mile to trailhead.

FEES: Car camping: $8-12/ vehicle.

FURTHER INFO: Lake Mendocino Manager's Office
(707) 462-7581.

OTHER SUGGESTION: You can also start this trail from the
SOUTH END at Overlook Picnic Area, near Trailhead #6. You
can CIRCUMNAVIGATE LAKE MENDOCINO by combining
this trail with Trails #5 and #6 and Marina Drive along the
north shore, but you would have to follow busy Highway 20
for 1⅛ miles to cross the East Fork Russian River at the
lake's inlet. This forms a 13½-mile loop.

dips right, then climbs before dipping through a gully with
buttercups at ½ mile. Contour south through a clearing where
invasive star thistles cluster on the left, surrounded by scattered
chaparral. Dip through another gully, where hairy honeysuckle
vine and vetch thrive beneath a large Douglas fir. Fawn lilies
and maidenhair ferns grow on the wooded slope beyond the
gully. Your path bends right and ascends, then dips slightly
across a broad gully. The trail winds past Sargent cypresses
toward the lake.

You have a sweeping view of the lake at ¾ mile, with brushy
Cow Mountain rising from the east shore. Cross a small gully
and descend gradually through patchy chaparral mixed with
cypresses. Contour through a shady gully then a sunny one.

Cross a bridge at one mile. Your trail bends left and heads toward the lake, descending gradually. As the path turns away from the lake, poppies thrive on a grassy hill beneath a large bushy knobcone pine. After crossing a bridge over another gully, climb briefly. The path bends right to contour south. Meander through a large grassy clearing. At the south end some antique farm equipment is covered with poison oak, with lupines nearby.

Meet a service road as you reach Ridge Point at 1¼ miles. The trail turns right to follow the road. (If you turn left and walk 300 feet east, you can explore the ruins of an old winery, source of the rusting machinery, out on the point.)

Follow the road southwest with grand views of the lake and Coyote Dam on the far shore. Descend along a sunny slope with dense chamise, then enter live oak woodland. Look for the trail forking right at 1⅜ miles, 30 feet from the shore at maximum lake level. (The road continues along the lake.) Turn right, ascending the path into the woods. Climb gradually in and out of woodlands, then contour until a sudden winding descent meets the end of the road at 1⅝ miles.

Your path winds through woodlands above the lake shore. Blue-eyed grass grows on a sunny slope above a gravel beach. Wind in and out of woodlands and brushy clearings, contouring around small coves along the shore, passing lomatium, hound's tongue and Indian warrior.

Your trail descends to wind around a cove lined with blue oaks and madrones. The inlet is favored by fishermen, mallards and grebes. Silvery paintbrush grows with sticky monkeyflowers on a steep, sunny bank. Traverse a deep shady gully where snowberry grows at the head of the cove, then cross an old road at 2 miles. The next 200 feet of trail may be muddy in winter, especially when mountain bikes have traveled it recently.

The path makes a winding ascent through woodland, then undulates through brushy grasslands. Round a grassy point above the lake shore at 2¼ miles, then wind around another cove, passing buckeyes and toyons around a large white oak. Veer right at a wooded promontory, then ascend south. Descend to cross a small bridge at 2½ miles.

Your trail soon begins a moderate climb. At a fork at 2⅝ miles, go right to climb southwest. Dip through a patch of chaparral, then ascend gradually through cool oak/buckeye woodland. Soon your path levels in open grasslands with white oaks and manzanita. Climb slightly to reach the edge of Overlook Picnic Area at 2⅞ miles. Pass a restroom and drinking fountain, coming to trail's end at the paved road before 3 miles.

If you would like to extend your hike by a short climb to a hilltop vista, you can take a footpath behind the restroom. It ascends gradually north for ⅛ mile, then moderately steeply past a water tank to a white "X" on the hilltop called Lorenzo.

The 981-foot summit has a grand view over Lake Mendocino and west across Ukiah Valley to the western flank of the Coast Range. Return to the picnic area and retrace your route north along Shakota Trail to your starting point.

5.

EAST SHORE
THROUGH LAKE MENDOCINO'S WILDLIFE AREA

This fire-road hike explores the wild east shore of Lake Mendocino. Ideal for mountain bikes, its up-down roller coaster course traverses the 689-acre designated Wildlife Area. You are most likely to see some of the abundant bird species, including waterfowl, raptors, wild turkey and valley quail. With a little luck you might also spot black-tailed deer, gray fox or other mammals. Keep in mind that hunting is permitted (shotguns only) from the third Saturday in October through the last Sunday in February.

You might plan to stay overnight at Miti Campground, accessible only by boat, foot, bike or horse, 2 ½ miles from the trailhead. The 18 sites have tables, fire pits, pit toilets and superb lake views. Water must be hauled in or purified from the lake.

From the small parking area north of the entrance kiosk, go ½ mile on the left fork of the paved road past Bu-shay Campground to the trailhead. At the end of the pavement, where a sign says "FIRE LANE," follow the level road south 400 feet. It bends right, passing a white iron gate, and descends steeply past cypresses and extensive poison oak.

Your track switchbacks left, descending across a seasonal creek where California buckeyes and blackberries thrive. Climb gradually out of the canyon past maidenhair ferns, horsetail, toyon, manzanita and bedstraw beneath deciduous valley oaks and evergreen blue oaks.

The track contours south beyond ¾ mile, overlooking the lake. Grasslands rise on your left. Oak woodland fills the steep slope above the lake on your right. The trail winds left through a gully, then dips through a larger gully, crossing a seasonal creek. Climb steeply to 1⅛ miles, passing shooting stars and milkmaids in early spring beneath oaks and buckeyes.

Your fire road contours along power lines to 1⅜ miles, then bends right on a winding descent to approach the lake shore. Climb steeply for 200 feet, then return to lake side, passing a clump of rushes on the left at 1⅝ miles. The track, which may be muddy here in winter, winds around a small bay. Veer right to ford a seasonal creek.

Your path soon bends left on a moderate climb, coming to a fork near a barn at 2 miles. The left fork is marked private property. Turn right and head west to a hilltop, where a side road forks right. Take the main road to descend gradually, then steeply. Your track winds around a small bay at 2¼ miles, then ascends through blue oak woodland.

Your road levels at 2⅜ miles, where a side track goes left. The main track contours northwest to the first sites of Miti Campground, beneath oaks in 300 feet. Two pit toilets are on the left at 2½ miles, with a junction just beyond. The main trail goes left, heading south. (If you plan to camp you can continue west past another dozen sites and more honey houses on the ¼-mile path to the peninsula's end. Shooting stars bloom here in February, then mule ears, poppies and other wildflowers.)

East Shore Trail heads south from the junction, crossing a grassy flat with coyote bush and manzanita. Pass a road on the right, then return to oak woodland. In 100 feet, veer right on the narrower of two tracks, climbing south-southeast to top a steep hill where your path bends left to head east. After a spur on the right, climb gradually to overlook the largest bay along the trail.

Another track crosses your road at 2⅞ miles. Continue straight

EAST SHORE:

DISTANCE: **4½ miles** (9 miles round trip); 2½ miles to Miti Camp, 4⅛ miles to Deerwood junction.

TIME: All day or overnight.

TERRAIN: Short but strenuous ups and downs along lake shore, climbing to hilltop views.

ELEVATION: TH (trailhead): 840 feet. Gain/loss: to Miti Campground: 440 feet+/480 feet-, total: 1200 feet+/880-.

BEST TIME: Early spring for wildflowers.

WARNINGS: Watch for poison oak and rattlesnakes.

DIRECTIONS TO TRAILHEAD: Turn north off Highway 20 at M.36.6 onto Inlet Road (3 miles east of Highway 101). Drive 1.2 miles to parking area just north of kiosk. (When road is open—April to October—you can drive .25 mile beyond kiosk to pleasant Mesa Day-use Area, then walk east through campground to join paved road portion of hike. It is nearly as long and rather confusing.)

FEES: Car camping: $10/vehicle.

FURTHER INFO: Lake Mendocino Manager's Office (707) 462-7581.

on a short, steep descent, then through roller coaster dips. Cross a gully at one inlet of the bay, then climb through grasslands. The path bends right and descends through the large glade, nearing the lake shore. Ascend briefly, then make a winding descent.

You ford the only year-round creek along the trail at 3½ miles. A large oak snag spreads bleached limbs above the crossing. The track winds southwest, passing two large valley oaks on the right that shade a riot of daffodils in spring. Climb gradually, then moderately through oak-studded grasslands to a summit at 4 miles. Your track bends right and descends briefly, then resumes climbing.

Come to a hilltop junction beyond 4⅛ miles. The track descending south leads to the Deerwood neighborhood of Ukiah. Turn right and climb steeply west. Ascend past the unsigned end of Kaweyo Horse Trail around 4¼ mile to reach East Shore Trail's highest point at 4⅜ miles. The view from this 1140-foot knob is best in winter when the oaks are leafless. Then you might see snow on 6873-foot Hull Mountain 26 miles northeast. Lake Mendocino sprawls among the wooded hills left of the peak, with Coyote Dam and the intake tower to the west. Ukiah Valley hides behind oak-covered hills.

The trail descends to a saddle, then climbs steeply to another knob at 4½ miles. This hilltop, shrouded in chaparral of manzanita, chamise and toyon, has views of Ukiah Valley.

If you want to continue the rest of the trail is described in Trail #6. Otherwise retrace your route around the lake to the trailhead.

van. 92

6.

KAWEYO HORSE

ACROSS DAM AND SPILLWAY TO WILD SOUTH SHORE

Our described trail leaves from the north end of Coyote Dam. (A spur heads 200 feet northeast—passing mariposa lilies in spring—to a wheelchair-accessible restroom and drinking fountain. A staging area for equestrians is ¼ mile west of the dam trailhead.) The level first ⅝ mile of the trail is ideal for an easy walk, jog or family jaunt, and offers wheelchair access as well. The paved road continues for another mile to overlook the spillway. The described trail leaves the pavement to meander along the shore to the lake's southeast corner, then returns along ridges, linking with East Shore Trail (Trail #5).

KAWEYO HORSE:

DISTANCE: **5⅜-mile loop** (or more); ⅝ mile across dam, 1⅜ miles to spillway, 3⅛ miles to East Shore Trail.

TIME: Three or more hours.

TERRAIN: Contours across dam; descends to shore, climbs gradually, then moderately before dropping to cross spillway; climbs steeply to summit; descends to spillway and returns.

ELEVATION: TH: 760 feet. Gain/loss: to spillway: 180 feet+/240 feet-, loop: 1040 feet+/1040 feet-.

BEST TIME: Spring for wildflowers.

WARNINGS: Watch for poison oak and rattlesnakes. Unsafe to cross spillway when lake approaches flood stage.

DIRECTIONS TO TRAILHEAD: Exit Highway 101 north of Ukiah onto Lake Mendocino Drive (M.27.6 from north, M.27.2 from south). Go east 1.9 miles (jogging north briefly on North State Street) to Kaweyo Staging Area on right, trailhead for equestrians. Hikers and bikers continue .1 mile past Che-ka-ka Campground to parking area on right, overlooking dam.

FEES: Car camping: $6/vehicle.

FURTHER INFO: Lake Mendocino Manager's Office (707) 462-7581.

OTHER SUGGESTION: SHAKOTA TRAIL (Trail #4) can be hiked from its south end at Overlook Picnic Area. Take left fork just before trailhead.

Head south on the level paved path across earth-fill Coyote Dam as the horse trail enters from the right. Lake Mendocino sparkles on your left. A wooded island at ¼ mile is a haven for geese. Soon the intake tower stands on your left, with the channelized East Fork Russian River below on your right. Pass a rest bench and continue to the end of the dam.

Where the paved road swings right on a gradual climb at ⅝ mile, turn left on the signed dirt horse trail descending along the shore. The lush vegetation includes toyon, California mountain mahogany, coyote bush, ceanothus, honeysuckle, scrubby white oak and poison oak. Various brodiaeas, red larkspur, Indian pink, yellow globe lily and shooting star add color in spring. As you follow the shore, huge soap plants on your right have leaves two feet long, with four-foot flower stalks in spring. Look across the lake to 6873-foot Hull Mountain.

The narrow path veers right on a short steep climb, passing berry vines, hound's tongue, milkmaids, blue-eyed grass and Indian warrior. Traverse short ups and downs through woods of madrone, oak and Douglas fir above the shore.

Descend to a junction in a gully with maidenhair fern, wild grape, bedstraw, Chinese houses, checker lily and bunch grass at 7/8 mile. Take the right fork on a gradual ascent along the gully beneath California buckeyes. Cross the gully and climb by two switchbacks, then ascend gradually along another gully.

You soon reach a ridge, joining a dirt road where the road bends right in 100 feet. Veer left on the horse trail, descending gradually, then steeply. Your descent eases around 1¼ miles. Climb briefly to rejoin the road and descend to the spillway, where you veer left on the narrow path heading northeast. It ascends to 1½ miles, then descends to the lake shore.

The trail climbs through woodlands with madrones, blue and white oaks, then contours through scrubby woodland where the grassy understory has mule ears, buttercup, yarrow and poison oak. Descend into a small gully, then a larger one. Your path turns right to ascend the second gully. Switchback to the right for a winding contour above the shore around 1¾ miles.

Dip through a gully and climb 50 feet to a fork. (The left fork ends in 200 feet.) Take the rutted right fork, climbing moderately, then gradually through woodlands.

Your road ends around 2 miles. To continue around the lake, take the trail contouring northeast through grasslands with scattered oaks and manzanitas. After crossing a small gully, descend gradually through grasslands rich with lupine in spring. Descend a ridgetop at 2⅜ miles, with a view across the lake to the dam. The path bends right, leaving the ridge on a moderate winding descent. Level and pass through a fence line, then ascend east through grasslands.

The path ends at a broad road beyond 2½ miles. (If you go left the road ends at the shore in ⅛ mile.) Turn right to climb steeply on the road. A broad trail forks left at 2⅝ miles. (It descends east to East Shore Trail in about ¼ mile.) Stay on the road that climbs moderately to a hilltop with a grand view. Your road descends to a saddle, then contours on the ridgetop.

Climb to a junction at 3 miles, where a broad path descends on the right. Continue straight, ascending moderately on the ridge road. It ends at East Shore Trail before 3⅛ miles, where you can go left or right. (If you go left, it is 3¾ miles to Bu-shay Campground at the lake's northeast corner.) Our described hike turns right, climbing briefly to a 1140-foot knob, the highest point on the loop. The road dips to a saddle, then climbs to a second knob, overlooking the Ukiah Valley.

Your road descends along the ridgetop, then contours to a confusing junction beyond 3⅜ miles. Turn right and descend 75 feet to a second junction, where you turn left. This road climbs briefly, then descends west to 3½ miles where a firebreak is on your left. Take the horse trail that bends right, descending. It soon winds left, passing the bottom of the firebreak, then bends left, descending in a spiraling plunge. At a steep bend right, you overlook the spillway, then continue the spiral descent.

The track bends right to contour north before a moderate winding descent to the spillway at 4 miles. Cross the broad channel and bear right to retrace your steps on the trail you came out on. Be careful not to take wrong turns on the way back. Some spur trails end at coves with impassable terrain beyond.

7.
LOW GAP PARK LOOP
NATURE IN THE CITY

A principal Northern Pomo village called Komli (meaning "soda spring") was located north of Orr Creek on the west side of Ukiah Valley, not far from where Low Gap Park is today. The valley was claimed by both the Northern Pomo and the Central or Yokaia Pomo, for whom the valley and town were named. Pomo oral history says this feud erupted into battle in the early nineteenth century, causing the people of Komli to move to Scotts Valley west of Clear Lake.

Oak woodland habitat, like this trail traverses, was extremely important in Pomo life. Not only were acorns the staple of their diet, but most other plants and animals the Pomo depended upon thrived in oak woodlands, a habitat more predominant before the changes wrought by European settlers.

Sam Lowry became the first outsider to settle in the valley in 1856. After a year he sold out to A. T. Perkins, who became a permanent resident. When the settlement was chosen as Mendocino County seat in 1859, only 100 white people lived in the whole Ukiah Valley.

Low Gap Park, established 1973, comprises 80 acres along Orr Creek. The park, managed jointly by the City of Ukiah and Mendocino County, is popular for varied recreational activities. The park was once the site of a county dump and a small lumber mill. Today more than half the park remains in a natural state. Its wild corners offer an accessible respite from the bustle of Ukiah. County Parks Director Art Kramer asserts the park has over 6 miles of trails. This loop and the two "OTHER SUGGESTIONS" sample about half of them. You can vary the

LOW GAP PARK LOOP:

DISTANCE: 1⅝-mile loop, plus options.

TIME: One or two hours.

TERRAIN: Through woods along creek, then climbs and descends steep hillside.

ELEVATION: TH: 720 feet. Gain/loss: 240 feet+/240 feet-.

BEST TIME: Early spring for wildflowers. Hot in summer, although pleasant in early morning.

WARNINGS: Watch for poison oak and flying frisbees. No horse or bike riding on park trails.

DIRECTIONS TO TRAILHEAD: From Highway 101, take North Ukiah/North State Street exit (M.26.2 from north, M.25.9 from south). Go .6 mile south to Low Gap Road, then west one mile to park entrance on left.

FURTHER INFO: Mendocino County Parks (707) 463-4267.

OTHER SUGGESTION: LOWER ORR CREEK TRAIL turns left after bridge over Orr Creek, heading downstream ¼ mile to end at golf course. GOLF COURSE TRAIL descends east across tributary of Orr Creek, then loops through northeast corner of park. Park offers bikers good staging area for weekend rides up LOW GAP ROAD; watch for vehicle traffic.

described loop by taking one of the many secondary paths interweaving the park's trails.

Incidentally, Ukiah Valley was a hub of native trails heading in the four cardinal directions, including the easiest route to the coast, west over Low Gap and along ridges between the Navarro, Albion and Big Rivers. Today Low Gap and Comptche-Ukiah Roads generally follow the old coast trail.

From the parking lot, walk west to the turnstile beside the green gate signed "RECREATION AREAS ACROSS ORR CREEK." Descend the paved path, cross a bridge over Orr Creek and meet a junction. (Lower Orr Creek Trail is on the left.) Take the broad paved trail on the right, climbing gently along the creek.

Fork right at ⅛ mile on narrow, dirt Orr Creek Trail. Descend gradually across a grassy area to a directional sign. The path parallels the creek upstream, traversing woodlands with oaks, bay laurel, California buckeye and toyon. Soap plant and buttercup thrive in the shady understory. As you ascend

43

vaw. 92

gradually, you might see shooting stars blooming as early as February and lilies, including mission bells, in March and April. (A spur on the right descends to the creek before ¼ mile.)

Your trail continues up the creek past California mountain mahogany, bedstraw and hairy honeysuckle beneath blue oaks and manzanita. Brodiaeas bloom March to May. Soon a large Fremont silktassel shrub is on your right. Climb briefly by a rock outcrop draped with leather ferns and mosses, with wood rose and columbine nearby. After a brief descent, plunge through a tunnel of vines beside the creek. Contour upstream past bear grass, maidenhair fern, redwood and live oak brush.

Climb moderately through a stand of madrones to a junction. (The left fork returns to the park's center.) Bear right across a small bridge and ascend a sunny path lined with buckeyes and blue oaks. This West End Loop doubles as a fitness course.

Descend briefly to contour through a small meadow. Pass a picnic table on the left as you parallel the creek, returning to woodland. Reach the park boundary at ½ mile. Your path bends left and climbs gently. Although blue oak dominates the woodland, five other oaks grow nearby: evergreen canyon and interior live oaks, deciduous white, black and valley oaks.

Cross the top of the small meadow, then wind up a hill for a view west up Low Gap Canyon. Descend to the end of West End

44

Loop beside a sundial at ⅝ mile. Bear right on the broad path lined with manzanita, madrone and coyote bush. At another junction in 200 feet, continue straight on a moderate ascent. (The left fork leads to the park's center.)

You soon enter a grassy clearing. Go straight where a path forks left to a picnic table and drinking fountain overlooking Ukiah. Go 50 feet, pass a madrone, turn right and ascend moderately. This narrow footpath, Canyon Creek Trail, is lined with hound's tongue in spring.

Just beyond ¾ mile (250 feet from the last junction), the trail forks. Bear left on the steep path switchbacking left and right, climbing through oak/madrone woodland. Switchback left as the ascent eases through a clearing, then switchback right, climbing into forest. Bear left at another junction and ascend southwest. After crossing a dark gully, your trail bends left. Ascend moderately by short switchbacks through a small stand of young redwoods, then past more madrones, ignoring several side paths.

The trail levels amidst chaparral dominated by chamise and manzanita. A rest bench on the right offers a great view of Ukiah Valley with Cow Mountain beyond. Sanhedrin Mountain (6175', snow-capped in winter) rises north-northeast. Your path descends gently through scrubby forest with yerba santa and sticky monkeyflower in the understory.

Ford a seasonal creek beyond one mile, then veer left to contour east. Fawn lilies flower in spring beneath California nutmeg, madrone, bay laurel, oak and redwoods. Wind away from the creek, descending moderately. Where a path forks left to the upper picnic area, continue straight, descending through open woodlands mixed with grasslands.

Canyon Creek Trail ends at 1¼ miles. (The trail to the right ascends into a "mini-wilderness" in the park's southeast corner. Watch for poison oak if you explore the fork of Orr Creek there.) The described loop turns left, descending north. You may find wildflowers around a tiny vernal pool in spring. Descend gently, enjoying views of the valley below and the highlands beyond.

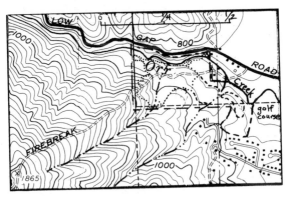

After a small footpath merges with your broad path, continue your descent. Fork right in 120 feet (passing Disc Golf Tee #15) and descend east along the park boundary.

The trail meets the end of a paved park road around 1⅜ miles. If you turn right, a restroom is behind the park caretaker's residence, with a picnic area beyond. (The side trail descending east over the creek is the Golf Course Trail.) The described loop turns left to descend the paved park maintenance road, coming to a "T" intersection in the heart of the park at 1½ miles. If you are not staying for a picnic, turn right and descend past the start of Orr Creek Trail in 200 feet, then retrace your steps for another ⅛ mile to the parking lot.

COW MOUNTAIN
RECREATION AREA

Cow Mountain, the high ridge east of Ukiah, is the northern end of the Mayacmas Range, which extends southeast 70 miles to end near Sonoma. This part of the range was created by folding and coastal uplifting, while portions to the south are of volcanic origin. The range was named for the Mayakmah (or Wappo) people who inhabited the range south of Cobb Mountain. The Pomo controlled the north end of the Mayacmas Range.

The Northern Pomo had a village called Smewakapda (meaning "wolf water creek") near the forks of Mill Creek, about two miles west of Mayacmas Trail. The people of the village spent the long wet winters at this home base. In summer they camped on the Russian River, catching abundant fish and enjoying the breezes. In autumn they roamed the hills, working hard to gather food for the winter. A native trail over Cow Mountain led to Pomo villages at Scotts Valley and Clear Lake. The modern trails on Cow Mountain follow portions of the traditional route.

Cow Mountain was named for the longhorn cattle early American settlers found running wild in these hills. The cattle were offspring of a herd brought to the Clear Lake area in 1839 by Salvador Vallejo, brother of Mariano Vallejo, the commander of Mexican forces at Sonoma.

The U. S. Congress set aside 50,000 acres on Cow Mountain in 1927. Now managed by the Bureau of Land Management's Ukiah office, today's Recreation Area includes 60,000 acres, predominantly chaparral on steep slopes, with pockets of knobcone pine and old-growth Douglas fir forest. Motor vehicles are restricted to roads within the area explored by the described trails. About 23,000 acres of Cow Mountain Recreation Area are open to off-road vehicles. (The OTHER SUGGESTION for Trail #11 is a hike in the area open to off-road vehicles.)

8.

MAYACMAS FROM WILLOW CREEK
STREAMSIDE OASIS AMIDST MOUNTAIN OF BRUSH

This hike, part of a projected 4½-mile Mayacmas Trail scheduled for completion in 1994, traverses some of the most lush, botanically diverse terrain on Cow Mountain. It is heavenly in spring, when the riot of plants along Willow Creek bursts forth in response to winter rains.

From the cul-de-sac at road's end, go through a low stile and walk north 100 feet to a split in the trail. Go left across a small bridge in dense woods of willow, Oregon ash and knobcone pine. You quickly climb above the creek into chaparral with chamise, California mountain mahogany and buck brush. Look for soap plant, wood rose, bedstraw, Ithuriel's spear, fork-toothed ookow, Chinese houses and mugwort in the understory.

Your path turns northeast paralleling the creek. Pass poison oak, mule ears, yellow globe lily, paintbrush, ground cone, blue field gilia, angelica and red larkspur amidst scrubby bay laurel and live oak. Disregard a side trail on the left. Mayacmas Trail passes above a cattail-lined pond where madrones and large live oaks grow. In spring hound's tongue, fat solomon's seal, deadly nightshade and narrow-leaved mule ears line your path above the pond.

Begin a gradual descent at ⅛ mile, passing snowberry, gooseberry, starflower and Oregon grape. After a brief climb, descend past checker lilies, also called mission bells. In spring you may also spot vetch, buttercups, miners lettuce, fairy bells and slim solomon's seal. The trail approaches tiny Willow Creek as the ground becomes rocky. Sword and other ferns, moss, celery-leaved lovage and alum root grow between the trail and

DISTANCE: **1⅜ miles** (2¾ miles round trip).

TIME: One or two hours.

TERRAIN: Descends gently along lush canyon, then moderately through forest to overlook confluence of Willow Creek and North Fork Mill Creek.

ELEVATION: TH: 2440 feet. Gain/loss: 60 feet+/700 feet-.

BEST TIME: Spring for wildflowers.

WARNINGS: Watch for rattlesnakes and poison oak.

DIRECTIONS TO TRAILHEAD: Exit Highway 101 at Talmage (M.23.7 from north, M.23.3 from south) south of Ukiah. Go east 2 miles, then right on Eastside Road. In .3 mile, go left on Mill Creek Road. In 2.7 miles turn left on steep, winding dirt Road 203C (no trailers or RV's). In 2.5 miles, go left to Willow Creek Recreation Site. Take left fork in .15 mile and drive .2 mile to trailhead.

FURTHER INFO: Bureau of Land Management (707) 462-3873.

OTHER SUGGESTION: Especially for equestrians, VALLEY VIEW TRAIL, 2.2 miles from Eastside Road, climbs steeply (+1300 feet) for 3 miles from Mill Creek County Park to meet the described hike at ¼ mile. OTHER TRAILS IN MILL CREEK PARK climb steep slope south of ponds.

the creek.

A trail forks left at ¼ mile, climbing into chaparral. (That is the Valley View Trail, which climbs to an overlook before descending west and south 3 miles to Mill Creek County Park.) Stay to the right on the trail along the creek.

The next section of lush creekside vegetation has many California buckeye trees, among the first deciduous plants to leaf out in spring. Look beneath their bright green foliage for trillium, maidenhair fern and cream bush.

Your trail fords to the north side of the seasonal creek, where oaks and bay laurels grow forty feet tall. Before returning to the south bank in 250 feet, pass more lilies, desert elderberry, cow parsnip, Indian pink and lovely Clarkia. Climb briefly into chaparral above the creek, then drop to another ford. Delicate coffee fern thrives on the moist, sunny south bank.

Your path climbs gently, angling away from the creek along slopes favored by large live oaks and buckeyes. A surprising array of wildflowers in spring include tongue Clarkia, lace pod and narrow-petalled sedum. You soon pass chamise and toyon.

A view opens up down steep North Fork Mill Creek Canyon and across Ukiah Valley to the high hills beyond. Descend past the yellow flowers of houndstongue hawkweed and arnica, yellow- and white-flowered lomatiums and shooting star. At ½ mile you overlook a wooded side canyon with California nutmeg. The Pomo used its roots in their beautiful baskets.

Your trail, easy to this point, becomes steeper and rougher. Switchback left, descending past wood rose, vanilla grass and trail plant. Drop down a steep slope by ten rough steps. As the path switchbacks right, you overlook Willow Creek. An 80-foot-tall nutmeg at the switchback is approaching the limits of the

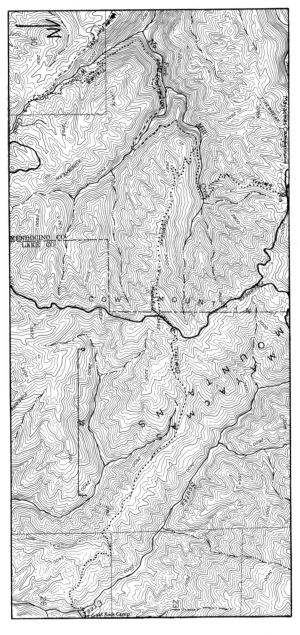

species. The creek, lined with bigleaf maple, oaks and bay laurel, tumbles steeply down a jumble of various-sized rocks.

Cross a tributary of Willow Creek lined with elk clover. The path bends left and drops gradually along Willow Creek through hardwood forest with abundant nutmeg. Large woodwardia ferns grow in Willow Creek beyond ¾ mile. Descend more steps as the stream plunges steeply away from the trail.

The path beyond this point is more rugged, steep in spots. You have views down the canyon as you descend steps past manroot vines. Descend across a sunny, mostly bare slope where fiddlenecks and tiny vari-leaf nemophila grow.

Switchback left and approach Willow Creek once again at one mile, then switchback to the right to follow it downstream. Traverse a steep slope on tread prone to rock slides, passing very large bay laurels and live oaks. Descend more steps along the steep slope as the creek drops steeply. Ascend past poison oak, vetch, buttercups, brodiaeas, Purdy's iris, and the delicate white flowers of woodland star.

At 1¼ miles your trail bends right as it enters the larger, steeper canyon of North Fork Mill Creek. Vegetation is lush on this north-facing slope. Use caution if you continue on the rough trail up the canyon. Poison oak grows profusely here. You may also see inside-out flower and western coltsfoot.

The trail, marked with red plastic flagging, becomes rough and indistinct by 1⅜ miles, traversing a precipitous slope. BLM plans to improve the trail by 1994, joining it with Upper Mayacmas Trail (Trail #9). We recommend you turn back here until the trail has been extended. (In May 1992, trail work was in progress from 1¼ to 2 miles.)

9.

UPPER MAYACMAS

FROM BRUSHY MOUNTAIN TO WOODED CREEK

Mayacmas Camp offers solitude and beauty in steep, wild terrain only 12 miles from Highway 101 near Ukiah. The winding dirt access road (unsafe for trailers or large recreational vehicles) climbs steeply. You will leave most of civilization's trappings behind whether you go for the day, a weekend or a week. The pleasant camp offers nine sites beneath large black oaks along a grassy ridgetop overlooking the surrounding steep and wild terrain. The price is right, too—it's free. Bring your own water. The Mayacmas Trail, projected for completion by 1994, will be part of an extensive trail network linking with Glen Eden and Valley View Trails. If you stay at Mayacmas Camp, be sure to explore the Upper Glen Eden Trail (Trail #10), about 1½ miles back along the access road.

UPPER MAYACMAS:

DISTANCE: 1¼ **miles** (2½ miles round trip).
TIME: One or two hours.
TERRAIN: Descends chaparral-covered ridge to wooded creek.
ELEVATION: TH: 3000 feet. Gain/loss: 20 feet+/600 feet-.
BEST TIME: Spring for wildflowers.
WARNINGS: Watch for rattlesnakes and poison oak.
DIRECTIONS TO TRAILHEAD: Exit Highway 101 at Talmage
   (M23.7 from north, M. 23.3 from south) south of Ukiah. Go
   east 2 miles, then right on Eastside Road. In .3 mile, go left
   on Mill Creek Road. In 2.7 miles turn left on steep, winding
   dirt Road 203C (no trailers or RV's). In 2.5 miles go right (left
   to Willow Creek). Go 4 miles, then take left fork (rough in
   spots) .75 mile, where trailhead is on left, beside water
   trough at Mayacmas Campground entrance.
FURTHER INFO: Bureau of Land Management (707) 462-3873.
OTHER SUGGESTION: DIRT ROADS AND FIREBREAKS in this
   area offer miles of opportunity for mountain bikers; you can
   continue north on the main road for 3 miles.

Follow the trail southwest from the water trough, winding over
a small rise before beginning a gradual descent along a ridgetop.
Drop through chaparral that includes manzanita, chamise,
toyon, interior live oak, soap plant and extensive poison oak.
Two ceanothus species thrive here, white-flowered buck brush
and blue-flowered warty-leaved ceanothus. Views expand to
the deep Ukiah Valley on your right and the western flank of the
Coast Range beyond. You can see several of Cow Mountain's
summits, including Mendo Rock on the left.

Continue your ridgetop descent beyond ¼ mile, where
pennyroyal and yerba santa grow in your path. Coyote bush
joins the chaparral as the descent steepens. Switchback right
and left as the path narrows dropping toward North Fork Mill
Creek Canyon. Notice the conifer forest on the steep north-
facing slope beyond the creek.

Your path levels beyond ⅝ mile, then bends right. Brush soon
crowds the trail. Switchback left around ¾ mile, passing
California mountain mahogany as you angle southeast on a
gradual but steady descent. Your path winds right, then quickly
switchbacks left as the brush gets deeper.

The track bends to the right, pointing down-canyon at 7/8 mile, where the conifer forest is not far across the ravine. You may hear the creek burbling as you descend, switchbacking left, right and left. After a short straightaway, drop steeply by two more switchbacks.

At one mile you overlook the confluence of the side canyon to your east with the canyon of North Fork Mill Creek. The path switchbacks right and left, leaving chaparral for scrubby forest where hedge nettle, brodiaea and bedstraw grow in spring.

After reaching the lip of the side canyon, your trail turns sharply left and descends beneath live oaks and bay laurels. In spring the understory has sword fern, shooting star, red larkspur and lilies. Cross the side canyon and descend along its east side past buckeye, nutmeg, wood rose, trail plant, gooseberry and tiny pink starflower.

As you come to the main canyon, the trail turns left and heads upstream briefly. Cross another side canyon and veer right to ford North Fork Mill Creek before 1¼ miles, where miners lettuce, giant trillium, and yellow stream violets thrive along moist, shady banks. The trail turns downstream, paralleling the creek past Douglas firs four feet wide mixed with madrones and oaks. Snowberry and poison oak inhabit the understory.

The path gets progressively rougher as it wanders downstream. You meet the west end of Glen Eden Trail as it descends the steep wooded hillside to your south. Use caution if you continue downstream, watching for poison oak and steep drops along the steepening creek. The creek plunges 700 feet in the next 1½ miles. BLM plans to link this with the rest of Mayacmas Trail by 1994 (see Trail #8). Until then it is best to turn back and explore another wild corner of Cow Mountain.

10.
GLEN EDEN FROM MENDO ROCK
OLD POMO TRAIL REVIVED BY LAKE EQUESTRIANS

This trail follows an ancient Pomo route used for travel between villages in Ukiah Valley and the Clear Lake area. It was part of a longer route between Clear Lake and the coast near Big River, the main artery of Northern Pomo trade. Glen Eden Trail has been rebuilt primarily through the efforts of the Clear Lake Horseman's Association. This volunteer group has done much of the trail work as well as lobbying BLM to finish the trail. The Association hopes eventually to extend the trail to the coast. You can camp overnight at the confluence of Scotts and Black Oak Springs Creeks, an area particularly beautiful in spring.

GLEN EDEN FROM MENDO ROCK:

DISTANCE: **6½ miles to Scotts Valley Trailhead**; 2⅝ miles to Scotts Creek, 2¾ miles to Goat Rock Camp (5½ miles round trip).

TIME: Half day to overnight.

TERRAIN: Descends brushy ridge, then switchbacks down to creek and camp.

ELEVATION: TH: 3400 feet. Gain/loss: 120 feet+/1480 feet-.

BEST TIME: Spring for wildflowers and flowing water in creeks.

WARNINGS: Watch for rattlesnakes and poison oak. Steep climb back to trailhead. Creeks may be dry by late summer. Mountain bikes only allowed on upper 3 miles; watch for/yield to equestrians and hikers.

DIRECTIONS TO TRAILHEAD: Exit Highway 101 at Talmage (M.23.7 from north, M.23.3 from south) south of Ukiah. Go east 2 miles, then right on Eastside Road. In .3 mile, go left on Mill Creek Road 2.7 miles, then left on steep dirt Road 203C (no trailers or RV's). In 2.5 miles go right (left to Willow Creek) 3.1 miles to trailhead, on right near green gate.

FURTHER INFO: Bureau of Land Management (707) 462-3873.

OTHER SUGGESTION: Across Road 203C from trailhead, GLEN EDEN TRAIL now HEADS WEST, climbing along ridgetop before descending to meet Upper Mayacmas Trail (Trail #9) in 2 miles. You can also take GLEN EDEN TRAIL FROM SCOTTS VALLEY (east end—Trail #12).

Your trail, unmarked at the trailhead, ascends east through chaparral past a green gate and around a 3400-foot ridgetop knob. Begin a steady descent along a brushy ridge at ⅛ mile, enjoying a grand view of Clear Lake and Mount Konocti as you pass scattered knobcone pines. You can see Cobb Mountain (4722') 30 miles southeast. The plumes of the Sonoma County geysers may be visible to its right on cool, clear days.

The trail bends left at ¼ mile as the descent steepens. Chaparral along the path includes poison oak, live oak, manzanita, chamise, yerba santa, white-flowered buck brush and blue-flowered deer brush. Drop steeply by 13 short switchbacks, then descend moderately along the ridge. In spring you may see the bright green leaves of lomatium, a plant with edible parts.

Descend through a stand of knobcone pines on the ridgetop

at ½ mile. The path winds out of the pines, then returns to them briefly as you head east. Ascend a small knob at ¾ mile. Your trail turns southeast, paralleling a canyon on the right as the descent turns gradual.

Ascend briefly at one mile, then contour past madrone, blueblossom, wood rose and toyon as the canyon on your right gets deeper. On your left Cow Mountain rises beyond the canyon of Scotts Creek. As you descend gently along the ridgetop, the canyon on the right merges with a larger, more wooded canyon. The path winds down the ridge, then climbs to a pine-covered knob at 1½ miles.

Resume descending as views expand of Scotts Creek Canyon to the north and the canyon of Black Oak Springs Creek to the east. Pennyroyal and the multiple white star-shaped flowers of star zygadene grow along the path. As you pass a rock outcrop on your right at 1⅝ miles, look for delicate hairy star tulips. Your path contours through a grassy area along the ridge.

The trail bends sharply left at 1⅞ miles, leaving the main ridge for a steady, winding descent on a spur ridge dense with chamise. Scattered ceanothus and manzanita, then a cluster of knobcone pines join the chaparral. Descend steeply at 2¼ miles. Return to the top of the spur ridge by 2⅜ miles, dropping gradually through chamise.

You soon make a sharp left turn, leaving the ridge to descend toward the large glade at the confluence of Scotts and Black Oak Springs Creek, winding down through dense chaparral on the most recently cleared portion of trail. Switchback to the right at 2⅝ miles and ford Scotts Creek, which may be dry by late summer. Serviceberry, fairy bells and wood rose grow beneath alders and bay laurels along the stream.

Your trail climbs east into the grasslands, passing below large, arresting Goat Rock jutting from the hillside. Pass a four-foot-diameter oak, then descend south to ford Black Oak Springs Creek at 2¾ miles. Two tables and a fire pit on the north bank constitute Goat Rock Camp. The valley is lush green and sparkling with wildflowers in spring. By summer the fire danger is extreme and the creeks slow to a trickle or dry up altogether. Black Oak Springs Creek is also known as Jack Hurt Creek, after an early settler.

Glen Eden Trail continues 3¾ miles to the Scotts Valley Trailhead, climbing east over Little Cow Mountain, then descending steeply. This eastern portion of the trail crosses private property on a restricted easement over which mountain bikes are not allowed. Trail #12 details the eastern portion of the route. Save some energy and plenty of water for the arduous ascent back to the trailhead on Cow Mountain Ridge.

54

iw.92

11.

FETZER VALLEY OAKS GARDEN
ORGANIC FARM FOR WEEKEND STROLLS

Valley Oaks, established as a livestock farm in 1910, was purchased by Fetzer Vineyards in 1984. The Fetzer family manages the 1400 acres at Valley Oaks as an organic farm, foregoing pesticides and using natural fertilizers and cover crops to demonstrate that medium scale agriculture can thrive with properly applied non-chemical methods. Fetzer operates the 4½-acre Garden Project, where over 1000 varieties are grown throughout the year. They use the biodynamic, French-intensive system Alan Chadwick popularized at the University of California, Santa Cruz campus and later at the Covelo Garden Project. This system uses naturally enriched soil in raised beds, companion planting and optimum spacing to achieve maximum yield, quality and flavor.

From the parking area, walk south through a shady picnic area and past the restrooms. Stop in at the Visitor Center, register and pick up a brochure and map of the Garden Project. Go out the front door, turn left and head south on the road that soon becomes dirt, passing old vineyards bright with yellow mustard in spring. Cross a small stone bridge, reaching the signed Garden Project beyond ⅛ mile. Jog right at the intersection and head toward craggy Duncan Peak. In 75 feet a sign explains the garden rules and defines the term "organic."

Fork left on the lamppost-lined path into the garden, taking the first right turn to signs explaining raised beds and drip irrigation. Go south on the brick path through the plum/herb crescent, a semicircle rimmed by plum trees.

At the end of the brick path, jog left, then go right on the path circling the garden clockwise. Palmette espaliered apples are on your right. On the left a mixed flower border beneath fuyu persimmon trees adds bright colors.

Reach an intersection at ¼ mile. (The path on the left explores

55

FETZER VALLEY OAKS GARDEN:

DISTANCE: ⅝-mile loop plus options, totalling 2¾ miles.
TIME: One to three hours.
TERRAIN: Level paths on valley floor.
ELEVATION: TH (trailhead): 500 feet.
BEST TIME: Any weekend.
WARNINGS: Open weekends and holidays only.
DIRECTIONS TO TRAILHEAD: Turn east off Highway 101 at
  Hopland, opposite Fetzer Tasting Room (M.10.9), onto
  Highway 175. Go .7 mile to entrance to Valley Oaks (at East
  Side Road). Go .5 mile to parking area.
FURTHER INFO: Fetzer Valley Oaks (707) 744-1250.
OTHER SUGGESTION: On weekdays, SHELDON CREEK
  CAMPGROUND in southern end of Cow Mountain Recreation
  Area has undeveloped hike, bike and equestrian choices. Turn
  right off Highway 175 onto Old Toll Road (2.7 miles from
  Highway 101). Go 7.3 miles, then left on road signed
  "SHELDON CREEK RECREATION SITE." Go one mile to creek
  and wheelchair-accessible toilet. Take left fork .1 mile to park
  beside water fountain (water must be purified). A ROUGH
  PATH heads west across a gully to join old road. Road ends
  before ⅛ mile, where you must scramble up steep hill to the
  trail climbing north through a steep glade to a ridge. Go right
  on fire road beyond ¼ mile, climbing steeply to hilltop
  junction at ⅝ mile, where a left turn heads east to main ridge
  of Mayacmas Range. Avoid in summer (too hot) and autumn
  (crowded with hunters and off-road vehicles).

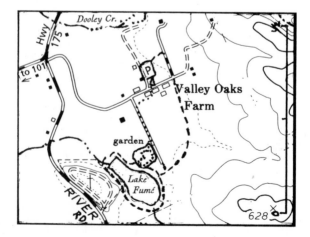

guavas, table grapes and a kiwi/blackberry trellis in the first 75 feet, then leads to the compost area, surrounded by immense, graceful valley oaks.) Continue on the path toward Duncan Peak, soon coming to the culinary demonstration kitchen beside Lake Fumé. The lake is graced by a black swan and used by coots and ducks. Red-wing blackbirds favor the cattails south of the kitchen.

Our described loop, the wheelchair-accessible path, goes right. (You can turn left for a ⅜-mile loop through the apple orchard back to the garden entrance or a ¾-mile loop through the vineyards and back to the parking lot—see map.) Head north between lake and garden for 100 feet, where the path on the right returns to garden's center.

(If you want a longer, slightly rougher hike, veer left on the concrete path around the edge of the lake. Where the path ends in 400 feet, scramble across the lake's rocky outlet. A ranch road on the west bank heads south around the lake. In about ½ mile, veer left and head east across a bridge at the head of the lake, passing soap plant and poison oak, then willows and a stand of tall slender oaks. Turn left and walk 200 feet, then go left around the lake to complete the one-mile loop.)

Follow the path through the center of the garden between rows of espaliered apples. At the intersection in 200 feet, a drinking fountain is on the north corner. Turn left past an assortment of vegetables, meeting another path before ⅜ mile.

Turn right and go 50 feet to the rest benches beneath a huge valley oak. This shady spot has a view of Duncan Peak. The edible flower crescent before you has at least ten varieties of palatable blooms, including nasturtium, borage, day-lily, calendula and mint. Feel free to taste a flower from that bed.

Continue east until the path comes to a "T" intersection. Jog right for 40 feet, then go left before another drinking fountain and return to the lamppost-lined path. Go left and retrace your route to the parking lot, completing a basic loop of ⅝ mile.

12.

GLEN EDEN FROM SCOTTS VALLEY

OVER LITTLE COW MOUNTAIN TO GOAT ROCK CAMP

A group of Northern Pomo called Moal-kai lived on the fertile land of deep Scotts Valley. Their main village, Norboral, was two miles south of the trailhead, but several small villages were nearby. The Moal-kai spent most of their time around Scotts Valley, but also had camps on Clear Lake, where they would take their tule canoes out to fish. The entire Scotts Creek watershed upstream from Blue Lakes was their territory, including Cow

GLEN EDEN FROM SCOTTS VALLEY:

DISTANCE: **3¾ miles to Goat Rock Camp** (7½ miles round trip), 6½ miles to end of trail.

TIME: Full day or overnight.

TERRAIN: Climbs steeply through woodland, then moderately on ridge to mountain top; descends through glades and woodlands to confluence of creeks.

ELEVATION: TH: 1380 feet. Gain/loss: 1880 feet+/1340-.

BEST TIME: Spring for wildflowers. Nice October to May, generally too hot in summer.

WARNINGS: Watch for rattlesnakes and poison oak. Creeks may be dry by late summer. No mountain bikes on this end of trail. Stay on trail (on private property) for first 2⅛ miles.

DIRECTIONS TO TRAILHEAD: FROM WEST: Exit Highway 101 onto Highway 20 east (M.30.6 from south, M.30.7 from north). Go east 15 miles to Scotts Valley Road (M.3.6, Lake County), then south 2.6 miles to signed trailhead on right. FROM SOUTH: Take Highway 29 to Lakeport. Exit at 11th Street (M.42.9, Lake County) and go west on Scotts Valley Road 9.5 miles to trailhead on left.

FROM EAST: Exit Interstate 5 near Williams onto Highway 20 West. Go 65 miles, then left on Scotts Valley Road 2.6 miles.

FURTHER INFO: Bureau of Land Management (707) 462-3873.

OTHER SUGGESTION: You can also take GLEN EDEN TRAIL FROM MENDO ROCK (west end—Trail #10).

Mountain's eastern slopes. Today's trail approximates an old Pomo route that crossed Cow Mountain and continued to the coast.

The first 2⅛ miles of the modern trail cross private property on an easement six feet wide. Please stay on the trail and respect adjacent private property. The easement also specifies no mountain bikes. Motorized vehicles are also forbidden. This trail is open thanks to the efforts of the Clear Lake Horseman's Association, a volunteer group. A pleasant picnic area with a hand-pumped well lies across the road from the trailhead. A private campground, Kelly's Kamp, is to the north, with other private campgrounds around Blue Lakes.

From the sign on the west side of the road, your trail climbs steeply west beneath valley oaks. Watch for poison oak as you ascend moderately, switchbacking left and right. Live oaks and bay laurels soon mix with the valley oaks. Switchback left and contour west briefly past honeysuckle vines. The path bends left to climb gradually past bedstraw and lilies. You soon switchback right, ascending past deer brush, California mountain mahogany and mule ears, then switchback left to climb through stands of manzanita and toyon.

By ¼ mile you reach the edge of a brushy canyon jammed with chamise and yerba santa. Your trail switchbacks right, climbing past large madrones. Starflowers carpet the ground in spring. Switchback left and right, climbing steeply past redbud and buck brush. The path bends left to ascend moderately. Soon the route is densely lined with invasive star thistle. Watch for its sharp spines, deadly to livestock.

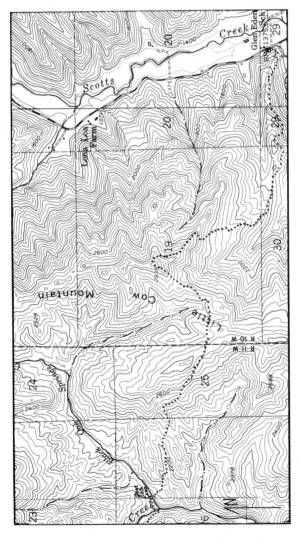

A sign warns of private property as the trail joins an old road bed, leaving woodlands to climb moderately through chaparral. Descend briefly, then resume a gradual ascent where currant, toyon, California nutmeg and buckeye tangle in brush. Beyond ⅝ mile your road parallels a brush-choked canyon on the right.

Come to a gate before ¾ mile. Please close it behind you. The road climbs southwest on a ridge, with a few dips as chamise dominates the chaparral. Ascend steeply on the winding ridgetop track beyond one mile. Descend briefly, then climb through a stand of oaks before 1¼ miles. Their cool shade provides welcome relief from the hot ascent. You pass a water trough on the left, then leave the road on a path climbing northwest through alternating pockets of oak, grassland and brush.

Chaparral dominates again as you make a winding ascent with views expanding to Clear Lake and Mount Konocti. After rabbitbrush joins the vegetative tangle, your route rejoins the old road on a winding ascent.

Beyond 1⅝ miles the track merges with a dirt road still used by ranch vehicles. Stay left, continuing a steady climb. The road levels atop Little Cow Mountain at 1⅞ miles, then descends slightly with grand views of Clear Lake.

Before the road resumes ascending, veer right on a trail that descends west, shaded by madrones and live oaks. The path levels briefly, then descends, switchbacking right and left. Your trail bends right to cross a gully at 2⅛ miles where wild grapes grow. Ascend gradually, then steeply. After a switchback left, the path climbs gradually.

Your trail bends right, ascending moderately past gray pines. Reach a ridgetop with views north to the mountains of Mendocino National Forest. Your track dips and rises, heading south along the ridgetop. Turn west through scrubby oak woodland at 2⅜ miles, then resume a southward ascent.

The trail crosses a road at a right angle and climbs briefly to a ridgetop, then descends beneath oaks. The path drops through grasslands with scattered oaks. A winding, moderate descent passes patches of chaparral, then junipers, mule ears and poison oak. Your trail makes a big bend left at 2¾ miles to descend south by three switchbacks. Oaks and grasslands are above you, with chamise-dense chaparral on the left.

Contour, then resume a gradual winding descent. Your trail levels briefly beyond 3 miles, then descends through more chaparral. The trail bends left and ascends, then makes a winding contour to 3¼ miles. Descend past more junipers, then turn west to descend gradually through grasslands with turkey mullein and naked stem buckwheat, following a gully.

Cross the drainage at 3½ miles and descend along its southeast side where deer brush, California mountain mahogany and live oaks grow. Cross the gully again and ascend its north slope briefly, then descend moderately. The big outcrop ahead is called Goat Rock.

The descent ends at Black Oak Springs Creek at 3¾ miles. Ford the creek (may be dry in late summer and fall) to the pleasant camp on the north bank, where two tables and a fire ring sit, with milkweed growing nearby. This valley is brilliantly green and dappled with wildflowers in spring. Fire danger (and often temperature) is extreme by June.

Glen Eden Trail continues, fording Scotts Creek and ascending a ridge, coming to Cow Mountain Ridge near Mendo Rock in another 2¾ miles. For details of the western portion of the trail, see Trail #10.

13.
DORN NATURE LOOP
OAK WOODLAND RAMBLE WITH VIEWS AND FLOWERS

The Clear Lake area was formed by an island of volcanic activity much younger than and unrelated to the Sonoma volcanic area to the south. Starting about two million years ago, molten rocks heaped atop the ancient, tectonically uplifted ocean floor that remains the earth's surface to the north and west. Mount Konocti, the potentially active 4299-foot composite volcano towering over Clear Lake, last erupted about 10,000 years ago.

In California, only Lake Tahoe exceeds Clear Lake in size. Geologists surmise Clear Lake was formed from smaller lakes by two major geological events. A lava flow on the east shore dammed the outlet to Cache Creek, raising the lake level and merging two or more lakes. The resulting larger lake drained west into the Russian River via Cold Creek for a few millennia. A few thousand years ago, a massive landslide from Cow Mountain's north slopes dammed Cold Creek west of Blue Lakes, raising the lake level until it overflowed the lava plug, reopening the Cache Creek outlet. Indian legend and geological evidence corroborate these theories.

Lake County remains active geologically. A magma chamber 13 miles in diameter is centered four miles beneath Mount Hannah, nine miles south of the park. It keeps various hot springs around the county percolating hot mineral water.

Ancestors of the Pomo people have lived around Clear Lake at least since the last eruption. They shared the name Konocti (meaning "old woman mountain") with three tribes who moved here more recently. The major Pomo village, Bidamiwina (meaning "close to creek"), was a mile west of Dorn Loop on Kelsey Creek, with four secondary villages nearby. The Lileek, an offshoot of the Mayahkmah or Wappo people, settled between Cole Creek and Mount Konocti about 200 years ago.

Clear Lake's immense size moderates the climate and

DORN NATURE LOOP:

DISTANCE: 1⅜-mile loop.

TIME: One or two hours.

TERRAIN: Climbs through oak woodlands to lake overlook; continues ascent east, then winds west traversing rocky sidehill to return to trailhead.

ELEVATION: TH: 1340 feet. Gain/loss: 120 feet+/120 feet-.

BEST TIME: Spring for wildflowers. Autumn for deciduous colors. Summer can be hot, but shady trail pleasant year round.

WARNINGS: Watch for poison oak and rattlesnakes.

DIRECTIONS TO TRAILHEAD: FROM SOUTH OR WEST: Exit Highway 101 onto Highway 20 East (M.30.6 from south, M.30.7 from north). Go 20 miles, then right on Highway 29 (M.8.3). Go 10 miles south to stoplight (M.40.1), then left on Soda Bay Road 5 miles to park entrance on left. In .75 mile, turn left to Visitor Center parking.

FROM EAST: Exit Interstate 5 north of Williams onto Highway 20 West (M.18.5 from south, M.19.1 from north). Go 38 miles, then left on Highway 53 for 8 miles. Go right on Highway 29, for 14.4 miles. Go right on Main Street to Gaddy Lane, then left 3 miles to Soda Bay Road.

FEES: Day use/parking: $5/vehicle. Car camping: $12-19/night.

FURTHER INFO: Clear Lake State Park: (707) 279-4293.

OTHER SUGGESTION: INDIAN NATURE TRAIL, beyond entrance kiosk, is an informative ¼-mile loop on a pleasant, rocky hillside. Twenty stops in the park map/brochure describe plants and native culture. Wheelchair-accessible VISITOR CENTER (Saturday & Sunday, 10-4, other days in summer) offers fine exhibits on natural and native history.

encourages abundant bird and fish populations. Native cultures thrived in this abundance. Clear Lake's bounty allowed the Pomos (who called the lake Lupiyoma) to develop one of the most sophisticated native cultures in the west. They had highly developed religion and leisure activities, built buoyant canoes of rushes and traded widely. The sophistication of their basketry is renowned. Pomo prosperity and hospitality were so great that Lake Miwok, Patwin Wintun and Lileek Wappo peoples infringed on Pomo territory around the lake with minimal negative effect.

The encroachment of Anglo culture brought catastrophe. A few Mexican settlers from Mission Sonoma came first, bringing cattle in 1839. One of them sold out to four white men in 1847. Of the four, Andrew Kelsey and Charles Stone stayed to operate the ranch. They arrogantly presumed they could enslave the Pomos to do their work. The Pomos rebelled after two years, killing Stone and Kelsey. Six months later the U.S. Army sent troops from Benicia. They built the first road into Lake County for their wagons hauling howitzers and whale boats. They attacked the Pomo, who had retreated to an island, killing 100 men, women and children in the Bloody Island Massacre, one of the earliest and most shameful incidents of genocide in California history. Today the Pomo people still live in Lake County, about 2% of the population in a land where they long prospered.

Clear Lake State Park was established in the 1940s when Fred and Nellie Dorn donated 300 acres. Today the park includes 565 acres, with 147 developed campsites, including two hike and bike sites near the entrance.

You can reach Dorn Loop from six places in the park. This description starts at the Visitor Center parking area. (A picnic area lies northeast, a short walk over the Cole Creek foot

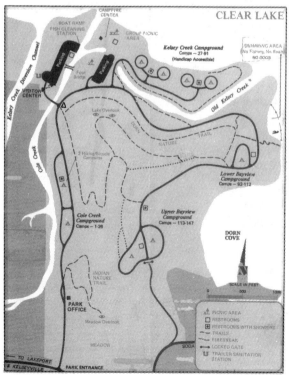

bridge.) Walk southeast from the Visitor Center on the access road to the main park road.

Cautiously cross the street and take the trail climbing southeast into a forest of California buckeye trees. Note a path on the left in 100 feet. If you follow the described loop, you return on that trail. Continue straight up the hill. Valley oaks dominate the forest, with poison oak, manzanita, redbud and soap plant in the understory. Tiny triangular goldenback ferns cluster around lichen-covered rocks on the hillside.

Your trail switchbacks left at ⅛ mile and heads north, Clear Lake visible in the distance. Maidenhair ferns, shooting stars and sticky monkeyflowers grow above the trail. The Pomo ground the monkeyflower seed into a fine meal called pinole, stored to eat year round. In spring miners lettuce grows beneath a knobby buckeye. The path switchbacks up to the right and left past California mountain mahogany, then squaw bush, a non-toxic relative of poison oak with similar leaves and edible red berries instead of toxic white ones.

Reach the top of a ridge at ¼ mile. A spur trail forks right, climbing to Upper Bayview Campground at the end of the park road. Veer left to contour north on Dorn Trail, passing several large bay laurel trees.

Descend briefly to the Lake Overlook. Its rocky knob, surrounded by valley oak, bay laurel and manzanita, surveys a grand view north and west, dominated by part of Clear Lake's

70-square-mile surface, the Mendocino Range rising beyond. The park's Visitor Center stands between Kelsey and Cole Creeks in the foreground, with vineyards and pear orchards stretching over the heart of Lake County. Hollyleaf coffeeberry grows beside the rest bench on the left.

Your path winds northeast along the ridge to a short spur that forks left to a second overlook, with a vista northeast. Return to the main trail to contour through oak woodlands with views east over the lake to the red hills beyond and southeast to Mount Konocti. Continue southeast past baby blue eyes.

Climb briefly at ½ mile, then start a gentle descent. A rest bench overlooks the lake. You may spot osprey nests in deciduous trees along the shore. Descend past a gray pine draped with the fruiting bodies of dwarf mistletoe. A large red elderberry bush is down slope. Buttercups thrive along the trail.

Your path soon turns east, leveling before reaching a junction at ⅝ mile. Go left and descend through oak woodlands where hound's tongue grows. Just before another junction at ¾ mile, a cypress is on the right. The right fork leads to Lower Bayview Campground.

Take the left fork and descend north, then northeast through mixed forest. In 250 feet, fork left again for Dorn Loop. Descend gradually with vistas of Old Kelsey Creek and the lake beyond. Climb briefly, soon coming to a shady rest bench. The path descends past miners lettuce, lady and maidenhair ferns beneath buckeye trees.

Around one mile your trail winds up and down among large mossy boulders. Contour west, then dip and rise among more mossy rock outcrops. You may spot gray squirrels darting from tree to tree. The path continues along cool and mossy rocky slopes, not far above the road and creek.

At 1⅜ miles your path descends to complete the loop. Turn right for the short descent to the park road. Then retrace your steps on the road past the Visitor Center to your car.

14.

ANDERSON MARSH
10,000 YEARS OF HARMONY WITH NATURE

Some of California's earliest known sites of human habitation were around Clear Lake's southeast corner, where Anderson Marsh State Park contains 33 known Native American sites. The Southeastern Pomo people controlled the lower lake, while the Lake Miwok or Tuleyome dominated Cache Creek's south bank and the region to the south. Lileek Wappo lived a few miles west and Patwin Wintun to the east, not far down Cache Creek.

Koi, the Southeastern Pomo's primary village, was one of several villages on Indian Island, where up to 1000 people lived during the height of Pomo culture. This complex society made tule boats and buildings, fishing nets, bows, arrows and a wondrous array of beautiful baskets. They had abundant obsidian from nearby Mount Konocti, a key currency in their extensive trade with tribes near and far. A reconstructed village on the trail is the site of a Pomo Festival each spring.

European hunters and trappers explored around Clear Lake in the 1820s, but white immigrants did not settle around Anderson Marsh until 1855. Achilles Fine and John Melchisadeck Grigsby, brothers from Tennessee, built the central part of the ranch house during their stay from 1855 to 1870.

In 1865 the Clear Lake Water Company built a dam downstream on Cache Creek. Clear Lake rose to record levels, flooding the ranchers and precipitating a diphtheria epidemic. In 1868 J.M. Grigsby sued the water company. Grigsby won the case, then lost when the California Supreme Court reversed the decision on technicalities. In November 1868, 300 neighbors joined the Grigsbys in seizing the water company officers and dismantling the dam, stone by stone. Details of the ongoing struggle are not recorded, but Grigsby sold out to the Water Company in 1870.

John Anderson, recently arrived from Scotland, bought the ranch house and adjacent lands in 1885, adding the tall west wing to the house in 1886. He and his wife raised six children there while they operated a cattle ranch. The youngest daughter lived in the house until 1966.

The State of California acquired Anderson Marsh for a park in 1982, after a campaign by archaeologist John Parker and many others saved it from subdivision. Today the park includes 940 acres. The Audubon Society owns 540-acre McVicar Wildlife Sanctuary, bordering on the west. The local chapter leads bird walks the first Saturday of each month at 9 a.m. Abundant and diverse bird life reaches its peak during winter and spring migration seasons. Birders have identified 150 species here. A checklist is available at the ranch house. As you hike, remember that you are passing through an important archaeological area; please do not disturb any artifacts.

Head west from the parking area on the level trail through a meadow, walked by humans for 10,000 years. You soon parallel the fence along the park's southern boundary. The double track traverses flat pasture land, liberally sprinkled with immense valley oaks. Mount Konocti rises to the northwest, the Mendocino Range to the north. The trail forks beyond ⅛ mile. Anderson Flats Trail is on the right. Go left on the path that jogs with the fence, climbing gently.

You soon approach a partially reconstructed Pomo village on the right. The display includes a round house within a wooden

ANDERSON MARSH:

DISTANCE: **2½-mile loop,** plus 3- to 5- mile side trip in McVicar Sanctuary.

TIME: Two hours to all day.

TERRAIN: Gentle ramble through meadows and oak woodlands, with long side trip along edge of marsh.

ELEVATION: TH: 1340 feet. Gain/loss: 80 feet+/80 feet-.

BEST TIME: Nice anytime. Winter may bring bald eagles. Spring brings white pelicans, ospreys and wildflowers.

WARNINGS: Watch for rattlesnakes and poison oak. Portions of trails (notably McVicar Trail) may be wet after major storms.

DIRECTIONS TO TRAILHEAD: On west side of Highway 53, .75 mile north of Highway 29 at Lower Lake. When gate is closed, park off highway opposite entrance and walk in.

FROM WEST: Exit Highway 101 onto Highway 20 east (M.30.6 from south, M.30.7 from north). Go east 20 miles, then right on Highway 29. Go 31 miles, then left on Highway 53 to park.

FROM SOUTH: Take Highway 29 for 60 miles north from Napa (33 miles from Calistoga).

FROM EAST: Exit Interstate 5 north of Williams onto Highway 20 West (M.18.5 from south, M.19.1 from north). Go 38 miles, then left 7 miles on Highway 53 to park on right.

FEES: Day use/parking: $5/vehicle.

FURTHER INFO: Anderson Marsh State Park (707) 994-0688, 279-4293.

OTHER SUGGESTION: GARNER ISLAND TRAIL at end of Lakeview Avenue, off Old Highway 53, 1.4 miles north of park, heads west to island in northern park, 1½ miles round trip.

fence, used for dances and other ceremonies, and several dwellings. The structures have willow frames and tule walls. The round house roof is rebuilt each spring for the Pomo Festival. This pleasant hillside on the edge of oak woodland overlooking the meadow also offers picnic tables.

Your trail heads south to ⅜ mile, then bends right, again following the fence. Climb gently past abundant blue oaks and manzanita. The path levels and veers right, leaving the fence.

Come to a junction in a clearing on the ridge at ⅝ mile. Ridge Trail continues straight. Go left, descending west on McVicar Trail. An interpretive sign in 200 feet tells about the bald eagles that visit Anderson Marsh from December through March.

At a vague, unmarked junction near the sign, you must make a choice. For a shorter loop of 2½ miles, turn right and climb north along Marsh Trail—skip the next 6 paragraphs if you do. Our described trip continues straight on McVicar Trail, exploring the Wildlife Sanctuary along the south and west edges of Anderson Marsh, a 3- to 5-mile side trip.

McVicar Trail descends to a grassy flat at the marsh's southeast corner, turning southwest across an area particularly wet and muddy after rains. Your meandering, level trail meets the fence line again, following it west. Wind through dense vegetation in moist habitat beneath oak trees, including California buckeye, willow, redbud, wood rose and thistle.

A sign at ⅜ mile indicates McVicar Audubon Sanctuary. Where

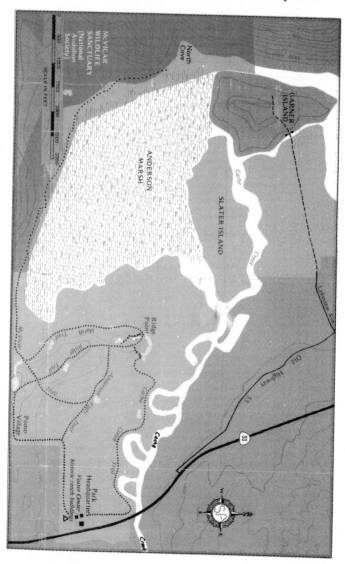

van . 92

several paths fork left, stay right on level ground. Dense vegetation has many poison oak vines. By ½ mile you can see the marsh and some open water on the right frequented by ducks. Pumice stones confirm the area's volcanic origins.

You soon reach an area on your right where trees have been cut, offering a broad view of the marsh. Look for water birds, including ducks, tundra swans, herons, egrets, grebes and coots, and raptors, including hawks, harriers, eagles, kites, kestrels and ospreys.

The trail turns northwest along the marsh's edge. Parallel a channel around ¾ mile with excellent views into the marsh. A commercial walnut grove is on the left. The path reaches a pleasant picnic area with tables at one mile.

Your trail winds west then turns north by 1⅛ miles, narrowing and turning vague as it follows the marsh shore. The Audubon Society has placed nesting boxes in the trees to encourage the residency of purple martins. Your trail leaves the oak woodland at 1¼ miles, continuing north through grasslands at the edge of the marsh. On a steep, densely wooded hill to your left, large gray pines tangle with oaks and buckeyes.

The path deteriorates further at 1½ miles. You could continue north between the hill and the marsh, although the path is indistinct. It is about ¾ mile to North Cove, one mile to the preserve boundary adjacent to Garner Island.

As I turned back toward the trailhead one day around sunset, three immense and graceful white pelicans soared over the marsh, soon joined by four more. They seemed to play follow the leader, silently sailing over dusk-graying water, turning in unison, then gliding elegantly to rest on the lake. White pelicans have wing spans up to ten feet! The huge birds arrive at Anderson Marsh in spring, leaving in September. Recently returned from the brink of extinction caused by the pesticide DDT, pelicans have changed little from their ancestors of 40 million years ago. They are highly evolved for catching large quantities of fish.

Returning to junction at the interpretive sign, climb gradually north on Marsh Trail's faint tread. Buttercup, soap plant and poison oak grow beneath blue oaks on rocky ground. By ¾ mile (not including McVicar side trip) you overlook the upper end of tule-filled Anderson Marsh. You may see black shouldered kites perching on willows amidst the marsh, occasionally diving for prey. Hawks and bald eagles also hunt here.

The trail descends gently, approaching the marsh's edge. A large valley oak on the left has dozens of acorn-filled holes, a woodpecker family's store house. The path leaves oak woodland, drawing near the edge of the marsh at one mile.

Your trail bends right at 1⅛ miles, climbing to Ridge Point. As you climb onto the ridge, the fragrant silver-green leaves of Douglas mugwort grow amidst the rocks on the left. The main path makes a big bend right, meeting Cache Creek Trail in 200 feet. But before you continue, look for the faint path on the right among the rocks on the ridgetop. Follow it south through an area where several grinding holes and a cryptic petroglyph mark the rocks around a rocky knob. Watch for prolific poison oak as you explore. The side path continues to two picnic tables at 1¼ miles, then meets Ridge Trail.

When you are ready to continue, return to Cache Creek Trail and follow it east onto the low grassland. It meanders through the level meadow, eventually turning toward the trees along Cache Creek. The path reaches the creek beyond 1⅝ miles.

Your winding trail turns east along the meandering creek, soon drawing alongside the muddy stream. If you approach quietly, you may see pond turtles sunning on the banks or on logs. Your path winds around one channel, crosses a sometimes muddy channel at 1⅞ miles, then winds left to return to the creek. Great blue and lesser green herons often perch in oaks, willows and cottonwoods across the creek. Look closely; they hide in the dense foliage. A side path forks left around 2 miles, exploring the creek side.

The main trail heads southeast, passing through an old fence line, then staying near the creek. Head east almost to the highway, winding through blackberry thickets and willows. Your path bends right to parallel the highway, then heads for the old ranch house. Draw near the road at 2¼ miles, then continue south. Wind around the ranch's cultivated blackberry patch, pass the house and reach the parking area at 2½ miles.

15.

BOGGS LAKE PRESERVE

RARE PLANTS AND BIRDS AT FOREST-LINED VERNAL POOL

The Pomo people and their ancestors have inhabited the southern Clear Lake area for at least 10,000 years. By the time of recorded history, the population was concentrated near the shores of the immense, bountiful lake. The village closest to Boggs Lake was an Eastern Pomo settlement on Kelsey Creek. The Pomo used the area around Boggs Lake as a hunting ground and a source of water when traveling. The Lileek Wappo also hunted here.

White people first settled here during the gold rush. Thomas Boyd built Lake County's first mill on Boggs Lake's south shore in 1858. Powered by steam, the combination gristmill and sawmill was purchased by Henry Carrol Boggs in 1868. Boggs attempted to deepen the lake by dynamiting its center. The blast quickly drained the lake, exposing underground caves created by the ancient lava flows that caused the lake. Boggs closed the mill for two years to plug the hole and let the pool refill.

Rumors of subdivision in the early 1970s prompted the California Native Plant Society to exhort The Nature Conservancy to acquire the land. TNC convinced the corporate owner to donate 101 acres, establishing the Preserve in 1972. Today TNC holds 153 acres. The California Department of Fish and Game protects adjacent acreage.

Birders have counted 142 species living at or visiting the sanctuary through the seasons. Over 200 plant species are present, including rare species of downingia, navarretia, hedge hyssop, Orcutt grass, watershield and the parasite called Indian lovevine or Howell's dodder. Please be careful not to disturb any plants.

On my first visit in April the lake was full, a large azure vernal pool of nearly 300 acres lined with pine forest. Upon a second visit in November, the lake bed was virtually dry. One had to look beneath tules and marsh grasses in the deepest channels to find water. No creeks or springs feed the pool; rainfall and runoff from the surrounding watershed fill it. The lake bed is an impervious layer of clay bordered by lava flows.

From the parking area head through a wooden stile and descend northeast past interpretive signs beneath a forest of black oaks, ponderosa and sugar pines. Your path bends right in 100 feet to head east. The forest understory has manzanita, California mountain mahogany, wood rose, chaparral honeysuckle vines and live oak brush, similar habitat to the Sierra Nevada or Yolla Bolly foothills at similar elevation.

Your path follows an old road briefly. The trail forks just 300

BOGGS LAKE PRESERVE:

DISTANCE: ⅞-mile loop.
TIME: One to three hours.
TERRAIN: Over and around gently rolling hills beside lake shore.
ELEVATION: TH: 2800 feet. Gain/loss: 60 feet+/60 feet-.
BEST TIME: For flowers: late April to May. For birds: January and
February for waterfowl, spring for herons and egrets.
WARNINGS: Please stay off lake bed; delicate area with rare
plants. No camping, hunting, collecting, fishing, mountain
bikes, motor vehicles, horses or pets. Watch for poison oak.
DIRECTIONS TO TRAILHEAD: FROM BAY AREA OR SANTA
ROSA: Exit Highway 101 north of Santa Rosa onto Mark West
Springs Road. Go 18 miles to Calistoga, then take Highway 29
north 18 miles to Middletown, where you go left on Highway
175. Go 10 miles, then left on Bottle Rock Road for 6.5 miles.
Watch carefully for right turn onto Harrington Flat Road.
Preserve parking is .5 mile on left.
FROM UKIAH AND NORTH: Exit Highway 101 onto Highway
20 east (M.30.6 from south, M.30.7 from north). Go east 20
miles, then right on Highway 29. Go 18 miles, then right
(M.32.4) on Bottle Rock Road. In 4.25 miles go left on
Harrington Flat Road .5 mile to parking.
FURTHER INFO: Nature Conservancy, Bay Area Preserve
Manager (415) 435-6465.

feet from the trailhead. Turn right and head south. Watch for poison oak as you descend to the flood plain of Boggs Lake and a floating boardwalk.

Walk 100 feet to the end of the ramp. You are amidst tall bulrushes (tules) at the edge of the open water on the deepest side of the lake. Four species of the uncommon, small blue-flowered plants called downingia grow in this vicinity, favoring moist pockets as the lake waters recede. The wooded peak of Mount Hannah rises gently to its 3978-foot summit a mile to the east. About a million years ago, lava flows issuing from the western flank of the peak converged to form this lake basin. Today a magma chamber 13 miles in diameter is centered four miles beneath Mount Hannah.

In winter the boardwalk is a good place to observe migratory waterfowl attracted by the lake. Wood ducks, hooded mergansers, mallards, geese, bald eagles and Wilson's phalaropes may drop in. Great blue herons and green-backed egrets often visit to feed on the large amphibian population, especially in spring. Red-winged blackbirds and coots nest in the tules. In spring and summer ospreys come to fish. (The pool has no native fish, but carp and catfish have occasionally been planted.)

Retrace your steps to the fork in the trail above the lake shore. Turn right and head north. Notice a trail on your left in 200 feet, your return path at the end of this loop.

Bear right for a brief ascent through uneven rocky terrain to a stony knob overlooking the lake basin at ¼ mile. Native bunch grasses, including fescue and the rare slender Orcutt grass, thrive here beneath black oaks. Perennial grasses grow in clusters that may be 70 years old. They dominated California grasslands until grazing by domestic animals decimated the perennials, replacing them with annuals. Your winding path descends, passing an immense black oak on the right.

The trail contours along the lake shore. Please stay off the delicate lake bed. Pass large pines killed by a flood stage in the lake's cycle. Young pines grow beneath the skeletal trees. Acorn woodpeckers have drilled many rows of storage holes in the dead trees. Each woodpecker family has its own tree. They wedge acorns from nearby black and canyon live oaks into the holes, fitting them so tightly that squirrels and birds with less pointed beaks have difficulty dislodging the cache. Pileated, downy and hairy woodpeckers also visit the Preserve.

Your path winds up to another wooded knob around ⅜ mile, overlooking a dogleg in the lake. When filled to capacity, Boggs Lake is larger than it appears from the road. When full it is 100 times the size of the largest lake in Yolla Bolly Wilderness.

The path contours briefly, then bends left on a winding descent past madrones. Stay to the left as a faint side trail forks right. Your trail heads north, meandering near the lake shore. The path bends left twice. Climb gently west past clumps of Douglas iris by ½ mile. Pomo women used the iris' strong fibers in their famous baskets. Bunch grasses also thrive here.

The path descends slightly, then levels, winding past monardella of the mint family and manzanita in grassy clearings

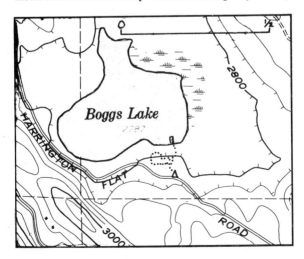

73

of the oak/pine forest. Your trail bends left, passing more woodpecker granaries. Look for white, ookow and harvest brodiaeas in spring. Coffeeberry also grows here.

Before ¾ mile you overlook a seasonally wet meadow on your right between you and the road. The pine-bordered grassland is habitat for yampa, a three-foot-high plant in the parsley family with narrow leaves and white or pink flower clusters in summer. It has an edible tuberous root high in food value. Small-flowered flax also grows in the meadow.

The trail becomes vague, bending left and right to complete the loop. Turn right at the junction and climb the gentle hill to the parking area.

16.
HOBERG LOOP
SOLITUDE IN BOGGS MOUNTAIN STATE FOREST

This middle-elevation ponderosa pine forest was the territory of the Lake Miwok people. Their nearest principal village was Oleyome (meaning "Coyote Home"), five miles downstream from Boggs Mountain at the confluence of Big Canyon Creek with Putah Creek. The Lake Miwok are related linguistically to the Miwok of the Sierra Nevada around Yosemite. Culturally they have more in common with the Pomo. The people of Oleyome journeyed through Wappo and Pomo lands once or twice each year to visit the Coast Miwok at Bodega Bay, where they collected or traded for salt, seaweed, fish, seal and otter pelts and the clamshells used for money between tribes. The trek to the coast took nearly a week, so they stayed a month or more before returning home, their baskets loaded with fresh supplies.

Early white settlers called this area Digger Jones Mountain. William "Digger" Jones was the only man legally hanged in Lake County, executed by Sheriff L.H. Boggs (Henry's brother) in 1883. Jones, who lived on Boggs Mountain with a native wife, was convicted of murdering his partner and son-in-law.

Henry C. Boggs acquired most of the land that is now State Forest between 1878 and 1884. His son Lilburn operated a sawmill at two sites on the northeast side of Boggs Mountain from 1880 to 1885. This forest was logged extensively then and again after 1945. When the State of California bought the land and established Boggs Mountain State Forest in 1949, virtually no merchantable timber remained. Thus most of the forest, now encompassing 3453 acres, has been logged twice, some of it three times.

The State Department of Forestry manages this forest to demonstrate "the productive and economic possibilities of good forest practices." On your visit you may see signs of logging,

HOBERG LOOP:

DISTANCE: **1⅝-mile loop,** plus ½-mile side trip to Vista Point.
TIME: One or two hours.
TERRAIN: Climbs through forest to high viewpoint near top of
    Boggs Mountain, then descends through forest.
ELEVATION: TH: 3040 feet. Gain/loss: 360 feet+/360 feet-.
BEST TIME: Spring for wildflowers. Accessible year round.
WARNINGS: Do not block fire road when parking. Deer hunting
    season August to September. Stay off private property
    adjacent to State Forest.
DIRECTIONS TO TRAILHEAD: On Highway 175, 10 miles north
    of Middletown or 9.75 miles south of Highway 29 (M.31.1)
    near Lower Lake. At Hobergs, turn east on Entrance Road
    (M.17.75) and go .1 mile to signed trailhead.
FURTHER INFO: Boggs Mountain State Forest (707) 928-4378.

*thinning or brush clearing. Still, the regenerated forest has
impressive stands of ponderosa pine and Douglas fir, and some
seldom visited corners. Miles of dirt roads offer extensive
possibilities for hikers, mountain bikers and equestrians. Ranging
from 2400- to 3750-feet elevation, Boggs Mountain State Forest
is accessible year round, except when an infrequent cold front
buries it in snow. Hoberg Loop is the easiest, most accessible trail
on Boggs Mountain. (The next trail report offers other choices.)*

*Hobergs, the little community near the trailhead, was born as
a resort in the early twentieth century, one of many resorts that
prospered in southern Lake County.*

From the signed trailhead, ascend gradually southeast on a
footpath through forest of ponderosa and sugar pines, Douglas
fir and black oak. Conifer seedlings mingle with manzanita
beneath an open forest canopy.

In 300 feet, turn left on a path that climbs north. (If you
continue southeast, the route is confusing in a tangle of
logging roads and other paths; the loop is easiest to follow
clockwise.) The trail soon crosses an old road and contours
north. Pine needles and squawmat carpet the forest floor.

A track on the right at ⅛ mile climbs steeply. Go straight on
the shady path behind some houses, soon resuming a gradual
ascent. Stay left at another fork, passing above a downed pine

and climbing moderately. Pass stumps in selectively logged forest as your ascent eases. The path bends right, ascending along a north slope dense with Douglas fir. Cross a path that descends steeply on the left and climb gradually on good tread.

Your track levels for a view around ⅜ mile. On a clear day you can see Snow Mountain due north. Mount Konocti is to its left in the middle ground with Mount Hannah and Mount Seigler in the foreground. Contour east and southeast, circling one of Boggs Mountain's several summits on your right. California mountain mahogany, coffeeberry and madrone grow in the understory. Climb gently past scattered television-size rocks.

Beyond a large stump, your trail makes a slow bend right. The path soon crests, then descends slightly as pines outnumber Douglas firs. Ascend slightly past blueblossom ceanothus at ¾ mile, then continue an easy climb past dead pines and bunch grass.

At a signed junction Hoberg Loop veers right. Our described hike turns left for a ½-mile side trip on Boggs Ridge Trail. Contour south briefly, then veer left across a gully and climb gradually east. Cedar seedlings, honeysuckle, coltsfoot and live oak brush grow amidst bunch grasses beneath the forest. Take the left fork before one mile, climbing gently. Ascend moderately on rocky tread to the wooded vista point.

An immense live oak overhangs the level knoll, a stand of

large Douglas firs surround it. The best view is northeast where, beyond the cliffy rock outcrop, the face of Boggs Mountain plunges 1000 feet into Big Canyon. You can see the town of Clearlake beyond, though intervening hills hide the lake. Desert-like country lies beyond along the canyons of Cache Creek.

Retrace your steps to Hoberg Loop, go left and ascend southwest, approaching the ridgetop by 1⅜ mile. Stay left at a vague fork. Ascend west, crossing three paths broader than the one you are on. Cross the ridgetop just north of a saddle. Hoberg Loop descends gradually west-northwest, crossing another skid trail before 1½ miles. Your path slowly bends right to descend northwest through a manzanita thicket.

Descend through pine forest, passing an immense black oak. Continue the decline through a stand of firs, then through open forest. A logged slope is below the path at 1⅝ miles. You soon make a big bend left to descend south-southwest through a dense stand of young Douglas firs. Descend gently until your

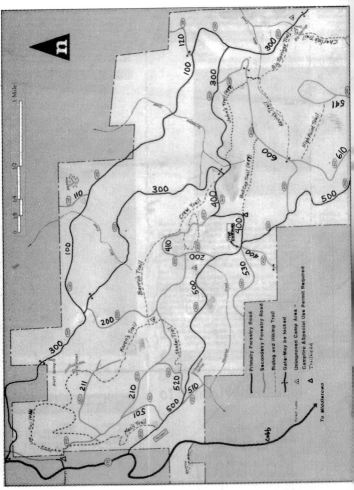

trail nearly levels at 1⅞ miles. Then descend across Road 210.

You quickly reach a confusing junction beyond the road. Ignore the maze of paths above on your left. Turn right and descend northwest 125 feet, then veer right on a gradual descent due north on a path crowded by young Douglas firs. Your descent becomes moderate. Stay left at the next junction and descend to the trailhead at 2⅛ miles.

17.
BALL CAP/ ROAD 600/ JOHN'S LOOP
ALMOST PARADISE FOR MOUNTAIN BIKERS

Boggs Mountain State Forest is heavenly for mountain bikers. Few hikers and equestrians use the 27 miles of back roads and 10 miles of designated trails. The benefits of the forest's shady, rolling terrain and fresh mountain air are offset only by occasional logging and the influx of hunters when deer season opens in August. Bikers must always watch for others along narrow trails and slow to a crawl on blind corners.

Hikers and equestrians can also enjoy this accessible, little traveled country. Three sites in the 3500-acre forest are open to rustic camping. There are only two reliable sources of water, Big Springs in the east and Houghton Springs in the southwest. You must obtain a campfire permit from a local California Department of Forestry office to camp, have a fire or use a gas stove. A campground 1 ½ miles from the highway on Road 500 has tables and fire pits.

This short loop samples two trails and a road in the heart of the State Forest. The report mentions several options to extend your adventure. Keep in mind that some trails here are difficult to locate and follow.

Ball Cap Trail heads south-southeast from a big bend on Road 400, .15 mile east of Five Corners intersection. The only sign indicates no motor vehicles allowed. Ascend gradually through forest of Douglas firs, ponderosa and sugar pines. The path soon turns east. Only a few live oaks, coffeeberry bushes and conifer seedlings grow in the understory.

The trail crests at ⅛ mile, then descends gently through dense vegetation. Squawmat and bunch grass grow beneath madrone and manzanita, then young Douglas firs crowd the path. Your trail bends right for a slight ascent, then contours. Veer left of a large black oak at ⅜ mile and begin a moderate winding descent through deep forest. Cross the headwaters of Spikenard Creek, then climb gradually.

Your trail levels at ⅝ mile where traditional camps are on the left. A rock outcrop beyond offers views north over steep

BALL CAP/ ROAD 600/ JOHN'S LOOP:

DISTANCE: 2⅜-mile loop plus miles of options.

TIME: One hour to all day.

TERRAIN: Undulates on path through forest, descends road, then returns on wooded trail.

ELEVATION: TH: 3400 feet. Gain/loss: 420 feet+/420 feet-.

BEST TIME: April and May for wildflowers. Pleasant anytime.

WARNINGS: Watch for poison oak. You must have a campfire permit to camp. Deer hunting season mid-August to September.

DIRECTIONS TO TRAILHEAD: On Highway 175, 9.75 miles north of Middletown or 10 miles south of Highway 29 (M.31.1) near Lower Lake. At M.18.25, between Cobb and Hobergs, turn east on Road 500. Drive 2 miles, passing California Dept. of Forestry Fire Station (campfire permits), to Road 400, then go left .15 mile to trailhead on right.

FURTHER INFO: Boggs Mountain State Forest (707) 928-4378.

OTHER SUGGESTION: Many other trails and fire roads offer miles of options. You can extend this loop by exploring KEVIN'S, HIGH POINT or BIG SPRINGS TRAILS or ROADS 100, 300, 410, 220, 200 or THE SOUTH END OF ROAD 500 AND ITS SPURS (see map).

country. Ball Cap Trail ends, meeting Road 600. The described loop turns left, descending along the road.

(You can go right to extend the loop. If you do, Road 600 climbs steeply, then levels around ¼ mile, soon passing signed Kevin's Trail on the left. If you turn left on Road 610 at ⅜ mile, you meet High Point Trail in 200 feet. It climbs to a ridge at ⅝ mile, then descends to Road 541 at ⅞ mile. For an easy climb to Boggs Mountain's highest point, turn right at the ridge on a skid trail ascending south. It passes 60 feet west of the summit before descending, a ⅝-mile round trip from High Point Trail.)

The described loop descends gradually on Road 600 to ¾ mile, then moderately as the headwaters of Malo Creek form on your right. Meet John's Trail before one mile. Our loop turns left on John's Trail, marked only with a no motor vehicles sign.

(You have other chances to expand the described loop at John's Trail junction. About 100 feet down Road 600, signed Big Springs Trail forks right, descending ¾ mile to Big Springs near the eastern Forest boundary. You can return by looping back on Roads 300 and 600. Or make a much longer loop, heading north and northwest on Road 100, then returning by Road 300, then right on Road 400 to the trailhead.)

John's Trail climbs northwest from Road 600 into dense young forest. Your narrow path soon levels with large trees scattered in young forest. The trail bends left at one mile to ascend gently where coffeeberry and bunch grasses grow year round. You may see star tulips in spring.

The path descends, then levels as the terrain becomes rocky. Watch for poison oak as you traverse a scree slope. Return to forest briefly, then traverse the base of another rock pile where poison oak, blueblossom, live oak and bracken fern thrive.

Make a brief steep climb to 1¼ miles. Your path broadens, contouring through forest with many madrones and live oaks. After a view northwest to Mount Hannah, the path bends right to descend slightly. Wind through a gully where a seasonal seep supports woodwardia ferns, hairy honeysuckle and wood rose.

Contour, winding through forest with many black and live oaks. Cross a ridgetop skid trail where Indian warriors bloom in spring. Contour through young forest on narrow, good tread. Cross the first of several headwater gulches of Spikenard Creek. The path bends right, then rolls up and down across a steep north slope. Cross another feeder gully before the rolling, winding path passes lupine, coltsfoot and more Indian warriors beneath black oaks and pines. Look northeast beyond the forest for glimpses of the wild desert-like country of eastern Lake County. Descend gradually through mixed forest where shooting star, hound's tongue and hedge nettle grow in spring. Descend to Road 300 at 1¾ miles.

Turn left and climb southwest on the road to a junction at 1⅞ miles. Road 400 climbs on the left, while Road 300 descends right. To complete the loop, bear left and follow Road 400 for ½ mile, returning to Ball Cap Trailhead at 2⅜ miles.

18.
CACHE CREEK WILDLIFE AREA
EAGLES AND ELK AROUND WILSON VALLEY

The Patwin branch of the Wintun people lived along Cache Creek, from Long and Indian Valleys near the headwaters all the way to its confluence with the Sacramento River. The Southeastern or River Patwin lived on the lower creek and the nearby river, while the Southwestern or Hill Patwin resided along the upper creek. Kuikui, the Southwestern Patwin village in Wilson Valley, was a ceremonial center for the tribe. Rugged Cache Creek Canyon provided refuge for many Patwin as they

CACHE CREEK WILDLIFE AREA:

DISTANCE: **7½ miles** (15 miles round trip); 2½ miles to Baton Flat ford, 5¼ miles to dry camp above valley, 6 miles to Rocky Creek and entrance to Wilson Valley.

TIME: Two hours to ford, full day to overlook, overnight to Wilson Valley.

TERRAIN: Contours through broad valley, climbs and descends over rolling hills to ford; ups and downs through more rolling hills until descent into broad, gentle Wilson Valley.

ELEVATION: TH (trailhead): 1000 feet. Gain/loss: to Baton Flat: 480 feet+/520 feet-, total: 1200 feet+/1300 feet-.

BEST TIME: March and April for wildflowers, December through February for bald eagles.

WARNINGS: Watch for rattlesnakes and poison oak. Seasonal closures to protect wildlife, especially mid-April through June for tule elk calving season. Stay a respectful distance from wildlife. Hunting allowed in season. Area subject to flash floods after major rainstorms; use caution at fords. Trails very muddy after rains. Very hot in summer.

DIRECTIONS TO TRAILHEAD: On south side of Highway 20 at M.36.98, 49.5 miles east of Highway 101, 33 miles west of Interstate 5. (5.5 miles east of Highway 53 junction near Clearlake Oaks.) Go .25 mile on gravel road to trailhead.

FURTHER INFO: Bureau of Land Management (707) 462-3873.

were forced off their lands during the Gold Rush. The Patwin recognized hawk as creator-spirit and envisioned the world originating from a turtle's dive into a primeval sea.

Cache Creek drains dry, semi-desert country with extreme seasonal variations. Wet winters result in a flushing of Clear Lake, sending extra water and abundant fish down Cache Creek, the lake's only outlet. These wet years bring numerous bald eagles to Cache Creek to feed on plentiful fish. This last happened in 1986, but can happen in any above-average-water year. The eagles favor secluded Wilson Valley at the end of this trail, but you might see them anywhere along the creek, skimming the water or perching in nearby gray pines. In dry years the creek remains small and only a few eagles might be seen. The lush green wildflower-dappled hills of spring disappear by the first of June, replaced by scorched, tinder-box dry grasses and parched chaparral. The land stays hot and dry until winter rains return.

81

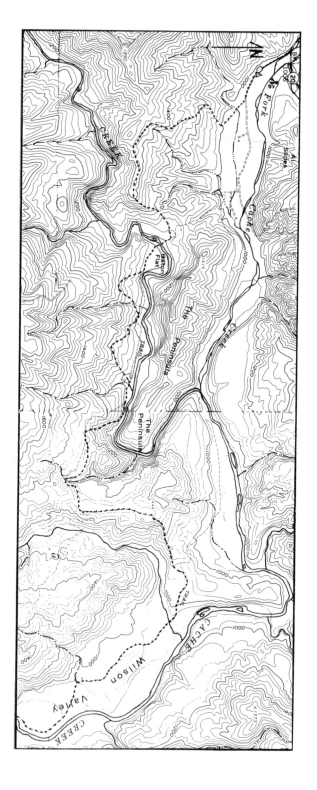

The best time to visit the 45,000-acre Cache Creek Wildlife Area spans winter and early spring. The area is subject to seasonal closure for the spring birthing season of the tule elk that live here, so call BLM before you visit.

Sign in at the trail register, where a map is usually available. Head southeast on the level road behind the locked gate. Cross a large meadow with oaks, buckeyes, gray pines and redbud, with North Fork Cache Creek meandering on your left. The tiny pink flowers of filaree carpet the meadow in spring.

Your road bends left to head east at ⅛ mile. Turn right where it bends left again before ¼ mile, following the hiker symbol on a grassy, two-rutted track. After fording a small seasonal creek, your trail narrows as it veers right, traversing the base of a wooded slope.

Before ½ mile the path begins a moderate ascent past manzanita, snowberry and California mountain mahogany. Switchback right and climb west, soon ascending a steep hill that can be very slippery after rain. In spring look for hound's tongue, miners lettuce, bedstraw and yarrow beneath oaks and gray pines. Your trail turns left and descends through a gully, then resumes a winding climb. Buck brush and chamise join chaparral entwined with honeysuckle vines, abundant soap plant growing below. Other spring wildflowers include Indian warrior, buttercup and lomatium.

The path levels around ⅞ mile, then makes a winding ascent to look east over the canyons of Cache Creek. Contour, then climb gently as the trail winds southeast. Live oaks mingle with black oaks and gray pines as you wind through two small gullies. Begin one more steady climb at 1¼ miles. You soon reach a summit with a breathtaking view south over the main fork of Cache Creek, Clear Lake's only outlet. Grasslands and chaparral cover the rolling hills.

Your trail descends, winding along a ridgetop past white- and yellow-flowered lomatiums beneath white oaks. Climb briefly to the best view yet of Cache Creek's twisting canyon. As you descend along the ridgetop, look for yellow fiddlenecks, white popcorn flowers and tiny blue and white lupines in spring.

Descend moderately on the right side of the ridge at 1⅝ miles, passing filaree and phacelia. The path bends left and right, then descends in big sweeping curves. Return to the ridge briefly at 2 miles, where bright orange western wallflowers grow with generous patches of Indian warriors in spring. Your trail bends right, leaving the ridgetop on a winding descent, which eases around 2¼ miles.

Meet another path as you reach Baton Flat. Pass a sign asking you not to disturb archaeological artifacts in the area. The trail turns right, passing a knot of irises, and drops to the Cache Creek ford before 2½ miles. The crossing is usually only ankle

deep; then you may be able to rock hop across. It may be knee deep or even impassable after major storms, and up to three feet deep in summer when water is released from Clear Lake for downstream irrigation. Cattails, tules and willows line the stream. Camping is only allowed beyond the ford.

Beyond the ford your trail follows a jeep track across grassy Baton Flat, passing large valley oaks. Watch for the footpath forking right ⅛ mile from the ford. Ascend moderately on the path into oak woodlands. Gray pines and manzanita mingle with oaks as the trail switchbacks right, then bends left. Look for shooting stars, buttercups and yarrow in spring.

Your path levels after crossing a two-rutted track. Bushy lupines grow beneath blue oaks and gray pines. Descend briefly past redbud and mule ears, then traverse short gentle ups and downs, joining a double track briefly.

Your trail veers right as the double track drops left at 2⅞ miles. Descend gradually, then switchback left and dip through a gully to a flat along Cache Creek where mugwort grows.

At 3 miles you head east on a two lane track for 300 feet. Veer right on a signed path, climbing to cross a steep-sided gully, then winding through two more gullies, passing baby blue eyes. Reach a summit with views north to east at 3⅜ miles. The trail descends to the road just east of a private property sign.

Turn right and follow the road 125 feet to a gully. Veer left on the trail descending gradually into forest of gray pine, cypress and oak. Contour east briefly around 3¾ miles. Climb moderately through mixed woodland, overlooking Cache Creek as it winds around the brushy ridge called The Peninsula. Your trail turns south, ascending moderately. Switchback right and left and continue a steady climb through extensive poison oak.

Your path bends around a rock outcrop and ascends to the jeep track at 4⅛ miles. Bay laurel and coffeeberry grow at the junction. Go left, following the road briefly. Soon you veer left on a gradually descending path, passing toyon, soap plant and wild celery. Cross a small gully, then a seasonal creek. Descend through chaparral until the trail bends right and enters a glade. Before leaving the grassland, you might see the pink flowers of

84

rare adobe lilies clustering on your right.

The path contours east to 4½ miles, then bends right to climb gradually with the grassy clearing on your right and a brush-choked canyon on your left. When you meet the jeep road, turn left and cross the canyon's seasonal creek. The road bends left for a winding contour through chaparral with star zygadene.

Fork left on the signed trail leaving the jeep track around 4⅞ miles. As the path bends left, you can see broad, grassy Wilson Valley to the east. Contour north along a ridge through a sea of chamise. Climb briefly, then contour along the ridge.

Pass a sign for the Cache Creek Wildlife Area at 5¼ miles. (A spur just beyond forks right, heading east 300 feet to a glade and a pleasant dry camp overlooking the broad valley, a good vantage to observe wildlife.) Continue north on the main trail to another brushy overlook at 5⅜ miles. Stay back from the top of a steeply undercut landslide if you leave the trail here.

The trail bends left and right, descending toward Wilson Valley. Chamise dominates the chaparral-lined descent. Your path merges with a jeep track at 5⅝ miles. Climb east through oak woodland, then descend through grassland.

Cross Rocky Creek around 6 miles, entering the broad, gently sloping immense grasslands of Wilson Valley. The track contours southeast. Wildflowers thrive in spring. Reach an old homestead site marked by two locust trees at the edge of the woodlands overlooking the valley at 6¾ miles.

The path continues beyond a seasonal creek, winding east to Cache Creek, then meandering downstream until the canyon narrows at 7½ miles. The trail ends as the creek turns east, descending along a steep narrow canyon. Be careful not to make any wrong turns as you retrace your steps to the trailhead.

MENDOCINO NATIONAL FOREST

Of the 18 National Forests in California, Mendocino is the only one not traversed by a paved road or highway. Mendocino National Forest contains a million acres of ridges and canyons rich with solitude and tranquility. The Forest, ranging in elevation from 750 feet on the eastern boundary to 8092 feet atop Mount Linn (highest peak in the Coast Range), includes portions of six counties: Mendocino, Lake, Colusa, Glenn, Tehama and Trinity. This book explores trails in all those counties.

Between 1850 and 1900, many small sawmills operated in the area. Two copper mining boom towns, Copper City and Pacific City, withered before the turn of the century, now only place names on the map. Hullville, a small community of livestock raisers, was established around 1870 in Gravelly Valley, where Lake Pillsbury is now. Families began leaving by the 1890s because the land was overgrazed. The remains of Hullville were submerged after the Eel River was dammed in 1906.

The U. S. Forest Service was created in 1907 when President Theodore Roosevelt established the million-acre Stony Creek Reserve with similar boundaries to today's Mendocino National Forest. The name was changed to California National Forest in 1908, then to its present name in 1932. (When I first hiked the Yolla Bollys in 1975, a sign in a little-traveled corner of the wilderness read "California National Forest, Ruth - 29 miles.")

About one fifth of Mendocino National Forest is preserved in a natural state in Yolla Bolly-Middle Eel and Snow Mountain Wilderness Areas. Most of the trails in the rest of this book survey those pristine regions. The next two trail reports explore non-wilderness areas in the southern Forest near Snow Mountain.

More than 40 developed campgrounds, many of them free, offer pleasant overnight possibilities at elevations ranging from 1500 to over 6000 feet. Some have toilets and piped water, others offer only a table, fire pit and unadulterated nature. A dozen sites are open year round. With a campfire permit, you are welcome to camp virtually anywhere else in the National Forest.

The official Mendocino National Forest Map is extremely useful when navigating the maze of secondary roads that provide access to the trails and campgrounds. The map, updated in 1991 and available at ranger stations for $3, lists all the campgrounds and facilities available. It is always wise to check your itinerary with the Forest Service, especially when visiting in non-summer months. Even primary forest roads—designated by the letter "M" preceding the road number—may ford streams and occasionally be closed by landslides, snow or logging operations.

Drive especially carefully on your visit. Many roads are one lane, unpaved, and can be extremely dusty. Logging trucks sometimes travel on all forest roads. Some roads have water bars—shallow ditches cut across them to carry rain runoff.

When you visit Mendocino National Forest, always come with a full tank of gas and enough food for the length of your stay. The only commercial facilities within the Forest—at Lake Pillsbury—are open seasonally. Other places surrounding the Forest where you can get gas and food are Stonyford, Elk Creek and Paskenta on the east side, Potter Valley and around Clear Lake on the south, and Covelo on the west. In the north, where trails in Six Rivers and Trinity National Forests are described, you can get supplies at Ruth, Mad River and Wildwood.

Mendocino National Forest has recently improved several sites to be accessible to people in wheelchairs or with other mobility limitations. Hammerhorn Lake Campground, 2 miles south of Yolla Bolly Wilderness, has a ¼-mile access path along the shore, with several fishing platforms. Other wheelchair-accessible facilities are at Letts Lake and Dixie Glade in the Stonyford Ranger District.

19

BLOODY ROCK/COLD CREEK
EEL RIVER TO CREST OF THE COAST RANGE

This trail explores the southern edge of Corbin Creek State Game Refuge, a rugged area of about 40,000 acres north of Snow Mountain Wilderness Area. The Game Refuge is the only part of Mendocino National Forest entirely closed to hunting. Even the possession of firearms is illegal here. The trail offers wonderful day hikes (and mountain biking), especially in spring and autumn. You can also backpack to primitive camps along pleasant Cold Creek east of the Eel River.

This fork of the Eel River, above Gravelly Valley (where Lake Pillsbury is today), was home to the branch of the Yuki people called Onkolukomno'm (Land-on-the-other-side-of-the-valley people). They ranged east to the crest of Snow Mountain and were friendly with the Northeastern Pomo who lived beyond the crest. While we do not know what they called the magnificent rock outcrop now named Bloody Rock, it was likely a holy place for them. From its summit one can survey most of their domain.

After European settlers became plentiful in the Mendocino Highlands, they heard rumors from the Potter Valley Pomo (traditional enemies of the Yuki) that the Onkolukomno'm were plotting against the settlers. A party of white men pursued these Yuki into the heart of their territory. One account says "The smoke of burning villages and forests blackened the sky at midday . . . while the wails of dying women and helpless babes burdened the air."

It was therefore natural that, when the Yuki could fight no more, a party of thirty or so warriors retreated to the top of the towering rock, perhaps hoping for supernatural intervention into the disaster thrust upon them. When the pursuing vigilantes told the warriors to surrender, the Yuki began chanting their death song. They linked hands and, with one last spirited cry, leaped over the cliff to their deaths. (Perhaps their souls soared to the rocky crests of Snow Mountain.)

The passage of time being a great healer, when you walk through the immense pastoral glades surrounding Bloody Rock today, it is hard to fathom such a tragic and terrible scene. And yet the rock radiates an unexplainable power and presence of its own. We can mourn the warriors who made this sad choice, but we must also respect them for it. (While this story may be apocryphal—no known evidence exists—the genocide of local indigenous peoples is a harsh reality.)

The broad turnout at the trailhead (with a rudimentary camp) overlooks an immense glade rimmed with white oaks, buck

BLOODY ROCK/COLD CREEK:

DISTANCE: **8 miles to Low Gap** (16 miles round trip); ¾ mile (via spur) to Bloody Rock, 1⅝ miles to Eel River, 5¾ miles to waterfall, 9 miles to Windy Gap (upper end of Trail #48).

TIME: Two hours to river, full day hike or overnight to upper Cold Creek.

TERRAIN: Descends gradually to river, climbs moderately on wooded north slope to upper Cold Creek, then to Low Gap.

ELEVATION: TH: 2940 feet. Gain/loss: 2640 feet+/760 feet-.

BEST TIME: April and May for wildflowers.

WARNINGS: No guns or vehicles allowed. Watch for rattlesnakes. Use caution at ford during spring runoff.

DIRECTIONS TO TRAILHEAD: On Forest Road M6, north of Lake Pillsbury. FROM WEST: Exit Highway 101 onto Highway 20 east (M.30.6 from south, M.30.7 from north). Go east 5 miles, then north on Potter Valley Road (Road 240) 6½ miles. Go right on Eel River Road 7 miles to Trout Creek Campground, then 10 more miles to Road M1 near Lake Pillsbury. Go left 6.3 miles, then right on Road M6 for 2.7 miles to signed Bloody Rock Trailhead on right.
FROM EAST: Turn north off Highway 20 at Upper Lake, taking Elk Mountain Road (M1) 29 miles to River Road (still M1). Go right 11 miles, then right on M6 for 2.7 miles to trailhead.

FURTHER INFO: Upper Lake Ranger District, Mendocino National Forest (707) 275-2361. Stonyford Ranger District (916) 963-3128.

OTHER SUGGESTION: TROUT CREEK CAMPGROUND (May to October) offers pleasant camping in old growth forest along beautiful stretch of Eel River. LAKE PILLSBURY has several campgrounds and short trails.

brush and scattered gray and ponderosa pines. The glade rolls toward Eel River Canyon, Snow Mountain's Crooked Tree Ridge (see Trail #47) and Crockett Peak (6172') rising steeply beyond. Due east, on Snow Mountain's left, the deep canyon of Cold Creek drops to meet the Eel.

The signed Bloody Rock Trail (no guns or vehicles allowed) descends southeast and south through the glade. The double track passes tiny lupines and non-native clovers. The purple brodiaea called ookow is extensive in spring. Dip through a deep gully where the dark blue flowers of dwarf delphinium grow. After a brief steep climb, your path joins an old road at ¼ mile and descends gradually south through the rolling glade.

Soon your distinct path veers left as a vague track climbs south. (The right fork follows a ridge to the top of Bloody Rock—one mile round trip from here.) The main trail descends slightly, heading southeast to cross a small gully. The path follows the gully through oak woodlands at the edge of the vast glade. Star zygadene, star tulip and yellow-flowered lomatium and Douglas violet cluster on the right.

The large rock outcrop called Bloody Rock, topped with wispy gray (or ghost) pines, appears to your south at ½ mile. You might say a prayer for the Yuki people who died there. Climb briefly to a chaparral-dominated ridge with a better view, where you can see Bloody Rock's steep east face, carved long ago as the Eel River created its canyon.

Descend, then contour east along a ridge where brush crowds the trail. By ¾ mile the ridgetop path is lined with healthy forest of ponderosa pine and black oak, with native bunch grass, manzanita, soap plant and Indian warrior in the understory. Another large glade lies below, between you and the brushy river canyon on the right. Douglas fir joins the forest. Hawkweeds, wood rose and lupine grow on the forest floor.

The old wagon road descends southeast, then levels as madrone and California mountain mahogany join the forest. Look for a narrow path beyond one mile that forks left off the level road, descending east through a dense stand of Douglas fir saplings. This is Cold Creek Trail.

(The wagon track continues southeast, descending to Marble Cabin site at another large glade before turning south to cross the Eel and climb to Skeleton Glade and Lower Nye Campground on Road M3. The original Cold Creek Trail, still shown on most maps, forked east at Marble Cabin. It is now impassable because of slides and brush along the river canyon.)

Descend moderately along narrow Cold Creek Trail. The path drops steeply past mountain violets, then levels at a small glade of native bunch grasses. Your path undulates, climbing gradually past a big Douglas fir and blazed ponderosa pines, then descending slightly to 1¼ miles before another gentle climb and descent. Descend moderately through tall forest to 1½ miles, then gently southeast on good tread until the Eel River is close by on your left. Grasslands beneath oaks support red larkspur, Shelton's violet, popcorn flower and woodland star.

A tiny old wooden sign at the base of a steep climb says "TRAIL." That is the old, now impassable route to Marble Cabin. You need to go left, descending vague tread 200 feet to ford the river at 1⅝ miles. A medium-sized swimming hole is just above the ford, but a bigger one lies 300 feet downstream. Use caution and a stout stick to cross the ford, which is 100 feet across at moderately high water. (Do not cross if it is fast and deep.)

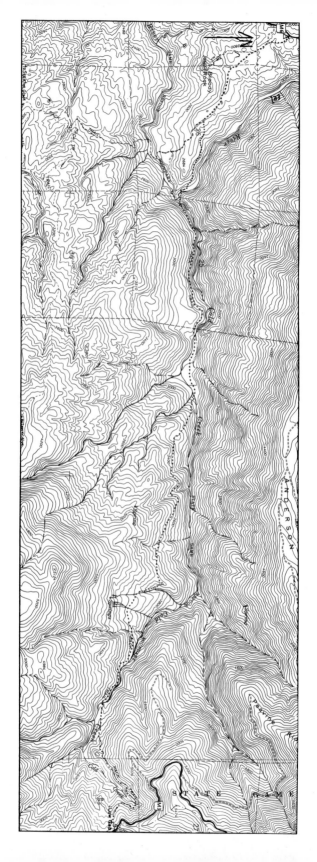

Douglas wallflower grows beside the obvious trail on the east bank. The sandy track leads to a pleasant camp in 150 feet. It overlooks the deep hole above the big bend where Cold Creek enters the Eel. The path east is marked with candy-stripe flagging. Make an easy ford of alder- and maple-lined Cold Creek at 1¾ miles. Climb the steep cutbank to another pleasant camp, just outside the Game Refuge, surrounded by Oregon ash, madrone and maple.

Cold Creek Trail climbs steeply east, switchbacking twice. Pass poison oak, trail plant, star tulip, starflower, serviceberry and Oregon grape beneath dense forest of Douglas fir and live oak. The tread improves after you climb over a deadfall tree.

From 2 miles your trail contours across a steep slope, winding along Cold Creek Canyon. Western white pine joins the forest with understory of pipsissewa and Indian warrior. Use caution on narrow tread across the top of a steep slide. Gradual climbs are interspersed with level tread beyond 2¼ miles. Look for wood rose, white-veined shinleaf, twisted stalk, spotted coral root and calypso orchids in spring. The trail crosses a gully, then a deadfall fir around 2⅝ miles, passing ponderosa and sugar pine, madrone and large-leaved lupine. Traverse the top of a slide that plunges 150 feet to Cold Creek, then contour east.

Before 3 miles your trail descends to cross a seasonal creek lined with red larkspur, bedstraw and miners lettuce. A gradual, winding descent continues to the broad rocky bed of Cold Creek in ⅛ mile. Your indistinct path heads up the south side of the canyon floor. Where the canyon becomes even broader, head east to ford Cold Creek. Follow a faint but flagged track on a gentle ascent past coffeeberry bushes on the broad, wooded canyon floor, staying left of the creek.

The path veers right at 3½ miles and descends to ford Cold Creek, just above its confluence with a small tributary on the far side. Since this is the last dependable water for 2¼ miles, take a break and refresh yourself. Angelica and raspberry grow abundantly at the ford.

Your trail climbs east, then switchbacks right and left, climbing from the canyon bottom. Ascend moderately, except for a steep hill around 3¾ miles.

The path disappears around 4 miles as it enters a glade. Cross the bottom of the clearing, contouring past a small pine to find the trail climbing east into forest. You soon cross a gully and climb into chaparral. Cream fawn lilies and the leafless yellow flowers of the saprophyte called fascicled broom-rape grow here in spring. You can see Hull Mountain northwest.

The trail ascends gradually, winding into forest. At 4¼ miles you encounter the first white fir on the hike, growing beneath Douglas firs. Scarlet fritillary grows nearby. Cross a small gully and make a winding contour through forest dominated by oaks.

Pass sugar pines as the path climbs gently southeast. You

have a good view up the canyon to the high country on the flank of Sheetiron Mountain (6503'). Your trail turns east at 4½ miles to cross a seasonal tributary. The track winds, climbing moderately, then gradually to 4¾ miles.

The trail undulates through gullies, then passes a sign marking the Game Refuge boundary. Ascend gradually across a gully, then through a small glade. After another gully crossing at 5 miles, climb moderately. Your path bends right at a six-foot-wide Douglas fir and ascends gradually. Climb along a gully, cross it, then make a winding ascent through another gully.

At 5½ miles the path levels high above a rushing tributary of Cold Creek. Turn south on a slight descent, soon entering a large glade. Ascend through the glade, then through mixed forest and grasslands. Descend briefly to a small waterfall on the spring-fed tributary, beneath incense cedars and Douglas firs. Ford the creek above the falls before 5¾ miles. Giant trillium and checker lily grow above the crossing in spring.

The trail makes a winding contour east, nearing upper Cold Creek at 6 miles. Climb moderately along the creek to 6⅜ miles. Ford to the north bank and follow the creek east to 6¾ miles.

Your trail turns northeast, climbing moderately up a gully following the Game Refuge boundary. Climb over a small ridge at 7 miles, then ascend along a seasonal creek, crossing it around 7½ miles. Your trail makes a winding ascent southeast and east to the crest of the eastern Coast Range. You meet Road M3 at Low Gap, about 8 miles from the trailhead. Upper Bearwallow Trailhead (Trail #48) is one mile south up the road.

20.

DEAFY GLADE

ALONG THE EDGE OF THE WILDERNESS FROM DIXIE GLADE

The Forest Service has developed a new campground in the pleasant, middle elevation pine and fir forest adjacent to the southern boundary of Snow Mountain Wilderness. The new Dixie Glade Campground, to be completed autumn 1992, offers basic car camping as well as wheelchair-accessible facilities, a group camp (by reservation only) and a corral and loading area for equestrians. It is also the new starting point for Deafy Glade Trail (the old trail started one mile west). The new trail is a very pretty addition to the old route. The trail enters Snow Mountain Wilderness Area beyond 1½ miles at the ford of South Fork Stony Creek.

Your level trail heads southwest from the parking area opposite the toilets. Skirt the upper edge of Dixie Glade and cross a tiny

DEAFY GLADE:

DISTANCE: **Dixie Glade to Deafy Glade: 1¾ miles** (3½ miles round trip).

TIME: Half-day hike or overnight.

TERRAIN: Climbs gently through forest, then descends to ford, followed by short steep climb to glade.

ELEVATION: TH: 3000 feet. Gain/loss: 860 feet+/160 feet-.

BEST TIME: A good hike whenever snow level is above 3600 feet. During spring runoff, ford may not be safe.

WARNINGS: Watch for poison oak and rattlesnakes. Use caution at South Fork ford; do not cross at high water.

DIRECTIONS TO TRAILHEAD: From Interstate 5, take Maxwell exit (M.26.6 from south, M.27.0 from north—Colusa County). Go west 32 miles to Stonyford. Turn left at Stonyford General Store (last gas and supplies). In .2 mile, go left on Fouts Springs Road (M10) 12 miles to Dixie Glade Campground (turnoff on right). Go .1 mile to trailhead parking.

FURTHER INFO: Stonyford Ranger District, Mendocino National Forest (916) 963-3128.

seasonal creek. The trail turns northwest and descends briefly. Gooseberry and redbud grow beneath the mixed forest. To the north, Snow Mountain's south flank rises beyond South Fork Stony Creek canyon.

Your trail climbs through the forest to ¼ mile, then meanders through rolling terrain where sugar pines join the ponderosas, knobcones, oaks and bay laurels. Cross the first of several small creeks and pass dogwood, wild grape and red larkspur.

Climb gradually through forest to cross a seasonal creek with Oregon grape, bedstraw and sword fern on its banks. The grade eases at ⅝ mile as the trail bends left and follows the cutbank of a year-round creek lined with bigleaf maple and large Oregon ash trees. Wild grape vines four inches in diameter entwine one tree.

Hound's tongue borders the trail where you ford the creek at ¾ mile. Climb out of the canyon into open forest. The trail levels before ⅞ mile, where the old Deafy Glade Trail enters from the left. Your mostly level path broadens, following an old road. South Fork Stony Creek roars (especially in spring) on your right as the trail draws near its canyon.

Climb gently through a forest, mostly Douglas fir with scattered incense cedar and pines, beyond one mile. As you pass through a clearing, seasonal springs provide moisture to support maples and honeysuckle vines. Your trail dips through a gully at 1¼ miles, then levels as views open north to Deafy Rock (3426') and the rushing creek in the gorge at its base.

Start a gradual descent at 1⅜ miles, nearing the creek. The grade steepens at 1½ miles, soon coming to the ford of South Fork Stony Creek just above its confluence with an unnamed creek from the north. The gravelly ford should not be attempted at high water in spring. Lilies, columbines and miners lettuce grow along the creek beneath large hardwood trees.

An immense live oak grows on the north bank. The rough trail climbs steeply out of the canyon by short switchbacks. It reaches the pleasant, steep clearing of Deafy Glade at 1¾ miles, rimmed by several nice campsites beneath Douglas firs, ponderosa pines and maples. The path climbs to the top of the glade, where Bathhouse Trail (Trail #49) enters on the right.

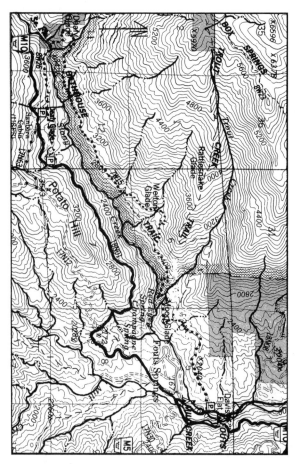

INTO THE WILDERNESS

Wilderness trips require more planning than short day hikes do, but you can have a wilderness experience without being a survivalist. If you are inexperienced in wilderness travel, start with a car camping trip, making day-hike forays into the wilderness. Many car camps border Yolla Bolly and Snow Mountain Wilderness Areas at or near the trailheads. You can move on to short overnight trips with a light pack. These wilderness areas offer many choices ideal for one or two night excursions. When you feel confident, you can make that long-dreamed-of week-long trip.

"YOU CALL THAT A TRAIL?"

Anyone heading into Yolla Bolly or Snow Mountain Wilderness Area, whether novice hiker or seasoned backpacker, needs to know some basic facts about these areas. They are in steep and rugged country, extremely isolated from towns and services, often so little traveled that you can take a trip without seeing anyone outside your party. As wonderful as this is, it holds inherent dangers you might not have encountered on that trip out of Tuolomne Meadows.

These areas are seldom patrolled by the Forest Service or anyone else. Assume your group will be on their own when solving any problems, whether it be forgotten gear, bad weather, serious injury or becoming lost.

No Forest Service official will know if you do not return on time. You do not need a wilderness permit to enter these areas. Even when you get a campfire permit (required to build a fire), no one is likely to check up on you, at least not until your vehicle starts looking abandoned.

These are truly untrammeled wilderness areas. While most of the trails described are maintained occasionally, that may be as seldom as once every ten years. Expect trails to be vague in places. You might even encounter tread that has disappeared altogether. What to do? First, don't panic; sit down and calmly think through your predicament. Second, use all your resources; are there blazes* on trees? rock cairns*? Did you make a wrong turn at the last bend, veering off on some deer path? Does *The Hiker's hip pocket Guide* mention anything that might help you understand and resolve what went wrong? Finally, don't be afraid to turn back; it is always easier to find the trail you came on than the unknown one ahead. Surely you can retrace your route or retreat to some known landmark.

Keep your party together whenever possible. Most mishaps occur when someone gets separated from their group. Two or more calm heads are better than one. We advise you not to travel solo. Be especially careful in every way if you do.

Study and know the Ten Wilderness Commandments before

you go. They have valuable safety information and methods of minimizing your impact on pristine habitats. When traveling in the wilderness, don't take unnecessary chances. Know where you are at all times. Stay on a known and planned route.

*TERMS YOU NEED TO KNOW

BLAZE. Two rectangular notches cut in a tree, one above the other, to indicate the route of a trail. (The term originated with the traditional candle and flame shape of the notches.)

BLOWDOWN. Trees that have fallen across the trail. "Deadfall" refers to the same thing.

CAIRN. A stack of rocks used to indicate the route through treeless country, especially where tread is vague (may also be called "ducks").

CONTOUR. When a trail remains at roughly the same elevation, i.e. stays within the contour lines on the map.

TANK TRAP. A pile of debris large enough to block a tank or other all-terrain vehicle.

UNDULATE. An undulating trail dips and climbs repeatedly, often through gullies.

TEN WILDERNESS COMMANDMENTS

When you visit the wilderness, make sure every action you take shows your respect for the pristine land and water you have come to enjoy. The following rules will help you realize this ideal and keep you safe.

1. ALWAYS DISPOSE OF BODILY WASTE PROPERLY. Go at least 100 feet from water and seasonal drainages for your toilet duties (200 feet is better!). Dig a hole six to eight inches deep to bury human waste. Then fill the hole, tamp it down to look as though no one has been there, and place a rock or branch on it. Burn or carry out the toilet paper.

2. NO TRACE CAMPING. You know that you must pack out whatever you pack into the wilderness. Never bury food or trash; animals will only dig it up. Camping with no lasting impact goes beyond that. Always camp on firm, dry ground, never on meadows or the soft areas at the edges of lakes or streams. Use only biodegradable soap and throw the waste water on rocks or trees 100 feet from lakes and drainages. Do not make "improvements" to your camp; if you build a fire ring, dismantle it before leaving. In most situations you do not need to dig a ditch around your tent; but if you do, fill it before breaking camp. If you bring livestock, keep them on a hitchline between two trees and at least 200 feet from water.

3. WATER. Fresh, clear mountain water is one of the unsung joys of the wilderness. You need to drink three quarts minimum

each day to compensate for the rigorous exercise of wilderness hiking. If your urine is darker than usual, you are not drinking enough water. Refill containers at every opportunity. Water is scarce on some trails (especially late summer), unavailable on others. Unless you are certain water is pure, purify it by filtering, using purification tablets or boiling for five minutes.

4. PLAN AHEAD/BE PREPARED. Plan your trip before you go. Inquire about trail conditions and weather before entering the wilderness. Write down your itinerary and when you expect to return for someone at home. Always carry flashlight, water, sufficient clothing and foul weather gear, first-aid kit, enough food. Carry map and compass and know how to use them.

5. WEATHER changes rapidly in the mountains. In summer, thunderstorms develop quickly on hot days, bringing dangerous lightning, especially on high ridges. When thunderstorms approach, get down from high ridges, peaks and other open areas. Avoid isolated trees. Low forests of short trees are the safest place, even better if in a valley. You must always be prepared for freezing temperatures and snow, which can occur in any season, but be especially watchful on non-summer trips.

6. TRAIL SENSE AND COURTESY. Never take chances at stream crossings. Remember that fords will be lowest in early morning, highest in late afternoon. Be reasonably quiet and respect other people's wilderness experience. Don't cut switchbacks. Horses have the right of way on trails.

7. LOST. If you feel you are lost, don't panic. Sit down and calmly think through your situation. Take out your map and compass and try to orient yourself, looking for familiar landmarks. Where were you last certain of your location? Can you backtrack to that place?

8. INJURED OR ILL. Blisters are a minor inconvenience, but treat them with moleskin as soon as you are aware of them, or they can become excruciating. Other health problems also need to be dealt with before getting out of hand. Make sure someone in your party knows first aid. The two most dangerous conditions in the wilderness are heat exhaustion and hypothermia. Caused by external conditions, the former is an increase in body temperature, the latter a decrease. Both are life-threatening and require immediate action. For conditions you cannot treat, like snakebite or broken bones, you must seek help. If you send for help, be sure the sufferer will be safe.

9. FIRE. Be very careful with it, clearing the area around your fire and extinguishing it completely before leaving camp. Use a stove for cooking. Conserve wood when it is scarce. You are required to have a fire permit to build fires outside developed campgrounds (that means anywhere inside the wilderness).

10. KNOW YOUR LIMITS. Don't carry too much weight or push too hard when backpacking. Take it easy and enjoy the experience. **ALWAYS TAKE RESPONSIBILITY FOR YOURSELF AND YOUR PARTY.**

YOLLA BOLLY-MIDDLE EEL WILDERNESS

The designated Yolla Bolly-Middle Eel Wilderness Area currently comprises 153,404 acres in Mendocino, Trinity and Six Rivers National Forests and adjacent Bureau of Land Management lands. Elevations range from 2000 feet in the canyons to over 8000 feet on South Yolla Bolly Mountain. This guide also covers adjacent lands north, west and south of the designated wilderness, pristine areas worth incorporating into the official wilderness. Earth First! estimates about 100,000 additional acres around the wilderness worthy of inclusion. *

The United States Forest Service first set aside portions of the Yolla Bollys for protection in 1931. Congress formally protected over 100,000 acres of the Yolla Bollys in the Wilderness Act of 1964, then added acreage in 1984.

The California Wilderness Coalition regards the Yolla Bollys as one of the best wildlife strongholds in California. The wilderness harbors abundant mammals like black bear, mountain lion, bobcat, black-tailed deer, wolverine, mountain beaver, ringtail, river otter, mink, marten and fisher, and 150 bird species, including rare and endangered golden and bald eagles, peregrine falcon and Northern spotted owl.

Geologically, the Yolla Bollys began forming 150 million years ago, during the Age of the dinosaurs. As the Pacific oceanic plate collided with the North American continental plate, the pressure pushed the former ocean bottom upward, folding it and lifting it high above the sea. This same pressure compressed the sandstone of the ocean floor, changing the sediments into metamorphic rock called schist. A great mass of granitic rock (batholith) underlying the sandstone was uplifted along with it. The uplifting continued for millions of years, forming the western Coast Range around 30 million years ago. Today the two plates continue to collide. Earthquakes periodically rattle the region as a reminder.

South Fork Trinity River follows a major fault through the Yolla Bolly region, separating the Klamath province to the north from the Coast Ranges to the south. The North Yolla Bollys are part of the Klamath Range. They are geologically distinct from

---

*Three unprotected areas and the lower Middle Fork Eel Canyon particularly deserve wilderness designation. The areas are 1) between Black Rock Lake and East Fork of South Fork Trinity River, 2) west and south from Rat Trap Gap, and 3) from Red Rock south along Leech Lake Mountain and Pine Ridge. In addition, the Middle Fork Eel River Canyon below 3000-feet elevation is designated a Wild and Scenic River but is not protected as wilderness. You might encourage the Forest Service and elected federal officials to incorporate these areas into the wilderness.

vaN.92

the rest of the Yolla Bollys.

Once the sea floor was uplifted to form the mountains in their present position, the erosive forces of wind, water and ice shaped the peaks we see today. You can see evidence of glaciation on the north sides of both North and South Yolla Bolly Mountains. This glacial erosion occurred mostly during the Pleistocene ice age (the most recent), between two million and 10,000 years ago. Water, however, has done the most extensive erosion. Millions of years of water-laid sediment now fill Round Valley to a depth of 800 to 1000 feet, creating an excellent aquifer for the valley's many wells. Water's erosive force gave the Yolla Bolly peaks their characteristic rounded shapes.

Native peoples have inhabited this region for unknown millennia. The name Yolla Bolly comes from the Wintun language, "yo-la" meaning "snow-covered," "bo-li" meaning "high peak." Various tribes of two distinct peoples called this area home long before any European people had set foot on this continent, let alone in California. The tributaries of the Sacramento River east of the main divide were home to the Nomlaki Wintun. West of the divide, the upper Eel River watershed was home to the Yuki people. The Yuki included eight or nine sub-groups. The northernmost of the Yuki were the Sukshaltatamno'm. They inhabited, and were spiritually linked to the watershed we today call Middle Fork Eel River. While all the Yuki inhabited mountainous terrain, the Sukshaltatamno'm people lived, hunted and gathered in the highest, most isolated *region of the Yuki territory.*

This isolation afforded these people some insulation from the first waves of European settlers. But after the immigrants found and began settling Round Valley in 1854, nothing could protect even the most remote indigenous people. A tragic and sordid period of genocide occurred from 1856 through 1864, after which the few remaining Yuki and Wintun people were confined to reservations.

When you visit the Yolla Bollys, you will see how isolated this pristine region remains even today. No matter which access road you choose, you wind and climb for miles from highways and towns. When you come to road's end and a trailhead, prepare to leave modern amenities and the technological world behind. Enter the wilderness with an open heart and mind, thankful that such solitude exists in such a troubled, complex world.

If you want a guided trip into Yolla Bolly Wilderness, Rollin' F Ranch offers guided horse trips from basic to deluxe, plus drop off service for hikers. For information, write them at 7355 Elphick Road, Sebastopol, CA 95472, or call (707) 829-7829.

PLEASE NOTE: *When referring to the Yolla Bolly Map in the back of the book, you must add twenty to the trail number on the map to get the corresponding trail number in the book. Thus Map Trail #1 is Trail #21 in the book and so on.*

21.

BLUEJAY MINE/
RED MOUNTAIN LOOP

LITTLE KNOWN ROUTE RICH IN HISTORY

This loop, one of the least known routes described in this book, explores the area most recently added to Yolla Bolly Wilderness. The loop connects with trails through even less traveled country. The virtually unknown North Fork Wilderness is to the west.

This loop is the only route in the Yolla Bollys entirely below 4500 feet. Its milder climate combines with harsh serpentine soils to offer vast contrasts in vegetation and scenery in a relatively short trip. Low elevation and the paved road guarantee access most of the year, though you must still be prepared for sudden storms, especially from October through April.

More history has been recorded about this western corner of Yolla Bolly Wilderness Area than about the rest of this high mountain region. The Lassik and Pitch Wailaki, southern Athabascan tribes, lived here. While much of the Yolla Bolly region is too high in elevation to have supported year-round residency, these tribes had villages on Red Mountain Creek and upper Mad River. They spoke Yuki as well as their native tongues, a result of much contact with the people to the south.

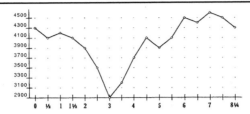

BLUEJAY MINE/RED MOUNTAIN LOOP:

DISTANCE: **6-mile semi-loop or 8¼-mile loop with 2¼-mile walk on road**; 1½ miles to Bluejay Mine, 3¼ miles to Red Mountain Trail, 4⅜ miles to Red Mountain summit.

TIME: Full day or overnight.

TERRAIN: Contours old road to mine site, then descends into creek canyons; climbs steeply over mountain, then down and up along ridge to road.

TRAILS INTERSECTED: Littlefield, 8E04.

BEST TIME: Early or late season; hot in summer. May be accessible year round.

WARNINGS: Watch for rattlesnakes and poison oak. Trail extremely vague where it climbs Red Mountain through burn.

DIRECTIONS TO TRAILHEAD: Take Highway 36 to Mad River (52 miles east of Highway 101, 80 miles west of Interstate 5). Turn south on County Road 501 joining County Road 504 before passing Ruth Store in 21 miles. In 5.9 miles turn right toward Three Forks on Road 504. In 4.1 miles County Road becomes Forest Road 27N02. Go 3.6 miles, then right on Road 26N32, signed "TRAIL", .2 mile to trailhead.

FURTHER INFO: Mad River Ranger District, Six Rivers National Forest (707) 574-6233.

OTHER SUGGESTION: For quicker access to RED MOUNTAIN TRAIL, drive 2.3 miles beyond Road 26N32 on Road 27N02 to signed trailhead on right. Unmaintained LITTLEFIELD TRAIL branches off Bluejay/Red Mountain Loop for a 6-mile loop with Trail 8E04.

Many modern trails in the area follow old native trails.

The Lassik and Pitch Wailaki suffered greatly in the tragic period of genocide brough on by white settlement. By 1863 the natives remaining on their home turf were constantly on the run, pursued by settlers from the south and the army from the north. By 1864 hostilities had ended and most surviving natives were on reservations or indentured.

Tyranny continued in the Red Mountain/North Fork area as rancher George White, later known as the "Cattle King," used hired gunmen to intimidate newcomers attempting to settle in the area. Jack Littlefield was murdered by White's buckaroos in 1895. This focused the attention of lawmen on this lawless area, soon making it safer for settlers to move in. The trail report has more of the area's history.

Bluejay Mine Trail heads southwest along an old road beyond a tank trap. The signed trailhead has no trail register. Descend gradually through fir and oak forest with a lush understory of hazel, ceanothus, sticky currant, raspberry and creeping snowberry. You soon wind across a moist gully crowded with bigleaf maples.

Pass another tank trap and continue a gentle descent as pines join the forest and elderberry, starflower and poison oak mix with the understory. The winding track passes a fire ring before ¼ mile, then a spur road on the right. The headwaters of South Fork Mad River gather in the deep canyon below.

Ascend gently before ½ mile, entering drier habitat than the first part of the trail. Climb to a fork where gray pines, buck brush and California mountain mahogany thrive. Turn right and contour west on a ridge that divides the Mad River and Eel River drainages. Pass manzanita, yerba santa and Fremont silktassel. By ¾ mile, where a large gray pine stands on the left, you have nearly crossed the dike-like ridge. Descend gradually.

By one mile your old road descends south along the east face of Hayden Roughs. Brush and hardwoods have claimed this area, burned in 1987. Wind through a gully, watching for extensive poison oak, then contour through shady mixed forest.

The road forks at 1½ miles. Take the left fork, descending into the burn area. In 250 feet the road forks again. The described route goes left, but the right fork is worth exploring. (It leads to a campsite in 125 feet, below a striking red rock outcrop, the site of Bluejay Mine, where manganese was extracted during the 1940s.)

The left fork descends moderately through chaparral, then into fir/oak forest. Soon the track bends left, reaching a shady campsite with a picnic table and concrete fire ring. Follow the road 150 feet to a spring on the right. In late season it is a putrid cattle hole. In spring one might find potable water.

Climb 250 feet on the deteriorating roadbed, then go left on a footpath descending south. The well blazed route descends gradually through grass and chaparral. Wind through a burn area where you see Red Mountain rising south-southeast with rugged country in between.

Beyond 2 miles the trail winds through a gully. Contour past madrone, live and white oaks, ceanothus, elderberry and poison oak. Descend, then climb briefly on gravel tread before descending past Oregon grape. The descent steepens through manzanita fields beneath scattered Jeffrey pines.

Reach a burned ridgetop at 2⅜ miles with views west to the ridge forming the wilderness boundary, south toward Red Mountain and east to the grassy ridge at the end of this loop. The trail leaves the ridge heading south-southwest on a steep winding descent. Then descend moderately in and out of mixed forest of Jeffrey pine, Douglas fir and incense cedar.

By 2⅞ miles you descend a ridge between two heavily wooded creeks. The trail bisects a grassy flat with much poison oak. At the lower half of the flat the trail becomes vague in the grasslands. To add to the confusion Trail 8E04 enters from the northwest. (It climbs the west ridge, meeting Trails 8E05 and 8E06 beyond the wilderness boundary.) Bear right near the bottom of the flat to parallel the creek on your right. Faint tread leads to a pleasant camp at the confluence of the creeks.

The trail fords Little Red Mountain Creek (on the left) just above its confluence with the unnamed creek. The creeks are lined with Oregon ash, white alder, hazel and bay laurel. Your path climbs to another grassy flat, more open than the last and rimmed by tall forest. Continue south on obvious track, soon leaving the clearing for forest with an open, grassy understory.

Your path merges with a deeply rutted jeep track and continues south, the creek on your right. Soon a camp sits on the right beneath an immense bay tree beside the creek.

Watch for a footpath forking left 250 feet beyond the camp. This is Red Mountain Trail, climbing southeast. The jeep track south is Littlefield Trail. Both were parts of the old Round Valley to Weaverville Trail, probably established in the 1860s. By the 1890s (if not earlier) travelers could stop here at Red Mountain House for a meal and a room. The inn was the site of a post office called Caution. During the early 1900s a school was over the ridge to the west.

Take the trail climbing southeast across grasslands, Red Mountain looming ahead. Within 250 feet the faint tread enters a burned area. Continue southeast over fallen saplings, passing left of a large grassy seep. The faint, unblazed route winds right and left, climbing generally southeast toward Red Mountain.

By 3⅜ miles the trail has climbed to a gently rolling grassland, a favorite haunt of cows and bears judging by the scat. Angle south-southeast for 125 feet to find a blaze on a burned double-trunk pine above the trail. The trail soon turns east following a finger of the large glade. Pass a blaze on a dead two-foot-wide pine on the left before 3½ miles. The nearly invisible trail continues east through the glade. Find another blaze 200 feet from the last. Your route climbs east-northeast 100 feet to a living pine blazed on both sides.

Climb north-northeast along the top edge of the glade. If you

vaN.92

are still on the route you will find a very steep, eroded red-dirt trail. It soon meets better tread climbing out of the burn area. Climb steeply northeast to a ridge by 3⅝ miles, where a blaze marks a large dead pine. You are out of the grasslands and onto the stark red dirt of Red Mountain. Better tread climbs northeast.

If you cannot match this description, you have gotten off this hard-to-find route. It would be safer to retrace your route via Bluejay Mine than to chance getting lost in this rugged, brushy country. If you have found the trail, continue up Red Mountain.

Climb steeply on a rocky, red-dirt trail. Fire burned this hillside in 1987, killing most of the Jeffrey pines. Manzanita, live oak and coffeeberry are revegetating the devastated area. Naked stem buckwheat, yerba santa, phacelia, poison oak, yarrow and cliff brake are also thriving. Climb past a surviving Jeffrey pine, then past live Douglas firs and gray pines. The path is very steep, then eases as it winds southeast.

A steep climb soon resumes, approaching the shoulder of Red Mountain. Beyond 4 miles the ascent eases as living trees offer shade. Climb moderately until the ascent eases heading east. The path turns northeast for another steep climb to 4¼ miles, with expansive views west and south.

The trail turns east, climbing gradually to the ultimate summit at 4⅜ miles, where views expand to the east. The trail descends northeast, then picks up a ridge. Look northeast to see the winding ridge you will follow to Jones Ridge and the road.

Duck under a deadfall pine and make a steep winding descent on a brushy, burned ridgetop to a saddle, then climb gradually. The path soon turns east and descends. The ridgetop trail undulates beyond 4¾ miles, with grand views of the stark terrain of western Yolla Bolly Wilderness.

Descend to a saddle, then veer to the right around a big knob on the ridge, crossing its steep east slope on slanting tread. Return to the ridgetop at 5 miles as tread improves. Terrain drops steeply on the left and right. Climb briefly, descend to a saddle, then climb over a small rise and drop to one last saddle.

Begin a steep climb toward the trailhead, a 500-foot gain. Ascend sloppy tread on a steep slope around 5½ miles. Your climb soon passes a seep on your left where scarlet monkeyflowers grow. You will find better water at the seep's source two bends up the trail. Climb moderately steeply through some brushy patches.

The trail climbs southeast past another seep. A brief steep climb soon turns moderate. Descend slightly across a red-rock scree slope. Manuever around a fallen pine and resume a gradual climb east. Cow paths in this area tend to obscure the real trail. Continue east to 6 miles, climbing to a ridgetop, then go left 100 feet to the road and trailhead. Your starting point is 2¼ miles north along Jones Ridge Road.

22.
ANT POINT/FOUR CORNERS LOOP
RIDGES AND CANYONS OF THE WESTERN WILDERNESS

This route explores wild, remote country where coyotes often howl in broad daylight. The trail from Jones Ridge Road to Ant Point, long known as Boundary Trail, follows the boundary between Six Rivers and Mendocino National Forests. The loop may be accessible most of the year, when higher trails are shrouded in snow. It offers an easy route to a pleasant camp at Little Butte Spring, then descends to seasonal Willow Creek. Beyond the creek the route becomes tricky to follow as it climbs to grand views atop 5406-foot Four Corners Rock.

Be especially careful not to lose the trail in this brushy country. A pleasant trailhead campsite offers splendid sunrise views over the wilderness. Bring water for the dry camp and first 2⅝ miles.

Your path climbs west from the signed trailhead, then turns southwest to ascend moderately through forest of Douglas and white firs, ponderosa pine, white and black oaks. The trail levels and meets an old jeep track. Follow the track south along a grassy ridgetop with brushy slopes through pine forest.

Ascend to a grand view at ¼ mile that looks south to the barren, dark rock of Ant Point, west to nearby Red Mountain and the King Range on the horizon, and northwest to Hayden Roughs and Grizzly Mountain near Zenia. A winding descent offers expansive views east over the rest of the wilderness. Yellow sulphur flowers line the open ridgetop.

A firebreak is on your left as the trail angles right. Your path climbs briefly, meets the firebreak, then undulates through a

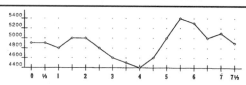

DISTANCE: 7½-mile loop (with 1 mile walk on road); 2 miles to Ant Point, 2⅝ miles to Little Butte Spring, 4 miles to Willow Creek ford, 5¾ miles to Four Corners Rock.

TIME: Full day hike or overnight.

TERRAIN: Follows wooded, then barren ridge; descends through forest to spring, then to Willow Creek; climbs to brushy ridge, grand view and road.

TRAILS INTERSECTED: Morrison, Four Corners Rock.

BEST TIME: May and June for water; may be accessible April through November.

WARNINGS: Watch for rattlesnakes. Willow Creek may be dry by July. Brushy and hard to follow approaching Four Corners Rock; take long pants, map and compass.

DIRECTIONS TO TRAILHEAD: Take Highway 36 to Mad River (52 miles east of Highway 101, 80 miles west of Interstate 5). Turn south on County Road 501 joining County Road 504 before passing Ruth Store in 21 miles. In 5.9 miles, turn right toward Three Forks on Road 504. County Road becomes Forest Road 27N02 at 4.1 miles. Go 8.5 more miles to signed trailhead.

FURTHER INFO: Covelo Ranger District, Mendocino National Forest (707) 983-6118.

OTHER SUGGESTION: FOUR CORNERS ROCK TRAIL leaves Road 27N02 1.9 miles beyond Ant Point Trail, descending 2 miles to River Trail near pleasant camp. MORRISON TRAIL leaves described loop near Little Butte Spring, climbing, then descending 4 miles to River Trail near Brown Camp.

broad clearing on the ridgetop. Intriguing rocks and wind-sculpted Jeffrey pines jut from the soil. A short steep climb ends in a barren clearing. The trail descends gently, soon bending right. Contour across a glade east of a ridgetop knob at ¾ mile.

Your path returns briefly to the ridgetop. Faint tread veers left to descend south in 150 feet, leaving the jeep track. The trail soon improves, winding up and down through young forest. Return to the ridgetop at a saddle and ascend through barren,

kW.92

rocky terrain with brushy patches and a few stunted trees. Top
a ridgetop knob at 1⅛ miles and descend to a saddle, then climb
gradually to the top of a long hill, where you look south to Ant
Point, with wooded Little and Big Buttes towering beyond.

The trail dips, rises and weaves along the ridge toward Ant
Point, crossing a large glade lined with white oaks. The landscape
turns vaguely moonscapish as a few stunted plants—white
oak, mule ears, rabbitbrush and naked stem buckwheat—are
the only suggestion that this is not some lifeless planet. The
terrain resembles an ancient, violently uplifted ocean floor.

Descend steeply at 1¾ miles, passing a short, fat juniper.
Wind toward Ant Point, traversing its steep west slope until the
path switches left to wind along the east slope. Return to the
ridgetop to complete the ascent, passing 50 feet northeast of
the 5058-foot top of Ant Point at 2 miles.

Your trail descends along bare rocky ridgetop. Climb over the
last of Ant Point's stark knobs and look for the vague tread
which continues south 150 feet before a steep descent leads to
better tread. The path bends sharply left to descend east. Your
descent eases, leaving bare ground for oak brush. The route
becomes very brushy as it turns south, then climbs southeast.

The climb eases, entering forest at 2½ miles and coming to
a triangular junction. The unmapped trail on the right descends
south. Take the left fork to contour northeast. In 300 feet you
reach a small grassy clearing with a trickling spring on the
trail's right shoulder. (A vague spur forks right just before this

spring, climbing 200 feet to pleasant campsites beside a small glade, Little Butte Camp. A path climbs 75 feet from the upper camp to a year-round spring—look for the iron pipe.)

The main trail climbs north briefly. The path becomes vague along the bottom of a glade (the camps are on its upper end), quickly reaching a junction. Morrison Trail heads east. Our described route goes left on Willow Creek Trail. Descend to another good spring on your right where the path becomes vague. Descend north to find clear tread descending northeast through the forest. The trail turns faint again as it heads north through a tiny glade, then becomes distinct, descending through mixed forest.

Descend a gully with white-veined shinleaf, snowberry and wood rose. By 3⅛ miles this small gully joins a larger one. Descend to a ford and pass a six-foot-wide Douglas fir. The gully has steep, heavily wooded slopes. You may find water here even when the rest of the creek is dry. Return to the left bank where the path is sometimes vague as it descends along the creek bed. Wind above the creek past a spring in a gully, then return to the creek.

At 3½ miles the path crosses to the east bank, then fords twice more. Soon your path ascends the east bank steeply, then contours a steep slope as the creek drops away on your left.

Your trail bends left around a fallen fir at 3⅞ miles, then descends gradually. The path turns east to ford broad Willow Creek. (Expect no water in late summer.) On the creek's north bank a wealth of cow paths may confuse. Look for a well blazed trail climbing gradually east. Top a rise and drop to another fork of Willow Creek at 4⅛ miles. The faint path heads north across the ford, then turns east in the middle of the broad stream bed before climbing southeast through forest.

The path soon bends left for a steep winding climb, then ascends a ridge east. Sporadically vague, brushy tread descends briefly, then climbs steadily, winding along the ridgetop. Before 4¾ miles your trail climbs east, leaving the ridgetop. Pass an immense black oak, then a cattle trough. Your trail climbs steeply east, quickly coming to a glade where the trail vanishes.

Fear not! Turn northeast and climb to the ridgetop, where you find a faint, blazed trail. Ascend the ridgetop northwest past a blazed 30-inch pine. Decent tread climbs from there. Your path drops off the ridgetop, angling northeast and soon resuming its climb. Veer left, climbing steeply around fallen snags.

Meet Four Corners Rock Trail at 5 miles. A trail sign points east, claiming 3½ miles to Sulphur Camp. (That rugged route, not recommended, descends east to ford North Fork Middle Fork Eel River and reach River Trail [Trail #43] in 1¼ miles.)

Turn left on Four Corners Rock Trail, climbing steeply west and northwest to complete the loop. The path winds to the right around a big fallen pine, then ascends the ridgetop gradually,

low .9 2

passing impressive pines and oaks. Make one short steep climb and a brushy detour right of another deadfall.

By 5¼ miles the trail becomes brushy with low white oaks. You do not want to continue without long pants. The brush situation deteriorates from knee-high to head-high. The trail splinters into many paths, some brushier, some straighter, all rough going. Stay on or near the ridgetop, heading generally north-northwest toward Four Corners Rock, visible ahead.

By 5½ miles the worst brush is over as you near Four Corners Rock. Watch for a sharp bend left down the ridge's west face. In 200 feet you switchback right toward Four Corners Rock. Climb steeply to the right as you encounter another wall of oak brush. Pick up another path just west of the ridgetop. It soon bends right and heads north, switching to the ridge's east side beyond 5⅝ miles.

Pause beneath the shade of one last tall pine, enjoying a fine view of Four Corners Rock. Continue toward the rock, climbing to its right and reaching its north face, where an easy scramble climbs 30 feet to the summit.

You can see most of the peaks in Yolla Bolly Wilderness from the 5406-foot summit. The Trinity Alps are due north, the Blue Trinity Mountains 10 degrees to the west. Golden eagles sometimes soar overhead. You can also see the trail north. What a relief to see it finds a clear path through the brushy oaks, soon joining an old jeep road. Continue north to an old turnaround at 5⅞ miles. The path forks just beyond. (The right fork descends to Four Corners Rock Trailhead in ¼ mile.)

To return to Ant Point Trailhead, bear left at the fork. The path heads northwest, descending then contouring along a faint old jeep track near the top of Jones Ridge. The track turns due west through oak forest, then angles southwest, dropping across the top of a large glade. By 6½ miles descend to Jones Ridge Road at a spot marked "STOCKWATER TROUGH." It is one mile west along Jones Ridge Road to Ant Point Trailhead.

23.
WATERSPOUT/YELLOWJACKET
BACK WAY TO HAYNES DELIGHT

Waterspout Trail offers one of the easiest and least traveled routes into Yolla Bolly Wilderness. Although the drive is long and winding (what drive to the Yolla Bollys isn't?), you can reach this trailhead in three hours from Eureka or Garberville. Waterspout offers access to upper North Fork Middle Fork Eel River, Sulphur Glade and Yellowjacket Creek. The trail becomes moderately steep before reaching Haynes Delight, a solitude-rich alternative to the overly popular route via Georges Valley (Trail #41). Moderate elevation and paved access make Waterspout an excellent choice for a short wilderness trip anytime the snow level rises above 4500 feet. I have visited in December and early May and found the trail open; inquire before off-season travel.

The trail descends southeast from the wooded trailhead. In 300 feet, ford a tiny seasonal creek in a grassy swale. Yellow buttercups and stream violets add color in spring. Ford the creek again by ⅛ mile. The path is vague in spots, but it follows the water downstream. After a blazed juniper on your right, your creek joins a larger creek. Cross to the left bank in 200 feet. Douglas and white firs, ponderosa pine, incense cedar and black oak grace the forest surrounding the grassy drainage.

At ¼ mile the trail descends to another ford. Climb a small rise, then drop to another ford and follow the creek's left bank. A fire ring at ½ mile is too close to the creek; better camps lie ahead. Ford the creek twice more by ⅝ mile, where a good camp on your right sits in a sunny flat above the creek. The trail fords to the right bank, then quickly back to the left.

Just beyond ¾ mile your path fords to the right bank and climbs above a rock outcrop along the creek. Descend through the forest, passing shooting stars and fawn lilies in spring. Drop to ford a wooded tributary. After a brief, steep ascent, switchback left and climb gradually to one mile where you have a view up the main creek's rocky canyon.

110

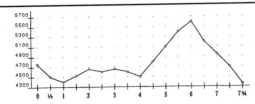

DISTANCE: **7¾ miles to Haynes Delight** (15½ miles round trip); 1⅛ miles to North Fork, 3 miles to Sulphur Glade, 5¾ miles to Buck Ridge.

TIME: Day hike or overnight to Sulphur Glade, one or two nights to Haynes Delight.

TERRAIN: Descends creek to river ford, follows canyon downstream to Yellowjacket and River Trails; Yellowjacket Trail climbs gradually to Sulphur Glade and Doe Ridge Trail, follows Yellowjacket Creek, climbs steeply to Buck Ridge, descends to Haynes Delight.

TRAILS INTERSECTED: River, Doe Ridge, Buck Ridge, Haynes.

BEST TIME: May and June. May be accessible into October.

WARNINGS: Watch for rattlesnakes. Expect bears at Haynes Delight; ford there may be dangerous in early season.

DIRECTIONS TO TRAILHEAD: Follow directions in Trail #22, then go 4.2 miles to signed trailhead on right.

FURTHER INFO: Trail: Covelo Ranger District, Mendocino National Forest (707) 983-6118. Road: Mad River Ranger District, Six Rivers National Forest (707) 574-6233.

Descending gradually, you soon see North Fork Middle Fork Eel River in its wooded canyon. Reach a broad, shallow ford of the river at 1⅛ miles, just below its confluence with the Waterspout creek. Climb steeply up the east cutbank to a terrace where a fire ring anchors a pleasant camp.

Waterspout Trail heads south down the canyon. Climb steeply away from the river, then parallel it downstream. As the climb eases, the dark green lanceolate leaves of pipsissewa line the trail. Descend with views of the river on your right, passing whitethorn and hound's tongue. Descend gently to a tributary, then climb gradually, angling away from the river.

At 1¾ miles the trail levels on an old river terrace where interior live oaks mingle with conifers. Wind across a side stream lined with sugar pines and cedars, then contour to ford another feeder creek. This one has dry slopes covered with white oaks and a rocky canyon upstream. Climb steeply for 300 feet, then dip through short ups and downs.

After a dry, shady gully, the trail climbs steadily away from the river to 2¼ miles, where you overlook densely wooded country. Descend to ford a seasonal tributary, then climb gently to cross a small gully. Your trail contours through mixed forest, then a dense patch of spiny whitethorn to a junction on a spur ridge beyond 2⅝ miles.

River Trail (Trail #43), signed "NORTH FORK - 11W05," descends southwest along the ridge. Our described route forks left on Yellowjacket Trail, contouring east through pleasant glades and tall forest. Cross a seasonal creek at 2⅞ miles and start a winding ascent into Sulphur Glade. Meet Doe Ridge Trail (Trail #24) at 3 miles. (It heads north 200 feet to a pleasant hilltop camp, one of several in these extensive glades. A spring northeast of the camp flows slowly year round. You can get better water in early season from nearby seasonal creeks.)

Yellowjacket Trail heads northeast, but soon descends east to ford a seasonal tributary of Yellowjacket Creek. Continue east across a corner of Sulphur Glade, very wet in spring. Blazed trees mark the route where the path is vague. Cross a gully, then another fork of Yellowjacket Creek. Follow the tributary downstream briefly, then leave it, descending gently through mixed forest. You soon overlook Yellowjacket Creek where white oaks mingle with conifers. Pass rock outcrops between you and the creek, then climb gently east. The trail crosses a tributary, then meanders back to the cutbank above Yellowjacket Creek passing pipsissewa, fawn lily, currant, lupine, wood rose, angelica, whitethorn and brushy white and live oaks.

Descend to ford Yellowjacket Creek at 3¾ miles at the confluence of its two main forks, the last dependable water for 3 or 4 miles. The trail climbs southeast up the right bank of the right fork. Wind into a side canyon, then climb gradually on the hillside above the creek, where Oregon grape grows. Your ascent steepens then eases.

At 4¼ miles the trail leaves Yellowjacket Creek to follow a small tributary on the right. You soon ford it and climb along the ridge between the tributary and the creek. Leave the ridge before 4⅝ miles on a steady winding ascent.

Regain the ridge at 4⅞ miles, turning southeast to continue the steady climb. The ridgetop turns brushy with manzanita and scrubby oaks. Your trail returns to the forest by 5 miles as the climb eases. The climb steepens as brush again dominates the ridgetop. A magnificent view unfolds as you climb: Doe Ridge and Shell Mountain rise to the north, while upper Buck Ridge on Shell's right stretches east. The barren slopes around Four Corners Rock rise five miles west. Scattered amidst the

van. 92

brush on the ridge are juniper, cedar, ponderosa and sugar pines, Douglas and white firs.

Whitethorn and manzanita crowd the trail beyond 5¼ miles, with squaw carpet and stonecrop scattered beneath. Climb steadily with occasional switchbacks. The climb eases beyond 5⅜ miles. At 5⅝ miles the trail bends right, leaving the brushy ridgetop to wind through fir forest.

Top the ridge and meet Buck Ridge Trail at 5¾ miles. Upper Buck Ridge Trail (see Trail #44) climbs east. Turn right, descending southwest, then west along wooded Buck Ridge. At 5⅞ miles the trail switchbacks left to descend southeast.

At 6 miles vague, unmarked Buck Ridge Trail (Trail #44) forks to the right beside a white oak, descending south. You continue southeast on Haynes Delight Trail. The descent steepens slightly. Cross two gullies that may have seasonal streams in spring. At the second one, in the shade of a large cedar, your trail turns south as the descent becomes steep, winding through mature forest. At 6¼ miles cross a seasonal stream then resume descending.

As the descent steepens before 6½ miles, a faint side trail on the left leads 100 feet to pleasant and shady Watertrough Camp. The spring, 75 feet above the camp, is seasonal. One cannot depend on it after June.

A seasonal creek parallels Haynes Delight Trail as it descends southeast. The path soon bends away from it on a moderate descent levelling briefly amidst stately forest. Resume your descent past a year-round spring in a stump hole on the right, with corn and other lilies. Descend to a wet meadow below the spring. A nice camp sits on the meadow's far side, about 350 feet southwest.

The trail descends gradually to a seasonal pond at 6¾ miles. Your descent steepens at 7 miles, coming to a ford below a small waterfall. Contour to 7¼ miles, then descend with the seasonal creek on your right. Switchback left away from the creek for a steep descent. After the sixth switchback, the trail heads south. In spring you may hear a creek burbling on your left.

Come to a large glade beyond 7½ miles, descending along its edge as a high ridge towers on the left. After leaving the glade, the trail bends right. Step to the left to overlook the steep, eroding canyon of an unnamed creek. Your trail soon switchbacks left and right into another glade overlooking the Middle Fork Eel River.

Welcome to Haynes Delight. One camp is on the left at the top of the glade. The trail descends to the lower end of the glade and veers left to pass another camp at 7¾ miles, then descends the steep cutbank to the river ford. Use caution at the ford during high water runoff. If it is fast and deep, it is unsafe to cross. A fine pool lies just downstream from the ford. Though people have camped along the edge of the stream, the nicest and most ecological camps surround the glade. Look east for the trail on the east bank (Trail #41).

24.
DOE RIDGE
TO SHELL MOUNTAIN AND DEAD PUPPY RIDGE

This short trail traverses a rich variety of habitats: immense Sulphur Glade, the invertebrate-rich pond of Mud Lake, stark serpentine slopes of Doe Ridge, majestic pine forest, dense snow-bent fir forests and a glacial basin. If that is not enough, take a short side trip to the barren top of 6700-foot Shell Mountain for the finest view in the western half of the wilderness, a chance to see the Pacific Ocean 50 miles west. Doe Ridge Trail climbs steeply enough to make it a better day hike than backpack, but determined packers will be rewarded for their efforts.

Doe Ridge Trail heads north from Yellowjacket Trail (Trail #23), 3 miles from Waterspout Trailhead. Climb through lower Sulphur Glade to a pleasant hilltop camp, then descend to a spur on the right leading to a year-round spring, more camps and a

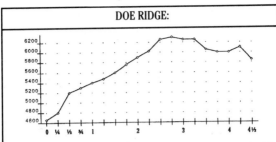

DOE RIDGE:

DISTANCE: **4½ miles to Long Ridge Trail** (9 miles round trip);
  3⅜ miles to Shell Mountain, 4⅜ miles to Dead Puppy Ridge.
TIME: Day hike from Sulphur Glade, one or two nights from road.
TERRAIN: Climbs ridge to shoulder of Shell Mountain, then
  traverses north slope to Dead Puppy Ridge.
TRAILS INTERSECTED: Yellowjacket, Buck Ridge, Dead Puppy
  Ridge.
BEST TIME: June and July. August and September also nice.
WARNINGS: Snow may linger on Shell Mountain's north face
  into June. Watch for rattlesnakes.
DIRECTIONS TO TRAILHEAD: Inside wilderness at Sulphur
  Glade, 3 miles from Waterspout Trailhead (Trail #23).
FURTHER INFO: Covelo Ranger District, Mendocino National
  Forest (707) 983-6118.

seasonal creek. The main trail ascends north through the
upper glade on faint tread, passing more cozy camps. Climb
right of a dark rock outcrop at the top of the glade. Junipers
grow beside the ponderosa pines most common around Sulphur
Glade. Ascend moderately, winding left of another dark rock.
Climb steeply past knots of whitethorn and white oaks in pine
forest. Your trail bends left to climb through a small glade.

Come to Mud Lake at ⅜ mile, a natural pond in a hollow on
your left. Pond turtles and invertebrates thrive in the soupy
water, but no fish. It is not recommended for drinking. The trail
turns north to climb steadily. Douglas fir, western juniper and
incense cedar mix with pine/oak forest. Make a winding ascent
through sparsely vegetated hills.

Views expand west to Jones Ridge and Four Corners Rock,
then southwest to Big and Little Buttes. Ascend along Doe
Ridge as the vista looks northwest to long, wooded South Fork
Mountain and Mad River watershed beyond. In spring and early

summer you may see violets, scarlet fritillaries and dwarf lupines. Your trail winds, climbing steeply along the ridgetop.

By ⅞ mile the climb eases as large ponderosa pines provide welcome shade. The trail becomes a bit vague. You actually have two choices here: continue climbing along the brushy ridgetop or follow a trail veering right of the ridgetop to ascend through stately forest of tall ponderosas. Either way you should be atop the ridge by one mile, climbing a narrowing ridgetop. Your view expands to the Trinity Alps in the north. The path levels briefly, then resumes its ridgetop ascent.

The climb becomes gradual as Shell Mountain looms ahead. The ridgetop turns barren. Pass the first of several large rock piles that might be God's own cairns, marking your way on often vague tread. The ascent steepens along the ridge's right side.

Return to the ridgetop, climbing steeply along the left edge of the ridge. Shooting stars and scarlet fritillaries grow beneath junipers and buck brush. White firs line the trail around 1½ miles. Jeffrey pines soon dominate the sparse forest as soils turn serpentine. Descend briefly on the barren ridge where tiny three-bracted onions thrive.

Climb gently, then contour until the trail ascends steeply from 1⅞ miles. The ascent turns moderate at a giant cairn at 2⅛ miles. Then contour on the ridge's south face. Rock outcrops on your left support stunted Jeffrey pines and junipers. Regain the ridgetop and ascend gradually, skirting a pocket of white firs. Your ascent increases at 2½ miles. Your path levels before 2¾ miles, heading toward Shell Mountain. Descend briefly, then climb the stark, rocky ridgetop.

At 3 miles Doe Ridge Trail leaves the ridge at a saddle, heading east into dense red fir forest where snow banks may linger into June. (You can make a cross-country ascent of Shell Mountain from the saddle—see box.) The trail descends, overlooking a rock outcrop and steep slopes to the north. Descend northeast past springs where swamp onions grow. Descend to 3¼ miles, then climb briefly before dropping steeply through fir forest with many deadfalls.

The descent becomes gradual through forest with a carpet of pinemat manzanita. At 3⅝ miles a wet meadow lies below on the left, with a huge gravel deposit between your trail and the meadow. Climb northeast to ford a seasonal creek, then climb gently toward Shell Mountain's towering north face.

The trail levels, then descends steeply to level again. Descend southeast to a mossy double ford of cascading streams just above their confluence. These are the headwaters of North Fork Middle Fork Eel River.

Doe Ridge Trail climbs northeast to 4 miles, then contours before a short, steep descent. Contour across the steep slope of the rugged basin, then climb to Buck Ridge Trail (Trail #44) at 4⅜ miles. You can turn left to descend ⅛ mile to Cutfinger/

Long Ridge Loop (Trail #25); turn right, climbing toward Buck Ridge and Cherry Camp; or return the way you came.

SHELL MOUNTAIN

From the saddle at 3 miles on Doe Ridge Trail, Shell Mountain offers a dramatic, reasonably safe, class-2 (no trail, steep terrain, no handholds necessary) ascent. Head south 200 feet to young cedars. Climb southeast through brush, steering to the right of the peak's cliffy north face. In ⅛ mile (where a spur ridge is below to the south), climb steeply east up an open, rocky face toward a scraggly Jeffrey pine. Take your time and make your own switchbacks. Reach the pine in 300 feet. Switchback left and climb steeply north-northwest to junipers. Then climb northeast to red rocks left of a snag at ¼ mile. Head east to the summit. An easy climb reaches the top, beside a juniper, in 300 feet.

Clockwise north to south you may spot Trinity Alps, Marble Mountains, Black Rock Mountain, Cedar Basin, North Yolla Bolly Peaks, Mount Lassen, Tomhead Mountain, Devils Hole Ridge, the South Yolla Bollys, Solomon Peak, Hammerhorn Mountain, Black Butte, Anthony Peak and Snow Mountain. Leech Lake Mountain is almost due south, then Red Rock, Castle Peak, Big Butte, Little Butte, Ant Point, Washington Rock, Four Corners Rock, King Range to the west, Jones Ridge and South Fork Mountain.

25.
CUTFINGER/LONG RIDGE LOOP
REMOTE ROUTE THROUGH CANYONS AND ALONG RIDGES

The trail expert for Covelo Ranger District said the start of Chicago Camp and Cutfinger Trails were a mess, devastated by a firebreak installed in 1988 when the Hermit fire threatened to engulf this corner of the wilderness. Despite his tips, I spent an afternoon finding Cutfinger Trail. So follow the start of this description closely. You should always have map, compass and the ability to use them on a route as vague as this loop. The firebreak is the first of four places on this loop where route finding is difficult, qualifying it as a difficult hike even aside from its elevation variations. Your reward will be solitude in rugged wilderness traveled more by wild animals (and ironically, cows) than humans. This is the shortest, but far from the easiest, route to Frying Pan.

From the perfunctory camp at road's end, your trail heads over a tank trap and climbs south through mixed forest on an old logging road. Gooseberry and creeping snowberry dominate the understory. The climb eases as the road bends left. In 200 feet a faint trail branches right (your return at the end of the

CUTFINGER/LONG RIDGE LOOP:

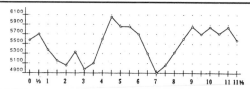

DISTANCE: **11⅜-mile loop** (16⅞-mile loop with trip to Frying Pan Meadow); ⅝ mile to Cutfinger Trail; 3¼ miles to first river ford, 4¾ miles to Long Ridge, 6¾ miles to second river ford, 8⅝ miles to Flournoy Cabin, 9 miles to Dead Puppy Ridge, 10¾ miles to Hopkins Camp.

TIME: Two or three days.

TERRAIN: Climbs through forest to ridgetop junction; descends brushy slope to river, climbs ridge to Long Ridge Trail (spur climbs to Frying Pan); descends Long Ridge to river, climbs to Flournoy Cabin and Dead Puppy Ridge Trail; latter descends ridge to Hopkins Camp.

TRAILS INTERSECTED: Chicago Camp, Long Ridge, Willow Basin Cut-off, Dead Puppy Ridge.

BEST TIME: June and July. Also nice August and September.

WARNINGS: Difficult to locate in several spots, especially junction of Chicago Camp and Cutfinger Trails. Watch for rattlesnakes. Water may be scarce in late season. Use caution at fords at high water.

DIRECTIONS TO TRAILHEAD: Follow directions in Trail #22 to Ruth Store. In 12.5 miles from store, paved road narrows, becoming Forest Highway 30. At 18.5 miles, turn right on Road 27N23. Go south almost 5 miles, then left on Road 27N23. Go 8 miles to logging landing, then right on Road 27N22 for 1.5 miles to trail register, 1.8 miles to trailhead.

FURTHER INFO: Yolla Bolly Ranger District, Trinity National Forest (916) 352-4211; Covelo R.D. (707) 983-6118.

OTHER SUGGESTION: You can join this loop's EAST END from Frying Pan; or its WEST END via Dead Puppy Ridge Trail from end of Doe Ridge and Buck Ridge Trails. WEST END OF CHICAGO CAMP TRAIL is a mess as it follows firebreak; if you can find trail at 2 miles where it leaves south edge of firebreak, decent path climbs gradually to Bearwallow Spring (poor) and Powell Ridge Trail. CHICAGO CAMP TRAIL continues east, climbing gradually to Devils Hole Ridge Trail at 5⅜ miles. At end of Road 27N23, seldom-maintained POWELL RIDGE TRAIL climbs to Bearwallow Spring.

118

described loop). Climb east on the road to a logging landing, then descend past a wilderness boundary sign around ¼ mile. Follow the road to a saddle, then follow a broad firebreak.

Ascend the south edge of the break for ¼ mile. Just before a knob on the ridgetop, look for small cairns beneath a lone pine on the right. Cutfinger Trail angles southeast, extremely vague until it leaves the firebreak in 200 feet, where blazes mark small pines. Continue southeast on faint, well blazed tread.

Begin a gradual descent, soon gaining a ridge, then descending its west face. Whitethorn crowds the path, but blazes and cairns mark the way. Descend moderately along the ridgetop beyond ¾ mile on improved tread. Your descent soon eases. Wind around some deadfall trees to descend steeply, then moderately on a narrow ridgetop with a view of Shell Mountain. Squaw carpet joins the understory.

Approach the bottom of the ridge at 1¼ miles, winding steeply past paintbrush entwined with willows and California mountain mahogany. Cross a gully, then parallel Cutfinger Creek down a lush green swath. The creek flows intermittently by late summer. The canyon broadens as your descent is broken by short climbs and brushy patches. Starflower and silktassel line the route.

Before 1½ miles a canyon enters on the right. Your trail turns east, then southeast with the creek. Cross a gully and continue downstream, soon fording to the southwest bank. Wind through willows along the gravel bed, passing trail plant, bleeding heart, large-leaved lupine and wood rose.

Your trail ascends a small ridge beyond 1¾ miles, then fords a gully with a basic camp on the left beneath Jeffrey pines. Ford to the northeast bank and continue downstream. As your canyon merges with a larger canyon on the left, the path bends left to cross the broad canyon. Turn south, climbing 100 feet above the creek, then descending sporadically.

At 2¼ miles descend to ford a side stream with a year-round flow. Good grazing and evidence of cattle are below the ford. You might want to walk upstream to tank up on water at a spring ⅛ mile above the crossing.

Faint tread climbs steeply from Cutfinger Creek. Ascend a spur ridge, then climb across the base of Stockton Ridge around 2⅝ miles. Contour, then make a winding, brushy descent southeast. Contour east along a dry brushy slope. Descend to ford Middle Fork Eel River at 3¼ miles.

At the ford, where willows and umbrella plants grow, look west for an obvious blaze on a Jeffrey pine. Your faint trail heads west to the next blazed tree, then climbs southwest up a gully. Veer left at 3⅜ miles to ascend steeply. Switchback up a ridge with sparse vegetation.

Climb gradually on the ridge's south side, where curl-leaved mountain mahogany grows beneath Jeffrey pines. Your trail switchbacks steeply left, gaining the ridgetop for a steep winding climb past Douglas firs and up a brushy, rocky slope. Long Ridge looms to the south; Windy Mountain peeks over its saddles. Be careful not to lose the vague tread. It generally stays just south of the ridgetop, passing a few blazed pines.

The path levels atop the ridge at 4¼ miles. Pause to enjoy views north to the North Yolla Bollys, and east to Lazyman Butte beyond Devils Hole Ridge. Your trail soon drops to a saddle with dead conifers, then climbs steeply as the ridgetop angles south. Climb the ridge's east face as Tomhead Mountain rises left of Lazyman Butte. The ascent eases as dense squaw carpet and pinemat manzanita line the path. Cutfinger Trail ends at Long Ridge Trail before 4¾ miles. Your loop turns right to descend Long Ridge to another ford of Middle Fork Eel River.

(You can make a 2¾-mile side trip [5½ miles round trip] to Frying Pan Meadow from here. Ascend east on Long Ridge Trail, then contour with grand views until the path leaves the ridge to climb steeply southeast. As you ascend along the base of the big outcrop called Spring Rock, look for bright knots of mountain pride. At ⅝ mile your trail turns south on a ridge. Contour on or near the ridgetop to 1¼ miles. Faint, well blazed tread climbs southeast to a saddle where Willow Basin Cut-off forks right, ascending steeply to Wrights Ridge [Trail #42]. Long Ridge Trail descends to ford Willow Basin Creek at a pleasant, isolated camp. Follow the creek downstream ¼ mile, then ascend east across the divide between Willow and Frying Pan Basins. Contour, then descend through mixed forest to beautiful Frying Pan Meadow at 2¾ miles. See the end of Trail #39 for more about Frying Pan.)

Our loop descends west from Long Ridge/Cutfinger junction on faint tread. The path soon improves, descending moderately on the ridge's south face. Level at a saddle, then climb gently along the south face to 5¼ miles. Contour along the ridgetop to 5⅝ miles, passing little prince's pine, three-bracted onion, yellow ground iris and dwarf monkeyflower.

The descent along the wooded south face starts gradually, turning moderate, then steep on bare rocky slopes. Angle northwest into forest as the descent eases. Regain the ridgetop, then switchback four times, descending moderately past blue field gilia. The grade steepens around 6¼ miles, winding steeply down the ridge. Look right to see Eel River snaking through its deep canyon. Pass a rudimentary camp at 6¾ miles, then wind 200 feet to the canyon floor and the ford beside a rock outcrop. Douglas firs and junipers grow here, with curl-leaved mountain mahogany on the dry banks, willows, alders and umbrella plants in the riverbed.

Long Ridge Trail becomes extremely vague and hard to follow for the next ½ mile. Splash your face (at least) and fill your water containers at the river. Be certain you are ready to continue on the nebulous, brushy route to Flournoy Cabin.

A small pine west of the ford has a blaze. Your vague trail climbs from the river following the north (right) side of an unnamed side creek. The route angles up and down the slope, dipping in and out of the creek bed. At 6⅞ miles a blazed Jeffrey pine is 20 feet north of the creek. The indistinct path descends to the creek bed. A blazed Douglas fir in the creek is 125 feet from the last blaze.

It is rough going with no tread as you pick your way along the tiny creek passing another blaze on a dead fir in 125 feet. Soon a vague tread angles up the north bank. It returns to the stream at a blazed pine around 7 miles. A vague track traverses the steep north bank, soon returning to the stream to pass a blazed Jeffrey pine on the north bank.

Your route follows the north shore as the tread improves, climbing gradually above the creek. Join another track and cross a gully with narrow-leaved mule ears. The tread improves substantially, paralleling the creek past pines and oak brush.

Where the canyon splits in two, your trail bends right to follow the smaller fork, climbing sporadically. Switchback left and cross the side canyon. Then ascend the ridge between the canyons, following distinct tread with some brushy spots.

Your path turns particularly brushy beyond 7½ miles. It soon bends left, improving to climb south, then west. After a very brushy stretch, good tread climbs northwest beneath mixed forest. Navigate a brushy patch below a rock outcrop, then ascend northeast briefly.

Leave the forest for patchy brush with scattered trees around 8 miles. The path bends left to ascend one of the brushiest parts of the route. Turn north, ascending to a ridge. Your trail bends left on a winding climb through forest on the ridge's south face. The ascent eases, following the ridgetop through patches of bitter cherry and whitethorn. The brush parts for a glade.

Climb moderately to ruined Flournoy Cabin at 8⅝ miles. The collapsed cabin was only 8 by 12 feet in its heyday. Now a picnic table and Forest Service fire pit sit incongruously beside it. It makes an odd but pleasant and remote camp, especially when the spring ⅛ mile up the trail is flowing.

Your trail climbs northwest through forest in an area where three springs flow freely in spring. By September they are undependable. (The most reliable spring is 50 feet above the trail, reached by a steep path.) Climb moderately, then steeply across a precipitous slope. Ascend north on faint narrow tread to Dead Puppy Ridge Trail at 9 miles.

This junction is at the north end of the Buck Ridge Trail (Trail #44), and only ⅛ mile from Doe Ridge Trail (Trail #24), offering choices for extended trips. Your described route turns right, descending gradually along Dead Puppy Ridge (signed "WILDERNESS BOUNDARY"). Descend through mixed forest, then climb briefly to the right of a rock outcrop.

Your trail switches from the right to the left side of the ridge and begins a steep descent. Drop to a saddle, then ascend gradually along the ridge's west face, where sulphur flowers grow. A brief steep climb ends at a knob at 9⅜ miles. Contour, then drop to a saddle where low brush crowds the path. Climb along the ridge's west face, then along the ridgetop through sparse grasslands with junipers. The glade offers a view of Shell Mountain's glaciated north face. Your path levels at 9¾ miles, becoming brushy. Ascend gently on the ridgetop, then climb steeply around the west side of a knob.

The tread suddenly turns vague before 10 miles. The route continues north, leaving the ridgetop to descend its east face steeply. The descent winds through low brush to a false saddle. Wind left and drop to a saddle at the head of Cutfinger Creek.

Climb steeply, then moderately on the west face of a ridge. Your trail soon descends along a west facing slope. The path undulates, then ascends to 10½ miles. Contour north, then descend gradually through forest to a firebreak.

Your path becomes indistinct as it follows the break north-northwest. Around 10¾ miles the break levels, then becomes very broad, with a large glade to the west. On your right (north) a five-foot-diameter pine stump stands on the edge of the firebreak. Look 30 feet southeast for a young white fir with a sign. (It points south for "SHELL MOUNTAIN, CHERRY SPRING, BUCK RIDGE"). This was the original junction of Dead Puppy and Chicago Camp Trails, now jumbled by firebreaks.

A vague but cleared path heads northeast 100 feet to mediocre Hopkins Camp, with a new metal sign. As your route heads east, you must wind left of two deadfall firs. The path jogs south 250 feet to meet good tread climbing east. Cross another firebreak, then contour east on a broad track. It soon descends gradually, then moderately through selectively logged forest.

The path levels briefly, then resumes descending. Cross a gully, then climb briefly before descending to complete the loop, meeting Chicago Camp Trail at 11¼ miles. Turn left on the closed road, descending to the trailhead at 11⅜ miles.

26.

HUMBOLDT FROM WEST LOW GAP

HISTORIC ROUTE ACROSS SOUTH FACE OF NORTH YOLLA BOLLYS

This western trailhead is the more rewarding and challenging of the Humboldt Trail's two access points. It provides quick passage to the spectacular, rugged south slope of the North Yolla Bolly Mountains and the immense glades and icy springs of Cedar Basin. The western access is steeper than the route from Tomhead Saddle on the east. At this writing, it is also challenging because

lew. 92

*of a confusing maze of cattle trails in severely burned forest on
the first mile. Follow the description carefully or chance getting
lost. The charred forest is stark, sometimes ugly. But the trail
offers opportunities to observe forest recovering from fire.*

*Humboldt Trail was an important supply route between
Humboldt County and the Sacramento Valley. Pierce Asbill
pioneered the trail in 1855, taking a pack train of tanned deer
hides from Hettenshaw Valley west of Ruth, to Kingsley's Trading
Post near Red Bluff. Before 1915, when a decent road linked
Humboldt with San Francisco, stockmen drove herds west along
the trail to sell on the coast. Today it takes almost as long to drive
the winding roads from one trailhead to the other as it does to
hike the 13½ miles.*

Humboldt Trail climbs east from the trailhead and trail register.
The distinct path ascends through grasslands along an edge of
the immense area charred in the 1988 Hermit Fire. In 250 feet
the trail bends right to climb through a forest of fire-scarred
trees, with many survivors here. Views expand over the headwaters of South Fork Trinity River. Then climb through forest
where no trees survive. Oaks sprout from stumps, silver lupine
and grasses thrive, but invasive thistles dominate the hillside.

As you approach a ridge at ¼ mile, the trail becomes vague.
Proceed to the wilderness boundary sign on a dead cedar on the
ridgetop. Large fire-killed trees have been cut right to the
boundary. Black Rock Mountain looms above the charred zone.

From the boundary sign, one trail descends southeast—not
the one you want. Your vague trail descends north toward Black

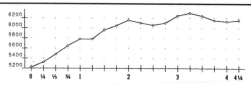

Rock Mountain beyond a small fire-fallen pine. The path soon
becomes distinct. Within 300 feet the trail begins a moderate
climb. Some surviving trees stand improbably green amidst the
blackened wreckage. As your trail traverses a steep slope,
survivors are scarce.

Humboldt Trail turns north as your climb eases on a dusty
path. At ½ mile another trail descends from the west to cross
Humboldt Trail—it may look more traveled but is only a cattle
track. Take the grassy trail ascending north-northeast. It

124

steepens, angling northeast past raspberry and mullein.

Your trail levels, then bends left to head north. Ignore another cow path on the right. Take the left fork climbing north-northeast. In 300 feet another misleading path veers to the right around a fallen pine and descends. The path you want is just uphill, hiding behind a foot-diameter fallen pine; it climbs steeply north-northeast. Continue north at another cow-path junction around ¾ mile (path forking left climbs to ridge). Your trail levels for 120 feet, then bends right on a gradual climb northeast. Scattered clumps of whitethorn, raspberry and bracken ferns are the only green plants.

Climb gradually, then cross a dry gully where the trail bends right on a gentle climb east above springs. A short steep climb ends at one mile, where you resume a gradual ascent. Your trail turns northeast, contouring above rushing streams.

The trail turns east again, then winds left at 1¼ miles into a drainage with California hazel, whitethorn and bracken fern. Pass two seeps, then cross a creek lined with thimbleberry, gooseberry, wood rose and checker mallow, a green oasis amidst charred forest. A camp is on the right in 250 feet.

Climb to a fire-scarred ridge, then turn east on a gradual climb. After an outcrop of green rock, the trail climbs into a drainage where the fire's chaotic path spared many ponderosas, white firs and cedars. Elderberry bushes thrive in the charred understory. Your trail climbs gently as surviving trees begin to outnumber victims. Cross two tiny streams and return to the edge of the burn, climbing gradually. Enter an area with no survivors; the naked forest offers views in all directions. Climb gradually past a huge, charred fallen cedar, then two seeps.

At 2⅛ miles a year-round creek is surrounded by burnt forest. The top of Black Rock Mountain towers 1700 feet overhead, ¾ mile north. The stream supports a riot of vegetation including angelica, leopard lily, sneezeweed, columbine, paintbrush and mimulus. Descend briefly past elderberry, gooseberry, phacelia and Indian pink. Your winding path contours, then descends slightly into a pocket of live trees. Such pockets play an important role in reforestation after a fire; they spread seeds over surrounding terrain, generating new forest.

Climb briefly to a cow-polluted seep, beyond which the forest holds no survivors. Pass another spring and contour to 2¾ miles. Where burned forest surrounds a rock outcrop on the left, begin a gradual climb through live forest with pussy paws. Pass a tiny seep, then cross a seasonal stream and climb through forest dominated by young cedars.

Climb through a large glade, wind through a gully, then climb gently through forest at 3¼ miles. Many trees are scorched here, but most survived. The fire must have raced up this slope. You soon traverse an immense glade extending to the very mountain top. The grasslands support rabbitbrush, wild

/eV. 92

cucumber vine, broad leaved lupine, sneezeweed and scattered pockets of cedar and fir. Your trail winds through the glade, climbing past four seeps and a stream to 3½ miles.

Soon a beautiful aspen grove lines the path, the only aspens in the Yolla Bollys. Cross a seasonal seep with rein orchid and paintbrush. Descend through the aspen grove to a pleasant camp below the trail, with aspens 18 inches wide. Nothing in the world sounds like the wind rustling their leaves. At the lower end of the grove, conifers mingle with the aspens.

Leave the grove, descending along a row of cedars and firs. Cross a shady gully where the trail winds, then climbs gradually through burned and living forest. Before 3⅞ miles the trail descends to a boulder-strewn gully, then climbs briefly along a rocky slope.

At 4 miles your trail traverses the base of a large rock outcrop. Climb gently across the top of a small glade, passing purple mountain aster and giant frasera, then crossing a wooded gully. The trail bends sharply right, then left, climbing gently through partially burned forest.

Veer left again and climb to meet Pettijohn Trail (Trail #27) at 4¼ miles. (It climbs north over the North Yolla Bolly Range.) Humboldt Trail continues southeast to Chicago Camp Trail (Trail #30) at 4⅜ miles, just before North Yolla Bolly Spring. Humboldt Trail continues east and southeast to Tomhead Saddle Trailhead, 13½ miles from West Low Gap Trailhead. (See Trail #33 for the eastern portion of the trail.)

27

PETTIJOHN
STEEP CLIMB OVER NORTH YOLLA BOLLYS

This popular trail offers quick access to the northern wilderness. Its north-facing slopes and high summit hold snow late into the season, however. Sometimes Pettijohn Trail does not open before July, although mid-June is more common. This route reaches Pettijohn Basin's springs, glades and forests, connects with side trips to lakes and peaks, and offers the shortest route to Cedar Basin and North Yolla Bolly Spring, as well as the heart of the wilderness beyond.

From the loop at road's end above Stuart Gap, climb south from the trail register along the edge of a partially logged area. The moderate climb soon enters virgin forest of white fir, ponderosa pine and incense cedar. The understory includes wood rose, gooseberry, strawberry, phacelia and bracken fern. The path bends right to climb west as white-veined shinleaf and creeping snowberry join the ground covers. Turn south before ¼ mile, climbing moderately through a small grassy clearing. The ascent eases through patchy forest with bitter cherry and whitethorn, then climbs along a ridgetop.

At ½ mile the forest thins on your right for a view of Black Rock Mountain's steep north face. Climb moderately on the ridgetop past yarrow and broad leaved lupine. The trail levels as red fir joins the forest. Trail plant, naked stem buckwheat, waterleaf and bedstraw mix with other understory plants.

Leave the ridgetop at ¾ mile and climb gradually. Corn lily and Douglas wallflower line the path. Pass an unmarked spur on the right before meeting the wilderness boundary, where elderberry and alder grow. Climbing moderately, you may see the dark blue flowers of snapdragon skullcap. The ascent eases as you wind through a grassy gully where mimulus, stream violets and hedge nettle grow.

Black Rock Lake Trail (Trail #28) forks right at 1⅛ miles. Pettijohn Trail climbs moderately through forest to a clearing with views of the steep North Yolla Bollys. North Yolla Bolly Lake Trail (see Trail #31) forks left at a signed junction.

Pettijohn Trail (signed "CHICAGO CAMP") climbs gradually through sparse mixed forest with hawkweed and grasses, then traverses the top of a large glade. You can hear the East Fork South Fork Trinity River collecting its headwaters below.

Cross a tiny, year-round creek at 1½ miles. Its alder-lined banks support seep-spring and primrose monkeyflower, purple monkshood, columbine, twisted stalk, currant and gooseberry. As the trail climbs south leaving grassland for forest, you may

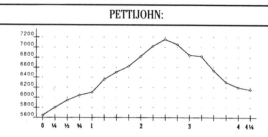

PETTIJOHN:

DISTANCE: 4¼ **miles to Chicago Camp Trail** (8½ miles round trip); 1⅛ miles to Black Rock Lake Trail, 2⅝ miles to summit, 4 miles to Humboldt Trail.

TIME: Full day hike or overnight.

TERRAIN: Climbs gentle ridge into Pettijohn Basin, then climbs steeply to ridgetop before dropping into Cedar Basin.

TRAILS INTERSECTED: Black Rock Lake, North Yolla Bolly Lake, Black Rock Mountain, North Yolla Bolly Mountain, Humboldt, Chicago Camp.

BEST TIME: July and August. September may be good. North-facing slopes mean short season.

WARNINGS: May encounter snow pack into June.

DIRECTIONS TO TRAILHEAD: Take Highway 36 to Forest Road 30, 2 miles west of Wildwood. Go 10 miles on paved Road 30, then left on Road 35 for 11 miles to Stuart Gap. Take Road 28N62 one mile to trailhead at end.

FURTHER INFO: Yolla Bolly Ranger District, Trinity National Forest (916) 352-4211.

OTHER SUGGESTION: You can reach NORTH YOLLA BOLLY LAKE and NORTH YOLLA BOLLY MOUNTAIN from Pettijohn Trail, but routes are steep and difficult. They are more easily reached from Rat Trap Gap (Trails #31 and 32). Outside wilderness, SOUTH FORK NATIONAL RECREATION TRAIL follows South Fork Trinity River upstream 18 miles, leaving from Hells Gate Campground on Highway 36 (2 miles east of Forest Glen); 2320-foot trailhead elevation assures year-round access to trail, with many pools for swimming and fishing in season; you can reach UPPER END, SOUTH FORK TRAIL just east of where Road 30 crosses the river.

see giant frasera, bleeding heart, miners lettuce, Shelton's violet, elegant brodiaea and pennyroyal. Your gradual climb turns southwest, soon crossing a seasonal creek and beginning a moderate winding climb.

The ascent steepens as you reach the first two switchbacks at 2 miles. Climb through rocky terrain in red fir forest to a rock outcrop with a view north to the Trinity Alps, with Mount Shasta and its secondary peak Shastina to the right. Western white pines join the forest. Another small outcrop at 2⅜ miles offers a view of North Yolla Bolly Mountain towering overhead.

Pettijohn Trail makes its final big ascent, with four short switchbacks followed by a long one. Climb out of the forest and into a large field of silver lupine, reaching the summit before 2⅝ miles. Pussy paws and bunch grass grow amidst the lupine. A sign on the largest fir around indicates faint Black Rock Mountain Trail on the right. At roughly the same place, an unmarked trail climbs east toward North Yolla Bolly Mountain. (See Trails #29 and 32.)

Pettijohn Trail descends gradually then steeply southeast on a tread of thick orange-brown dust. Expansive views of the wilderness unfold as you descend bare slopes with scattered rock outcrops amidst sparse grasses and phacelia. The path wraps around a cabin-sized rock with purple penstemon at its base, then winds through a gully with scrawny cedars and Jeffrey pines, California mountain mahogany and paintbrush. Descend through an expansive glade, looking toward the bald tops of the South Yolla Bollys.

A healthy spring burbles from a stone spring box above the trail before 3 miles. Its refreshing, icy water supports monkeyflower, sneezeweed, buttercup and corn lily. Pass wild cucumber, salsify and rabbitbrush below the seep. Your descent steepens through a field of corn lilies. A thicket at its lower end has twinberry, willow and frasera. Leopard lilies, ranger's buttons and broad leaved lupine grow at a spring beyond.

The trail undulates, then descends steeply. Pass two patches of dense vegetation where Douglas spiraea, mugwort and elderberry tangle. The path levels at 3⅝ miles for a short break

VAW.92

from your descent. The sweetly fragrant lavender flowers of a gilia cover drier areas of the glade. Descend across open slopes, past a seep in a gully and into sparse forest. Beyond 3¾ miles the trees have been scorched by fire. The descent eases briefly, then drops to Humboldt Trail before 4 miles.

Bear left on Humboldt Trail, climbing gradually, then traversing short ups and downs to Chicago Camp Trail at 4¼ miles. North Yolla Bolly Spring and Camp are 120 feet east of this junction. Trail #30 describes the trail south, while Trails #26 and 33 describe routes west and east (in reverse).

28.

BLACK ROCK LAKE
YOLLA BOLLY'S LARGEST

One might think the largest lake in the designated wilderness would be tucked safely away, miles from a trailhead and far from wilderness boundaries. The dismaying fact is that the wilderness ends just 200 feet below Black Rock Lake's outlet, where an immense virgin forest on a precipitous slope qualifies for protection by most anyone's definition of wilderness. The boundary urgently needs to be extended a mile north to include the canyon of East Fork of South Fork Trinity River. Action must be taken before some road-happy planner seizes the opportunity to plunder these pristine environs. The area is small, but the positive impact of a wilderness designation would be of great value, especially at Black Rock Lake!

The route follows Pettijohn Trail for 1⅛ miles, making a moderate climb along a wooded ridge (Trail #27 has more details). Enter designated wilderness and ascend to the signed junction, where Black Rock Lake Trail forks right.

Your trail descends gradually south as views open up to the craggy dark face of Black Rock Mountain and the glacially sculpted head wall of North Yolla Bolly Range. Descend through cedar/white fir forest with scattered ponderosas. Understory plants include bitter cherry, whitethorn, pennyroyal, paintbrush, yarrow and naked stem buckwheat.

Your trail switchbacks right to descend northwest and west. A spur at the bend leads south to a camp on the edge of the meadow near the tiny creek that becomes East Fork South Fork Trinity River. The main trail levels nearing the river. Pass a camp on your left where mountain aster and lupine grow.

The trail fords the river at 1⅜ miles. Alders shade the crossing, sheltering lady ferns, seep-spring monkeyflowers and rein orchids. The path winds west to ford a smaller stream, climbs

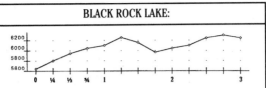

BLACK ROCK LAKE:

DISTANCE: **3 miles to lake** (including 1⅛ miles on Pettijohn Trail), 3⅛ miles to end (6¼ miles round trip).
TIME: Day hike or overnight.
TERRAIN: Pettijohn Trail climbs gentle ridge to junction; Black Rock Lake Trail traverses north slopes, descending to headwaters of East Fork South Fork Trinity River, climbing gently, then steeply, before descent to lake.
BEST TIME: July and August. June, September and October may be good.
WARNINGS: Snowpack may last into July. One of most heavily used trails in wilderness; expect crowds, be extra careful to minimize impact.
DIRECTIONS TO TRAILHEAD: Same as Trail #27.
FURTHER INFO: Yolla Bolly Ranger District, Trinity National Forest (916) 352-4211.

briefly, then contours through red fir forest before crossing a seasonal creek.

Descend through forest on a rock-strewn slope, paralleling the river briefly before the path bends left to contour west. The trail descends briefly, then contours. Descend to an alder-lined stream at 1¾ miles. Follow it downstream to a ford where purple monkshood grows.

The trail heads northwest into forest, soon beginning a moderate climb. Switchback left and right and ascend northwest. The climb turns gradual by 2⅛ miles, passing creeping snowberry, coral root orchid and white-veined shinleaf. Climb through mature forest with a carpet of pinemat manzanita.

Topping a ridge at 2¼ miles, your path bends left on a brief descent, then contours west on rocky tread. Cross a rocky gully, then climb moderately through red fir forest. Traverse a rock slide at 2½ miles and climb gradually. Your path levels, then descends across a steep slope, winding down to cross a gully. Climb gradually with some level stretches. At 2⅞ miles a large boulder stands on the left, as sugar pines mix with red fir forest.

Your trail promptly crests a ridge and you overlook Black Rock Lake. Make a winding descent to a pleasant camp at the top of a steep slope near the lake's outlet. Consider the frightening fact that the steep slope is outside the designated wilderness; the majestic red firs there could be clearcut! The beautiful lake merits a larger buffer zone. The lake's alder- and maple-lined outlet is marred by concrete, once hauled in by ambitious fools in a futile effort to raise the lake level by about ten feet. A rudimentary camp 100 feet west of the outlet offers the best view of the lake's glacial cirque and head wall.

A footpath heads south from the first camp along the east shore, lined with willows and golden chinquapin. Before 3⅛ miles it comes to three camps crowding each other beside a large fir snag at the lake's southeast corner. The path turns west, soon crossing a seasonal creek, Black Rock Lake's main tributary, lined with corn lily, mullein, Douglas spiraea, mountain aster, columbine, bleeding heart, cow parsnip, wallflower and paintbrush. The path continues 120 feet to a sheltered and secluded camp, squeezed between cliff and lake in dense vegetation. Red firs dominate the forest of the cirque basin, with scattered sugar and western white pines, white firs and incense cedars.

If you camp or picnic here, be especially careful to minimize your impact: haul out all trash (including tangled fishing line!), leave the lake basin for toilet duties and bury human waste.

29.
BLACK ROCK MOUNTAIN
CLIMB TO VIEWS OF THE COAST

The North Yolla Bolly Mountains form the southern flank of the Klamath Range, which also includes the Trinity, Marble and Siskiyou Mountains to the north. The North Yolla Bollys, older than and geologically unlike the rest of the Yolla Bollys, consist of greenstone, a crumbly gray-green rock metamorphosed from lava.

The trail up Black Rock Mountain explores the western flank of this rugged little range, offering dramatic views north over the rest of the Klamath Range, south over the entire Yolla Bolly Wilderness, and west to the Pacific on the clearest days.

When I first ascended Black Rock Mountain in 1976, the fire lookout tower was still active. After I admired the view in solitude for a while, the man in the lookout invited me up. Typical of the solitary fire lookout, this guy was experiencing some cabin fever. He talked my ear off for hours.

Suddenly I saw the sun sinking into the Pacific, visible 60

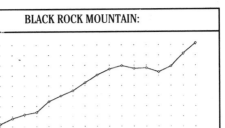

BLACK ROCK MOUNTAIN:

DISTANCE: **4¼ miles to peak**, with 2⅝ miles on Pettijohn Trail (8⅝ miles round trip).

TIME: Full day hike or overnight.

TERRAIN: Climbs Pettijohn Trail to summit; Black Rock Mountain Trail climbs gradually on open ridge and through forest, then steeply up bare face of mountain to peak.

BEST TIME: July and August. Late June, September or early October may be good.

WARNINGS: Snow may obscure trail into June. Stay off abandoned lookout tower; unsafe. No year-round water beyond 1½ miles.

DIRECTIONS TO TRAILHEAD: Same as Trail #27.

FURTHER INFO: Yolla Bolly Ranger District, Trinity National Forest (916) 352-4211.

miles west. I had left my flashlight in my camp six miles away. I said farewell and hurried down the mountain. Two things saved me from a miserable night. First, twilight lingers on high mountain ridges in early summer; I was half way to camp before darkness fell. The second was my faithful dog, Shango. In the pitch black night, he sniffed out the trail we had ascended, while I followed the jingling of his collar. When we made it to camp, I fell exhausted on my sleeping bag. (It never hurts to carry a flashlight, even when you do not expect to need it.)

Ascend Pettijohn Trail (Trail #27) for 2⅝ miles to meet Black Rock Mountain Trail at the summit. From the signed junction, the trail to the peak forks right, climbing west-northwest. Although the path is extremely vague for the first 200 feet, it ascends just north of the ridge, soon becoming a well beaten track. Climb moderately through patches of red firs with pussy

von.92

paws, rabbitbrush and naked stem buckwheat.

The trail crosses a field of silver lupine. As the path forks, take the more traveled right fork, climbing gently past purple penstemon, yarrow, pennyroyal, phacelia and gooseberry. Whitethorn abounds beside a large anthill. After passing a knob on the ridgetop, the trail descends gradually, joining the left spur and following the ridgetop through patchy red fir forest.

Your trail resumes climbing at 3 miles. Red firs grow to four feet in diameter in sheltered forest pockets along the ridge. Soon you leave the forest and climb along the rocky south face of the ridge past giant frasera, California mountain mahogany, paintbrush and sulphur flower. The path levels overlooking the vast wooded wilderness to the south, with the charred snags of the 1988 Hermit Fire not far below. A few pines and cedars struggle for survival in the harsh, rocky subalpine terrain. Purple mountain pennyroyal graces the rocky slopes.

Pass a charred Jeffrey pine at 3¼ miles. The trail climbs briefly, then descends as the top of Black Rock Mountain with its lookout tower appears. Cross scree slopes, then pass through an area where the big fire burned the top of the ridge. Chinquapin, sword fern and cliff brake hunker amidst the rocks.

Climb past bitter cherry to a saddle at 3⅝ miles. As the trail forks again, take the more traveled right fork, climbing moderately, then steeply past an outcrop of striated black rock. Make a winding ascent through dwarf forest. Return to open, rocky slopes as the trail forks again. This description bears right.

The trail follows the crest of the ridge, climbing on uneven, rough tread. The climb steepens, winding to the mountain's south face. Ascend through a low carpet of dense brush with scattered firs and cedars. Indian pinks add color in summer. The path soon heads north as gravelly tread makes your climb more difficult. The ascent steepens where the path bends left, a giant dark rock towering overhead. Wind past miners lettuce, Douglas wallflower and a surprising array of plants.

By 4 miles you have climbed above one set of dark rocks only to have another set tower overhead. The trail offers a brief level respite as it switches to the peak's northeast face. Resume a winding climb on faint, eroded tread, soon climbing to the big rocks. The lookout tower looms as you ascend steeply toward the peak. As the path splits again, take the steep right fork. Ascend through a carpet of pinemat manzanita with hawkweed and sulphur flower. The climb turns moderate as the path heads north.

Your path bends left past the old privy—no longer functional. Pass one last large tree and ascend toward the summit. In summer a wildflower garden attracts bees, butterflies and hummingbirds, which dart from one burst of color to the next.

Reach the decaying lookout tower 4¼ miles from Pettijohn Trailhead (1⅝ miles from ridgetop junction). Stay off the rickety, hazardous structure. A mountain hemlock grows beside the tower, with more along the peak's north face. Mountain hemlocks do not grow elsewhere in the Yolla Bollys.

Black Rock Mountain's highest summit rises west of the tower, marked by a metal pole. An easy scramble gains the top in 300 feet, where you have an unobstructed view over much of northwestern California. On a very clear day, you can see the Pacific Ocean beyond the King Range sixty miles west. Most maps designate the peak as 7755 feet, but a recent metric map shows it as 7792 feet. You cannot see Black Rock Lake from this peak, but the lake is visible from a lesser summit to the northeast.

30

CHICAGO CAMP/DEVILS HOLE RIDGE

SPINE OF THE NORTHERN WILDERNESS

This is the key route connecting the northern and southern portions of Yolla Bolly Wilderness, offering a moderate ridgetop course that avoids the deep canyons otherwise involved in such a traverse. South Fork Cottonwood Creek Trail (Trail #34), the other main north-south route, begins and ends at roughly the same elevation as this trail, but descends to 2700 feet. You can traverse the entire spine of the wilderness in 24 miles by combining this trail with Pettijohn and Summit Trails (Trails #27 and 39) never dropping below 5600 feet.

From the Chicago Camp Trail junction just west of North Yolla Bolly Spring, descend southwest through mixed forest. Climb briefly, then descend to a clearing with spectacular views east at ¼ mile. Descend moderately along a narrow rocky ridgetop to a saddle, climb briefly, then descend past white oak brush, salsify and yarrow. Drop to another saddle beyond ¾ mile, the lowest point on your route at 5690 feet. The ridge is grassy here, with patches of wood rose, whitethorn, bitter cherry and gooseberry.

Your path ascends gradually along the ridgetop, where Indian pinks grow in sunny clearings and black oaks mix with conifer forest. The trail makes a brief easy descent, then levels as the ridgetop narrows. Descend briefly before a short steep climb, then contour through forest where large pines and firs mix with small cedars. At 1⅜ miles the path climbs moderately, leaving the backbone ridge to traverse its steep west face. Your route levels, then descends briefly past numerous fir snags.

Climbing gently to 1¾ miles, you pass a vague junction with unmaintained Brooks Ridge Trail. A cairn may mark the intersection—if local bears have not been too mischievous. (The vague, well-blazed trail descends northwest, dropping 2000 feet to ford South Fork Trinity River, meeting Powell Ridge Trail before climbing to Road 28N40—neither trail is recommended.)

Chicago Camp Trail contours south before descending moderately through young, then mature forest. As the trail levels, watch for a faint spur on the right at 2 miles. It descends 75 feet to Chicago Camp Spring. Its flow is minimal by August, but should be potable after purifying. The main trail continues south, immediately passing Chicago Camp on your left beneath white firs and cedars.

The junction of Chicago Camp and Devils Hole Ridge Trails, marked with an old metal sign, is 150 feet past the camp. Both

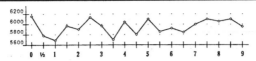

DISTANCE: **9 miles to Frying Pan** (13½ miles from Stuart Gap Trailhead, 27 miles round trip), 2 miles to Chicago Camp/Devils Hole Ridge junction, 3⅝ miles to lower Robinson Creek, 7¾ miles to Lazyman Trail.

TIME: Two to four days.

TERRAIN: Downs and ups along ridgetop, then descends Robinson Creek before climbing steeply to ridgetop for more ups and downs to Frying Pan Meadow.

TRAILS INTERSECTED: Humboldt, Brooks Ridge, Chicago Camp, Lazyman Butte, Knob Cut-off, Summit, Long Ridge.

BEST TIME: July and August. Also good June and September.

WARNINGS: If lightning approaches when you are on ridge, seek shelter in lowest gully you can find; avoid tall trees. Trail can be dry in late season.

DIRECTIONS TO TRAILHEAD: Inside wilderness at junction of Humboldt and Chicago Camp Trails. You can also hike from Frying Pan, following description in reverse.

FURTHER INFO: Yolla Bolly Ranger District, Trinity National Forest (916) 352-4211.

tracks are faint near the junction. (Chicago Camp Trail descends south and west 3½ miles to poor Bearwallow Spring and Powell Ridge Trail. The 1¾ miles beyond Bearwallow are difficult to follow along a ridgetop firebreak, finally reaching Hopkins Camp Trailhead—see Trail #25.)

Our described route bears left at the junction, climbing gradually southeast on unsigned Devils Hole Ridge Trail. The faint trail can be tricky to follow at first as it wanders through elderberry bushes in forest with a grassy floor. Soon the climb steepens, gaining a ridgetop at 2¼ miles. Ascend south along the ridge to a slate-like rock outcrop with a fine view of the North Yolla Bollys. Your winding path contours along the ridgetop.

Leave the ridgetop at 2½ miles, descending steeply through cedar forest. Dip through a gully, then descend through an area where wood rose crowds the path. Descend southeast to a

137

rudimentary camp on the right at the headwaters of Robinson Creek. You may find water here in early season.

The trail descends along the east bank of the creek, then fords and descends steadily above the west bank. Ford the seasonal stream four more times by 3⅛ miles. Descend moderately through white oak brush, passing miners lettuce, paintbrush and Fremont silktassel. Drop steeply to ford to the east bank. A white fir on the left has a yellow section marker indicating your location. Descend along the creek past whitethorn, creeping snowberry, phacelia, trail plant and twisted stalk.

As you ford a tributary at its confluence with Robinson Creek, look for twinberry, stream violet and leopard lily. An old sign on the far bank at 3⅝ miles points north for Chicago Camp. Your trail turns east to follow the tributary upstream, passing checker lilies and paintbrush. Ford the stream four times, then climb gradually until the trail bends right. Leave the creek on a steep, winding ascent north through forest with understory of white-veined shinleaf and pipsissewa. The precipitous climb turns southeast through wood rose, sticky currant and extensive pinemat manzanita beneath fir-dominated forest.

Top a ridge and descend along a gully at 4¼ miles. Descend steeply beneath scattered forest with the gully on your left. The trail climbs southeast beyond 4½ miles.

Pass a camp where the tread turns vague around 4⅝ miles. A spring lies uphill to the east, 20 feet to the right of the faint track. Tank up on water here, the last dependable source before Frying Pan. Leopard lilies, columbine, fairy bells and paintbrush grow lushly around the seep.

The winding trail improves, climbing southeast past broad leaved lupine and white California skullcap to a rock outcrop atop Grouse Ridge. Gently descend east on faint tread past curl-leaved mountain mahogany, purple penstemon and brodiaea. The trail turns southeast and levels with grand views south along Devils Hole Ridge at 5 miles.

Descend steeply east through a gully, then climb rocky tread along the base of a craggy outcrop. The path turns southeast. White oak brush and squaw carpet cover the tread in spots. Pass through a riot of purple penstemon. Dip to a saddle where junipers grow in mixed forest, with silver lupine, houndstongue hawkweed and yarrow in the understory.

Contour through sparse forest west of the ridgetop to 5⅜ miles. Climb gently to a dry knob on the ridgetop where many Indian pinks grow. Look east from the summit to see Lassen Peak left of Tomhead Mountain. On a winding descent, pass a drainage with California skullcap and purple verbena. Drop to a wooded saddle at 5¾ miles, then climb gently before contouring west of the ridgetop.

Your trail climbs gradually to another knob on the ridgetop, then descends through forest littered with sulphur flower and

law .92

wood rose. Beyond 6⅛ miles you reach a saddle with a grassy clearing which has a pond in spring and early summer. It generally dries up by August, when the vernal pool sports many tiny purple and white flowers.

Climb briefly, then contour past many cedars and the white flowers of California stickseed. Climb moderately through dense fir forest, then contour along the east side of the ridgetop, passing Douglas wallflower, purple penstemon, pussy paws, blue field gilia and pink stickseed. Descend gradually along the ridgetop to a Douglas-fir-shaded saddle at 6¾ miles.

Make a winding ascent, steep in places, to 7 miles. Then descend gently along the west face of the ridge, passing yellow trumpet-shaped flowers called fascicled broom-rape. Climb gently, winding with the ridgetop to 7¼ miles. Contour along the west face of a knob where pinemat manzanita grows with curl-leaved mountain mahogany. Descend moderately, then contour south before descending to a saddle.

Make a winding climb along the pinemat-covered ridgetop with a view east to Lazyman Butte. Climb moderately until the trail makes a big bend to the right, descending briefly to meet Lazyman Ridge Trail at 7¾ miles. (Lazyman Ridge Trail climbs briefly before descending east—see Trail #35).

Your trail climbs southwest along the ridgetop, then contours through forest. A rock on the left supports sedum and Sierra cliff brake. At 8 miles use caution on a brief steep descent across a loose talus slope with a precipitous drop on your left.

The trail promptly regains the ridgetop on a winding descent through sugar pine forest. At 8¼ miles the Knob Cut-off, a short-cut to Summit Trail, branches left as the main path veers right on a winding sidehill descent through fir forest. Cross the top of a small glade where scarlet fritillary and meadow larkspur grow, then ford two seasonal creeks. Reach the junction with Summit Trail (Trail #39) at 8⅞ miles. Turn right for a short, wooded descent to Frying Pan Meadow, 9 miles from North Yolla Bolly Spring and Humboldt Trail.

139

31

NORTH YOLLA BOLLY LAKE

GLACIAL CIRQUE BENEATH ROCKY SPIRES

If you look at a map showing the wilderness boundary in this northeastern corner of the Yolla Bollys, it appears that someone took a bite out of the wilderness. The bite was taken by timber harvest interests who could not bear to part with the dense fir forests above 6000 feet, even though they control most of Shasta-Trinity National Forest, the largest public provider of timber in California. The chewed off corner is only slightly larger than one square mile, but when you visit it, on this trail and the one to Barker Camp, the missing chunk clearly possesses wilderness values. It should be designated as wilderness to provide a buffer zone for the spectacular example of glacial geology offered by North Yolla Bolly Lake and the subalpine habitat of Beegum Basin. The loss to timber economy would be minute, while the addition to the wilderness is essential.

If you visit North Yolla Bolly Lake, be especially careful to minimize your impact on this fragile, subalpine environment. Camp at least 100 feet from the shore, pack out all trash and consider releasing any trout you catch. Try not to visit on holiday weekends, when visitors may crowd the lake basin.

From Rat Trap Gap Trailhead, follow Cold Fork Trail (Trail #32) uphill, signing in at the trail register. In 400 feet turn right on North Yolla Bolly Lake Trail, climbing southwest past a sign advising "TRAIL UNSAFE FOR HORSES." (The part dangerous

kW. 92

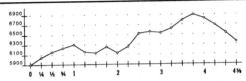

NORTH YOLLA BOLLY LAKE:

DISTANCE: 3 miles to lake, 4⅝ miles to Pettijohn Trail.

TIME: Day hike or overnight.

TERRAIN: Climbs steadily, traversing north slope, with several descents; climbs steeply into cirque basin to follow lake shore, then climbs steeply over ridge and descends.

TRAILS INTERSECTED: Cold Fork, Pettijohn.

BEST TIME: July and August. September also good.

WARNINGS: Snowpack may last into July. Lake often does not thaw until mid-June. Heavily used trail; expect crowds and be especially careful to minimize impact; avoid on holiday weekends and/or camp away from lake.

DIRECTIONS TO TRAILHEAD: Take Highway 36 to Road 30, 2 miles west of Wildwood. Go 10 miles on paved Road 30. Go left on Road 35 for 11 miles to Stuart Gap, then left 4 miles on Road 35 to signed trailhead at junction with Road 45.

FURTHER INFO: Yolla Bolly Ranger District, Trinity National Forest (916) 352-4211.

to equestrians is from 2 to 2⅞ miles.) Ascend steadily through red fir forest with scattered white firs and sugar pines.

The climb soon eases as a selectively logged area is on your right. Continue the gradual ascent, angling away from the cutover area to traverse a slope covered with pinemat manzanita and golden chinquapin. Ford a stream at ⅜ mile where western dog violet, gooseberry and currant thrive. Climb gradually, passing large white firs, with white-veined shinleaf and corn lilies in the understory.

Your trail tops a ridge and bends left to climb gently. Cross a corduroy bridge above an unreliable spring, then a split rail bridge wrapping around a large rock (watch for loose boards). Trail plant and wood rose join the understory. The gentle ascent continues past six-foot-wide sugar pines and Douglas firs.

Climb moderately through dense virgin forest, then drop to ford a creek lined with stream violets and currants. The trail

141

climbs steeply out of the drainage, passing little prince's pine, phacelia, coral root orchid and large lupine. After topping a ridge at 1⅛ miles, the trail contours through forest.

Descend southwest to a stream crossing around 1⅝ miles. The creek is lined with alder, elderberry, nettle and bleeding heart. Climb gradually through deep forest with red, white and Douglas firs, Jeffrey and sugar pines and incense cedar.

Top a ridge at 1⅞ miles, entering designated wilderness. A brief easy descent passes fairy bells, with greenish-white flowers maturing to scarlet berries by late summer. Climb across a rocky ridge where you overlook craggy country and the steep trail ahead.

Descend steeply past water-sculpted rocks, then giant frasera, naked stem buckwheat and hawkweed. A brief climb leads to a ford of the largest creek on this route. The stream, which drains Beegum Basin, is lined with pale pennyroyal, sticky currant, sneezeweed, leopard lily and the spherical white flowers called ranger's buttons.

The path heads along the creek, then bends left to climb past bitter cherry, pinemat manzanita and Sierra cliff brake beneath mixed forest. Climb steeply as the forest thins, offering grand views of the Trinity Alps and Mount Shasta. This rugged rocky area supports creeping snowberry, white oak brush, yarrow, whitethorn and California mountain mahogany, but few trees. Descend briefly through a patch of forest, then climb along a steep, rocky slope through spectacularly rugged, steep country with views of glacially carved, crenelated spires that tower above North Yolla Bolly Lake. Sedum and other succulents grow among the rocks with sulphur flower and western white pines. This steep, uneven trail is treacherous for horses.

From 2½ miles the tread improves somewhat, although you continue climbing, often steeply, through rough terrain. The path levels amidst a jumble of rocks and bowed, broken red firs. Resume a gradual winding climb through rocky terrain in fir forest with white and sugar pines.

Traverse a steep talus slope with Bridge's cliff brake, then ascend steeply through fir forest. Your path contours southwest along the base of a ridge topped with jagged rock pillars. Descend briefly, then head northwest.

Reach the outlet of North Yolla Bolly Lake at 3 miles. After a view-rich camp on the right, the path continues around the lake past the shallow north end, then turns southwest along the shore. Come to a roomy camp on the west shore, one of several camps on this bank. Red and white firs, whitethorn, pink Douglas spiraea, raspberry and gooseberry grow along the shore. Steep rock walls tower overhead.

The trail continues, climbing steeply over the cirque wall to the northwest, switchbacking through red fir forest. The steep ascent offers fine views of the lake basin and surrounding jagged terrain, then Lassen Peak and upper Sacramento Valley to the east and Mount Shasta and the Trinity Alps to the north. Climb steeply to the ninth switchback at 3¾ miles. Ascend gradually to the trail's summit for an extensive view.

The trail descends west, exiting the wilderness to cross another overlooked wedge of pristine country. Descend gradually, then moderately through red fir forest. After the path bends right, your descent and the surrounding terrain become more gentle. Continue a gradual winding descent past many broad leaved lupines. Reach trail's end at 4⅝ miles, at the junction with Pettijohn Trail (Trail #27).

van.'92

32.

COLD FORK/
NORTH YOLLA BOLLY MOUNTAIN
NORTHERN CREST OF THE WILDERNESS

This is the quickest route into North Yolla Bolly high country. Although steeper than Pettijohn Trail, it is much less traveled. You can ascend North Yolla Bolly Mountain on a long day hike for one of the finest views in the wilderness or pack in to Barker Camp and head out from there.

The area from the trailhead to Barker Camp is another foolish exclusion from the wilderness. It contains all the worthy elements for wilderness designation: pristine forests, headwaters of pretty creeks, high ridges and grand views.

Cold Fork Trail climbs from Rat Trap Gap Trailhead at the junction of three roads. Please sign in at the trail register in 150 feet. The path forks in another 250 feet. North Yolla Bolly Lake Trail (Trail #31) goes right. Take the left fork signed "BARKER CAMP." Climb moderately through forest with Douglas, white and red firs and scattered sugar pines. Whitethorn and rabbit-brush dominate a sparse understory.

The trail bends right, then left, climbing steadily on duff tread

143

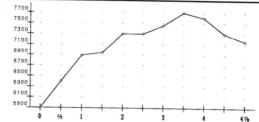

COLD FORK/NORTH YOLLA BOLLY MOUNTAIN:

DISTANCE: 4⅞ **miles** (5½ miles with main-peak side trip) to
Pettijohn Trail; 1½ miles to Barker Camp, 1⅝ miles to North
Yolla Bolly Mountain and Saunders Cut-off Trails, (3⅞ miles
to end of Cold Fork Trail at Humboldt Trail), 3⅞ miles to first
peak, 4⅜ miles to main peak.

TIME: Day hike or overnight.

TERRAIN: Climbs steadily through red fir forest to ridge, (Cold
Fork descends ridge and slope to Humboldt Trail); North
Yolla Bolly Mountain Trail climbs along ridge and south face
through forest, glades and barren clearings to view-studded
mountain tops, then descends to Pettijohn Trail.

TRAILS INTERSECTED: North Yolla Bolly Lake, Saunders Cut-
off, Humboldt, Pettijohn, Black Rock Mountain.

BEST TIME: July and August. May be good June and
September; inquire about snow level.

WARNINGS: Snow may cover north slope into June. Cold Fork
Trail is vague in spots beyond junction; unmarked at junction
with Humboldt Trail. Only reliable water at Barker Spring
and one mile before Pettijohn Trail. Trail is vague in places;
map and compass advisable.

DIRECTIONS TO TRAILHEAD: Same as Trail #31.

FURTHER INFO: Yolla Bolly Ranger District, Trinity National
Forest (916) 352-4211.

OTHER SUGGESTION: SAUNDERS CUT-OFF descends steeply
from ridgetop one mile to Humboldt Trail.

through deep forest. Ascend generally south, winding to ½
mile. You may glimpse steep canyons in the eastern wilderness
through the forest on your left. The ascent soon eases following
a ridgetop. Pass broad leaved lupine, hawkweed, pussy paws,
gooseberry and white-veined shinleaf as Shasta red firs
dominate the forest. The trail bends right to climb steeply at ⅞

mile. Cross the top of a mossy seep often defiled by cattle, where corn lily and blue western dog violet grow. Ascend gently beyond the seep. The trail climbs moderately at one mile, soon angling southwest through red fir forest.

Cross the outflow from Barker Spring at 1⅜ miles. The spring is in a small meadow above the trail. Beyond the ford, lined with young alders and aquatic red-rooted brooklime, the path meanders vaguely for 250 feet, then passes cool Barker Camp on the right beneath large red firs on the upper edge of the meadow. Bear bag your food if you camp here. Distinct tread climbs gently to the signed wilderness boundary. A forest clearing with an alder thicket overlooks the Sacramento Valley far below. (At night distant city lights twinkle as if underwater.) Climb moderately to a ridgetop junction at 1⅝ miles.

The three vaguely marked choices at the intersection may be confusing. First, on the right, North Yolla Bolly Mountain Trail climbs northwest; the balance of this report details that trail. In another 30 feet, the vague trail on the left, signed "EAST LOW GAP," is the continuation of Cold Fork Trail (see next paragraph). The trail straight ahead, marked "HUMBOLDT TRAIL," is Saunders Cut-off. It descends steeply, dropping 650 feet in a mile to Humboldt Trail (Trail #33) northeast of the start of South Fork Cottonwood Creek Trail (Trail #34).

(The rest of Cold Fork Trail descends the ridge east, meeting Humboldt Trail above East Low Gap. Recommended only if your destination is Tomhead Saddle, Cold Fork Trail follows the ridge to 2⅝ miles, then drops steeply along its south face. It regains the ridgetop at 3⅛ miles, staying south of the crest for ⅜ mile before joining an old jeep track. Double track winds down the ridge, obstructed by deadfall pines before meeting Humboldt Trail at an unmarked junction in a tangle of deadfall at 3⅞ miles.)

From the upper junction, climb gradually along the wooded ridgetop on North Yolla Bolly Mountain Trail. The ascent soon turns moderate. A break in the dense red fir forest offers views southeast to the South Yolla Bollys. The climb eases, crossing the top of a glade sprawling down the mountainside. Ascend the border between glade and forest, with grand views across the wilderness. Pussy paws, silver lupine, snapdragon skullcap and the fragrant pink flowers of a gilia abound.

The trail bends left, leaving the ridgetop to climb gently west through the immense glade spattered with red firs and Jeffrey pines. Gravelly ground supports little but lupine, yarrow and red fir. The path levels briefly at a cairn, then bends right, resuming a gentle climb through the glade.

At 2¼ miles your trail begins a long contour west along the south slope of a 7531-foot peak. Pass bitter cherry bushes, young cedars and larger red firs and Jeffrey pines. Contour through dense red fir forest, then descend briefly around 2⅝ miles as Peak 7531 is due north. Contour through forest at the base of jumbled rocks.

Return to open glade, contouring west to regain the ridge before 2⅞ miles, with a view north into Beegum Basin, North Yolla Bolly Mountain rising beyond. Occasionally vague tread winds through short ups and downs.

Climb moderately along the ridgetop as Mount Shasta rises north-northeast. The trail veers south of the ridgetop on vague tread. Return to the ridgetop beyond a stand of young red firs, one of the few stands of trees in the next ½ mile. The often vague trail generally follows the ridgetop, marked by cairns. Ascend the ridgetop, climbing steeply in places on rocky ground with sparse silver lupine and sulphur flower. Black Rock Mountain appears as you climb beyond 3½ miles.

Descend briefly to a saddle, then resume the ridgetop ascent toward the craggy south peak of the North Yolla Bollys. Short foxtail pines hunker amidst red firs on your right. Other plants include rabbitbrush and deltoid balsam root.

The trail swings left of the rocky summit at 3¾ miles, climbing steeply through sparse forest dominated by foxtail pines. Reach a saddle between two knobs of the 7700-foot-plus peak, where foxtail pines grow two feet wide and 50 feet tall. A tiny camp is on the right. The apex of the peak is 300 feet west. Descend west-northwest, then make a winding descent north into red fir forest.

At 4 miles you reach a saddle at 7500 feet. Turn around for a view of the cliffy face of the south peak, with Mount Linn 13 miles beyond. Read on before proceeding to avoid confusion.

Only the pull-out map in the back of this book has the rest of North Yolla Bolly Mountain Trail mapped correctly. The tread on the ground is too indistinct to help. In September 1991 three vague routes left this broad saddle heading west-southwest, west and north from various points, all marked by cairns and occasional vague tread. The first of these is the designated,

---

NORTH YOLLA BOLLY MOUNTAIN

From the saddle at 4 miles, consider a short side trip to the top of North Yolla Bolly Mountain, second highest peak in Yolla Bolly Wilderness. The vague trail climbs north from the saddle on a short, steep ascent of a windblown ridge. Veer right of the peak before ¼ mile to a saddle. Scramble west on a faint track up the dark rock, reaching the cabin-sized top in 250 feet. Foxtail pines grow 30 feet from the 7863-foot summit. The register on top, placed by the Mother Lode Chapter of the Sierra Club in 1988, resides in a metal pipe. It offers tales of ascents and a fitting rendering of Robert Service's poem Land of Beyond, *good reading while you admire the breathtaking view. Return to the 7500-foot saddle, completing a ⅝-mile round trip.*

poorly maintained trail descending to Pettijohn Trail.

From just south of the saddle, descend west-southwest 400 feet to distinct tread marked by a rock cairn. It descends west moderately, then west-northwest steeply. By 4⅛ miles follow distinct tread on a winding descent west through red fir forest. At 4¼ miles the descent eases as the trail approaches a spring at a small grassy meadow with a camp. The faint trail continues west, descending to Pettijohn Trail around 4⅞ miles.

33.

HUMBOLDT FROM TOMHEAD

HISTORIC TRAIL CROSSES SOUTH FACE OF NORTH YOLLA BOLLYS

The Humboldt Trail was a major supply route between Humboldt County and Sacramento Valley. Trail #26 describes the western third of Humboldt Trail and details its history. As Yolla Bolly trails go, this route is fairly level, varying only 1200 feet in elevation crossing the wilderness east to west. This eastern trailhead provides access to the more gentle, maintained part of the trail. The steeper west end is more spectacular.

Your trail starts just southwest of the small corral. Sign in at the same trail register as Syd Cabin Ridge Trail (Trail #35). Humboldt Trail heads northwest, descending slightly on soft duff tread. The path soon merges with an overgrown track from the register, then contours west around a rocky knob.

Descend moderately as white and Douglas firs, black oaks, ponderosa and sugar pines mingle in forest with an understory of whitethorn, manzanita, buck brush and silver lupine. In spring look for symmetrical white blooms of Piper's lomatium and tiny multiple purple flowers of three-bracted wild onion.

Descend gently on the ridgetop to level in a stately grove of large ponderosas at ½ mile. Descend slightly as incense cedar, red fir and live oak join the forest, with white-veined shinleaf, fawn lilies, snowberry and miners lettuce at ground level. Conifer seedlings, heavily browsed by deer, have a sculpted look.

Your path undulates along the ridgetop, passing California waterleaf, buttercup, gooseberry and spotted coral root orchid in mature forest. Climb gently at 1⅜ miles, then moderately. After a short steep ascent, climb gradually to a sign on a big ponderosa snag that says "MIDDLE RIDGE TRAIL." (The unmaintained route descends northeast, blazed but vague.) Climb gently along the ridgetop.

From 1⅞ miles the trail drops, climbs and dips again, passing a wooden sign pointing to Van Spring about ¼ mile downhill.

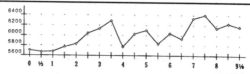

HUMBOLDT FROM TOMHEAD:

DISTANCE: **13½ miles to West Low Gap Trailhead** (27 miles round trip); 4¼ miles to East Low Gap, 9⅛ miles to North Yolla Bolly Spring, 9¼ miles to Pettijohn Trail.

TIME: Full day hike to East Low Gap, two nights for entire trail.

TERRAIN: Climbs gently along wooded ridgetop; descends to East Low Gap; climbs moderately, then contours wooded slope to N. Yolla Bolly Spring; ends at West Low Gap Trailhead.

TRAILS INTERSECTED: Syd Cabin Ridge, Cold Fork, Sanford Ridge, Saunders Cut-off, South Fork Cottonwood, Chicago Camp, Pettijohn.

BEST TIME: May and June. May be passable April to November; inquire first.

WARNINGS: Heavy blowdown Sanford Ridge to South Fork Trail.

DIRECTIONS TO TRAILHEAD: From Red Bluff (exit Interstate 5 at M.26.5 from south, M.28.6 from north, Tehama County), take Highway 36 west 15 miles. Go left on Cannon Road 5 miles to paved intersection. Go straight on what becomes Pettijohn Road (gravel) 15 miles to confusing junction, where you go left. Road 35 climbs 4.6 miles to Road 27N06. Go left one mile to Saddle Camp Guard Station. In .25 mile, take left fork, climbing steep, narrow road 4 miles to Tomhead Saddle Trailhead. (4 camps with tables, fire pits, pit toilets and corral; no water).

FURTHER INFO: Yolla Bolly Ranger District, Trinity National Forest (916) 352-4211.

OTHER SUGGESTION: SANFORD RIDGE TRAIL leaves Humboldt Trail beyond 4¾ miles, descending 2⅜ steep miles to South Fork Cottonwood Trail (also links with LONG RIDGE TRAIL, forming a loop with Syd Cabin Trail.)

You may glimpse the South Yolla Bollys and Solomon Peak through the forest as you climb past camps, then rock out-crops, reaching a knob on the ridgetop at 2⅜ miles.

Climb gently as the fir forest becomes dense, ponderosas becoming scarce. The ascent steepens, then turns gradual again on a very broad ridgetop. Descend slightly to a yellow section marker at 3 miles, where whitethorn and shooting stars thrive on the forest floor. The trail ascends gradually through dense forest with sugar pines and firs seven feet wide. After climbing moderately, the trail levels on the distinct double ruts of an old jeep road. Ascend the double track left of a high knob on the ridgetop.

Reach a summit at 3⅜ miles, just below 6300 feet. Your path contours, then descends a broad, occasionally double track. Descend moderately wrapping around a large, striking rock outcrop on the left where you can see peaks north, west and south. The descent continues to wooded East Low Gap Saddle at 4¼ miles, where wood strawberry, gooseberry and wood rose grow. A fire ring sits beside a rusting washtub and Fiestaware, remnants of a long history preceding the designated wilderness.

Humboldt Trail climbs northwest, then bends left to ascend steeply southwest. Meet vague, unmarked Cold Fork Trail (Trail #32) in a jumble of blowdown at 4⅜ miles. (Cold Fork climbs northwest up the ridge.) Take Humboldt Trail, climbing southwest, then west on a double track along a steep south-facing slope. Paintbrush grows beside a rocky outcrop with a view over Long Gulch and most of the eastern wilderness.

The path narrows to a single track, ascending moderately across a very steep slope with pussy paws and violets. Meet Sanford Ridge Trail beyond 4¾ miles. It leaves Humboldt Trail 50 feet before the sign marking the junction. (Sanford Trail makes an unrelenting descent south, dropping 2300 feet in 2⅜ miles to South Fork Cottonwood Trail near Burnt Camp. It meets Long Ridge Trail one third of the way down. Both are seldom maintained and brushy in spots.)

Humboldt Trail climbs gently from the junction, then contours before descending gently. The terrain and tread get rough around 5⅜ miles as the path undulates through young forest prone to blowdown. The forest alternates between large trees and young saplings, with scarlet fritillary, Indian pink and snowberry in the understory. Pass a rudimentary camp on your left, on a shelf below the trail around 5⅝ miles.

A spring in a rough wood box on the trail's right edge beyond 5¾ miles has cold clear water (may dry up late summer). Cedars surround the seep, with trillium, sneezeweed, strawberry, corn and other lilies. Pass another seep in 100 feet as the trail contours or descends slightly through dense forest. The tread improves as you climb past a large pine snag.

The trail contours west, crossing the headwaters of Deer Creek beside a large cedar where leopard lily, chocolate lily and frasera grow. Cross two gullies as you climb to 6⅛ miles, where two large pine snags stand on the left. Descend past large rocks and grassy clearings to another large pine snag. Contour on faint tread past many dead young trees. Descend across a gravelly gully, then climb steadily to the top of a rock outcrop at

6¾ miles, with red penstemon at its base. The ascent continues, crossing two small streams, then a glade.

Humboldt Trail levels beyond 7⅛ miles, then descends gradually through young cedar forest, winding through gullies and passing several small creeks and springs. One spring has a long, dilapidated corduroy crossing lined with leopard lilies. Climb briefly on vague tread through another glade.

The trail contours through a glade with tall elderberry bushes, across another seep and back into forest. Meet an unmarked junction just before a verdant creek at 7⅝ miles. The unmarked spur climbing north is Saunders Cut-off. (It ascends 650 feet in a mile to Cold Fork and North Yolla Bolly Mountain Trails.)

Humboldt Trail continues west across the creek, where broad leaved lupine and swamp onions grow. Descend briefly, make a winding contour, then descend through a glade and past a spring to South Fork Cottonwood Trail (Trail #34), which forks left heading southeast.

Humboldt Trail winds through a creek gully, then contours through cedar forest. Descend gently beyond 8 miles, passing an immense eight-foot-diameter ponderosa, then crossing the moist tongue of a large glade. Contour through forest of large firs, crossing another glade. The winding trail undulates, then contours through gullies. At 8⅞ miles large quadruplet incense cedars stand on your right.

Climb gently to the outlet of North Yolla Bolly Spring at a mossy water trough before 9⅛ miles. A shady camp on the right occupies the site of the old North Yolla Bolly Guard Station, which was razed after this became designated wilderness in 1964. A grand view of Shell Mountain, Brooks Ridge and Opium Glade Ridge is framed by cedars.

In 100 feet Humboldt Trail meets Chicago Camp Trail (Trail #30), which descends south along the backbone of the wilderness. Humboldt Trail continues west to Pettijohn Trail (Trail #27) at 9¼ miles, then contours through glades, forest and an aspen grove in Cedar Basin, traversing the steep south slope of Black Rock Mountain. It climbs, then finally drops to West Low Gap Trailhead at 13½ miles. For details of the western portion of Humboldt Trail, see Trail #26.

34.

SOUTH FORK COTTONWOOD CREEK

STEEP ROUTE THROUGH DEEP CANYONS TO SUBALPINE

Do not think of this trail as a recommended trip; it is not. Consider it a link between the trails it intersects, offering options for day trips and loops into some of the most remote, rugged terrain in Yolla Bolly Wilderness. Many parts of South

Fork Cottonwood Trail are wonderful, but backpacking its entire length would likely be a grueling chore rather than the pleasant adventure for which we head to the wilderness. I explored it on four different day hikes from camps inside the wilderness, with a light day pack rather than a backpack. If you backpack this trail, take it in small doses, say 3 to 6 miles a day.

This trail leaves Humboldt Trail 7⅞ miles west of Tomhead Trailhead, about one mile east of North Yolla Bolly Spring. A sign facing west marks the path where it angles southeast through cedar forest. After a brief level stretch, descend gently through a gully where water is generally available.

The trail soon traverses Saunders Glade. At the bottom of the glade, a sign on the right marks spacious Saunders Camp in the forest at the clearing's edge. The sticky saprophytes called pinedrops grow here. An old cut-off ascends the east edge of the glade. Your trail descends gradually east through forest, then switchbacks right to descend south. (Do not be deceived by the gentle start—the trail drops 2100 feet in 3⅝ miles to the South Fork.) Descend gently by three switchbacks to one mile, passing eight-foot-wide ponderosas in forest with firs and cedars. Gooseberry is the only plant thriving in the understory.

The forest thins on a long switchback where many large snags stand, offering views east to Tomhead Mountain and south to the South Yolla Bollys where this trail ends. Descend by six more long switchbacks to traverse the top of a steep glade around 1½ miles. Opium Glade Ridge towers above South Fork Cottonwood Creek Canyon to your south. Your trail picks up a ridgetop, descending moderately past manzanita, buck brush and silver lupine. Black and live oaks mingle with the conifers.

Switchback left to leave the ridge, soon descending a ridge nearer Bear Gulch. Wind through a clearing, then descend steeply. Switchback right to descend gradually in shady forest past fairy bells, wood rose, honeysuckle and California harebell. The trail soon descends the east side of the ridgetop, passing snowberry and bunch grass. Switchback left away from the ridge at 2½ miles, dropping through forest with a view up the steep slopes of the North Yolla Bollys. Switchback to the right around a large Douglas fir and descend gradually, dropping onto another ridge around 2⅞ miles. Follow it east briefly, then switchback right on a gradual descent.

Cross another ridge, then descend ten more switchbacks to Bear Gulch at 3⅝ miles. (A side trail on the left drops to a pleasant campsite in the gulch.) Your trail descends south above the stony cascades and pools of a creek. Good tread descends gracefully to the bottom of Bear Gulch at its confluence with South Fork Cottonwood Creek. The larger creek is shady and cool, lined with alders. Fill up on water here, especially in late season when the next water source is unpredictable.

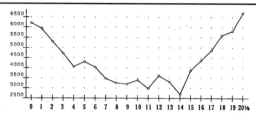

SOUTH FORK COTTONWOOD CREEK:

DISTANCE: **20⅛ miles one way**; 3¾ miles to South Fork at Bear Gulch, 5½ miles to second ford, 6 miles to Burnt Camp, 8 miles to last ford of South Fork, 9 miles to Lazyman Trail, 9⅜ miles to Syd Cabin Trail and Hawk Camp, 11⅛ miles to Buck Creek, 13½ miles to Slides Creek, 15⅜ miles to Thunder Camp, 17¾ miles to Brown Camp junction.

TIME: Two to four nights.

TERRAIN: Well-graded descent to Bear Gulch and South Fork Cottonwood Creek; climbs through forest, drops to ford; climbs east bank, descends to creek at Burnt Camp; climbs steep, south-facing slope; descends through glades and forest to follow wooded stretch of creek, fords to west bank and climbs through forest; descends to Lazyman Ridge and Syd Cabin Trails; up and down through forest, drops to Buck Creek; climbs steeply, then descends steeply to Slides Creek; climbs steeply through chaparral then steadily to Thunder Camp and up wooded Thunder Camp Ridge to Ides Cove Loop.

TRAILS INTERSECTED: Humboldt, Sanford, Lazyman, Syd Cabin, Scorpion Camp, Brown Camp, Ides Cove Loop.

BEST TIME: May and June. Upper creek dry in places by July; lower stretches of trail can be insufferably hot and dry.

WARNINGS: Seldom hiked as continuous trip, best used in short sections to link other trails. Total elevation change extreme. Upper creek may be dry by July. Watch for rattlesnakes, scorpions and poison oak. Use caution at fords, especially early season. Ford at 8⅛ miles is dangerous for stock.

DIRECTIONS TO TRAILHEAD: Inside wilderness on Humboldt Trail (Trail #33), 7⅞ miles from Tomhead Trailhead.

FURTHER INFO: Yolla Bolly Ranger District, Trinity National Forest for first 12 miles: (916) 352-4211. Corning Ranger District, Mendocino National Forest south of Buck Creek: (916) 824-5196.

OTHER SUGGESTION: SANFORD RIDGE TRAIL, steep, poorly maintained, offers shortcut from Humboldt Trail saving 6⅜ miles to Burnt Camp.

Beyond the South Fork ford, the trail climbs above the rocky canyon by two short steep switchbacks. Soon oak brush crowds the trail as you climb gradually, paralleling the creek downstream. Contour, then wind through a shady gully where elk clover and leopard lilies grow. Ascend two switchbacks, rising moderately through forest past fairy bells, solomon's seal, trail plant, paintbrush, sugarstick and hazel bushes. After a short steep descent, climb to 4¼ miles, then contour to 4¾ miles. Douglas firs dominate forest with pines, oaks and cedars.

Cross a glade at the base of Opium Glade Ridge, passing a damp seep (not a reliable water source) where sneezeweed, verbena, corn lily, hedge nettle and a riot of other moisture-loving plants thrive, concealing the trail briefly. Vague tread heads south across the lower part of the glade through many bracken ferns. The tread improves, contouring through more grasslands, then forest. Dip steeply through one gully, then climb to another where poison oak grows beneath maples. The trail ascends gradually, then levels at 5 miles. Descend steeply, then moderately through forest with a grassy floor. Switchback left as oaks begin to dominate the forest. Cross a small gully with bunch grasses and descend switchbacks right and left to South Fork Cottonwood Creek just beyond 5½ miles.

If the 15-foot drop from the eroded cutbank seems unreasonable, you turned right too soon. Walk upstream 50 feet to find the steep descent to the ford, where bleeding heart and mullein grow. The creek may be underground here as early as July. If the ford is dry and you need water, the creek is usually above ground ⅛ mile upstream.

Walk downstream 400 feet from the ford, where a pleasant camp sits on the broad, flat east bank. The trail climbs southeast up the cutbank from the camp to meet unmarked Sanford Ridge Trail, which climbs steeply northeast. Your trail, signed "SULPHUR SPRING," contours southeast along the top of the cutbank to 5¾ miles, then descends to an unmarked spur. (The path on the right descends steeply to Burnt Camp in ⅛ mile, on a broad wooded flat by the creek with red larkspur, checker lily and raspberry.) The main trail climbs south along the top of a slide into a large brushy glade surrounded by ponderosa pines, where another camp is on the right. The path descends, then undulates through shady forest to 6⅛ miles.

Your trail turns east across a south-facing slope, traversing steep dry terrain peppered with rock outcrops. The sunny clearing supports interior live oak brush, buck brush, redbud, soap plant and wild grape. Descend through the clearing past Douglas wallflower, yarrow, paintbrush, blue field gilia, star thistle, brodiaea, tarweed and phacelia in spring. The trail undulates over brushy slopes above the rugged canyon. Return to forest at 6⅝ miles as the trail descends, then climbs slightly through a glade. The purple blooms of godetia come early in this sunny spot, where poison oak also thrives.

Climb slightly to a ridge, where a vague spur forks left (ascends ridge steeply to Sanford Ridge Trail). Your trail bends away from the creek, descending steeply to ford a tiny side stream, then descends toward the South Fork. Turn southeast to contour along the bottom of a glade where you may hear the melodic song of hermit thrushes harmonizing with the burbling creek 100 feet below. Descend gently across a steep slope, then moderately along the base of a rolling glade.

As the canyon broadens at 7½ miles, drop to ford to the north side of South Fork Cottonwood Creek, following the shady, alder-lined canyon bottom to another ford. Walk the south shore past lilies and starflowers. After a lush grassy spot, the trail climbs gradually above the creek. Descend east paralleling the creek on faint, uneven tread. Watch for poison oak, plus mule ears, morning glory, red larkspur, lupine and lilies.

Descend steeply by three switchbacks to a ford, the final crossing of South Fork Cottonwood Creek by the trail that bears its name. The ford, slick bedrock, can be treacherous and is not advisable for stock. White alders and bigleaf maples line the stream. Look southwest for the steep path ascending the south bank by three switchbacks. Climb past white-veined shinleaf and pipsissewa. At 8⅛ miles your trail veers left to follow the canyon downstream, dipping in and out of several lush side canyons in mixed forest.

Cross a small seep on a rough corduroy bridge before 8⅝ miles. Wind past another seep where scouring rush and California waterleaf (also called squaw lettuce—you can eat the young leaves raw) grow. Climb gently through a gully, then contour through another gully and across a steep dry slope. Descend gradually past little prince's pine in shady forest.

Your trail levels at a junction at 9 miles. Lazyman Ridge Trail (Trail #35) is a faint path on the right, signed "LAZYMAN MEADOW, THE KNOB." Your trail descends southeast across the bottom of the glade. Switchback left, then descend moderately by three more switchbacks to another junction before 9⅜ miles. On the left Syd Cabin Ridge Trail (Trail #35) descends steeply to Hawk Camp on the South Fork in 250 feet.

South Fork Cottonwood Trail, on the right, climbs through a gully and into mixed forest. I saw a rubber boa snake climbing in the low branches of a fir tree here. Dip through another gully, then descend to a brushy clearing with buck brush, brodiaea and godetia. Contour through oak forest, then descend gradually before a gentle climb to 10 miles. Then contour through mixed forest on dry slopes with a diverse understory where squaw bush and the yellow flowers of fascicled broom-rape grow.

Descend gradually across several lush gullies, climb briefly to a ridge, then descend gradually. Switchback left, coming to the edge of Buck Creek Canyon with a view southwest to the South

W. 92

Yolla Bollys. Gray pines and oaks suddenly dominate the forest. Descend steeply through chamise by six switchbacks.

The trail turns north on a flat next to rushing Buck Creek at 11 miles. Descend to a wet ford, surrounded by several campsites and tall ponderosa and gray pines draped with wild grapevines. The trail climbs east on the far bank, passing a pleasant camp above South Fork Cottonwood Creek.

Your trail winds, ascending gently, then steeply. The climb eases along a ridge before rising steeply into mixed forest. The steep ascent continues past a small glade around 11¾ miles. Climb gradually east, then south past a spring with woodwardia and other ferns. Descend gradually, then steeply to a sulphurous spring on the left and another spring just beyond. The trail descends moderately, then bends right to drop steeply past a third spring to a creek crossing at 12⅜ miles. Your track climbs gradually through oak forest, then bisects a small glade before ascending to a ridge at 12¾ miles. The path levels near Prine Cabin site amidst tall mixed forest with scattered grasslands.

Begin a gradual descent as oaks dominate the forest. The descent steepens as the forest thins. At a ridge where gray pines join oaks and ponderosas, look south to the South Yolla

Bollys, much closer now. The trail bends left and descends steeply through chaparral. Be careful on loose gravel tread as you drop by five switchbacks to the broad gravel bed of Slides Creek at 13½ miles. At 2700 feet, you are at one of the lowest elevations in the wilderness. Watch for rattlesnakes! Walk upstream 150 feet to the ford, just below where the canyon narrows. Use caution if you cross during spring runoff, when surging water milky with snow melt obscures the uneven creek bottom. California buckeye lines the stream.

South Fork Cottonwood Trail ascends 4000 feet in the next 6⅝ miles to reach Ides Cove Loop (Trail #36), the hardest stretch on a difficult trail. Take it easy if you continue. The rough trail switchbacks steeply up the canyon's dry, brushy east wall. The grueling climb eases a bit after the fourteenth switchback at 13¾ miles. The climb steepens again by 14 miles, where shady forest provides relief from the hot climb. As the trail angles southeast, oak leaves obscure the tread in spots.

The trail levels briefly before 14⅜ miles. Come to a junction notable for the danger of taking the wrong path. A sign on a small black oak on your left points east for "COTTONWOOD CREEK." That is Scorpion Camp Trail (descends steeply to South Fork Cottonwood Creek).

No sign marks the trail you want. Its vague tread switchbacks sharply right to climb west-northwest up the ridge. It soon switchbacks left to climb steadily with fine views. At 15⅜ miles a small sign on the right indicates Thunder Camp, tucked beneath large black oaks. The trail climbs east and northeast ⅛ mile to a glade and Thunder Camp Spring, a torpid waterhole that will do in a pinch if you purify the water.

The trail climbs east out of the glade, then bends to the right into forest, heading generally south on a steady, winding ascent up the ridge. A sluggish spring is on the left beyond 16¼ miles. Ascend steadily, nearly leaving the wilderness around 16¾ miles.

Descend briefly to a junction at 17¾ miles. The left fork is Brown Camp Trail. (It contours southeast, leaving the wilderness to reach Harding Spring in one mile and Brown Camp in 2½ miles, its course disrupted by logging roads.) South Fork Cottonwood Trail forks right at the junction, climbing steeply, then contouring along the ridgetop.

Descend gently, leaving the ridge at 18⅜ miles, then climbing past outcrops of dark Franciscan rock. Head west to cross a seasonal stream, a great rest stop when it is flowing. Wind through an area jumbled by landslides, then head west onto a broad ridgetop, climbing past a mossy stream bed and across more seasonal drainages.

Descend briefly, then climb past a spring on the left at 19 miles. Resume a winding ascent up the ridge through dense forest to regain the main ridgetop. Continue your steady zigzagging climb to the 20-mile point as views expand of the towering South Yolla Bollys ahead and Mount Lassen, Tomhead Mountain, Mount Shasta, North Yolla Bollys and Trinity Alps to the northeast and north. Finally your trail contours through mixed forest to meet Ides Cove Loop (Trail #36) at 20⅛ miles. Turn right to descend to Burnt Camp on upper Slides Creek, or left to climb steeply to the start of the loop and the trailhead.

35.
SYD CABIN RIDGE/LAZYMAN RIDGE
STEEP TRAIL NOT FOR THE LAZY

Despite considerable elevation change, the trail to Hawk Camp on South Fork Cottonwood Creek is well graded, a long but reasonable descent. Beyond Hawk Camp the trail climbs moderately to Sulphur Springs, then steeply to verdant Lazyman Meadow, followed by a long dry climb to Devils Hole Ridge and Frying Pan (most difficult route into Frying Pan). This trailhead is easy to reach, offering access to sparsely traveled deep canyons and spectacular ridges.

The trail descends southwest from Tomhead Campground on the road's big bend. Sign in at the trail register, where Humboldt Trail (Trail #33) forks northwest. Take Syd Cabin Trail descending south into the wilderness with a view of wooded Syd Cabin Ridge and the South Yolla Bolly Mountains beyond. A winding sidehill traverse descends through forest of large ponderosa pines with scattered white firs. Perennials in the understory include whitethorn, rabbitbrush, scrubby white and live oaks, gooseberry and buck brush. You may also see paint-brush, pussy paws, lupine and miners lettuce.

Your descending trail winds left, then switchbacks right and left. Descend through a fine grove of seven-foot-wide ponderosa pines. Your path levels briefly among white firs as the tread becomes rocky, then resumes a gentle descent.

Dip through two gullies around ⅝ mile. As the trail bends right, a faint spur descends to the green grass and shiny wet of Tomhead Spring in a gully on your right (last water for 3½ miles). Climb gently through forest of Douglas fir, sugar and ponderosa pines, incense cedar and oak.

The trail turns southwest to follow Syd Cabin Ridge around ⅞ mile. Contour through deep forest with fawn lilies as the ridgetop descends toward the trail. Descend west to a clearing with views of the North Yolla Bollys. Your path soon levels.

Join the trail from Buck Camp (private) at 1⅝ miles and descend gradually along the wooded ridgetop. Oaks dominate

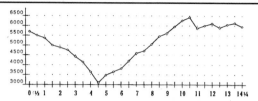

SYD CABIN RIDGE/LAZYMAN RIDGE:

DISTANCE: 14¼ **miles to Frying Pan** (28½ miles round trip); 4½ miles to South Fork Cottonwood Creek at Hawk Camp, 8⅝ miles to Lazyman Meadow, 13 miles to Devils Hole Ridge.

TIME: One or two days to Hawk Camp, three or four days to Frying Pan Meadow.

TERRAIN: Descends ridge to South Fork Cottonwood Creek; climbs to Lazyman Meadow; climbs Lazyman Ridge, with many ups and downs; descends to Frying Pan.

TRAILS INTERSECTED: Humboldt, Long Ridge, South Fork Cottonwood, Devils Hole Ridge, Knob Cut-off, Summit.

BEST TIME: May or June for first half, June or July for second half. Trailhead usually snow-free May to October.

WARNINGS: Watch for rattlesnakes, scorpions and poison oak. No water from Tomhead Spring (⅝ mile) to Hawk Camp; no water beyond Lazyman Meadow. Steep, difficult trail.

DIRECTIONS TO TRAILHEAD: Same as Trail #33.

FURTHER INFO: Yolla Bolly Ranger District, Trinity National Forest (916) 352-4211.

OTHER SUGGESTION: LONG RIDGE TRAIL climbs steeply from Long Gulch to Sanford Ridge Trail and Humboldt Trail.

the mixed forest, with manzanita, whitethorn, lupine, shooting star and bunch grass below. Climb gently across the north face of a ridgetop knob. Return briefly to the ridgetop, then traverse the side of a larger knob.

Begin a steady descent along the ridge's north side, passing Oregon grape and hound's tongue. The descent increases as the path bends north. Faint tread buried in oak leaves and pine needles passes purple meadow larkspur and striped coral root orchid. Switchback left before 2⅜ miles and return to the ridgetop, where broad leaved lupines grow densely.

The trail switchbacks right, leaving the ridge for good. (A faint spur winds south toward Plum Garden.) Your trail descends north, then switchbacks left to descend west through oak woodlands with pines and Douglas firs. A rolling glade sprawls on the right.

The trail bends left, winding across the top of another glade. Mountain violet, bedstraw, buttercup and squaw bush thrive here. In June you may see heart-shaped leaves and purple flowers of purple milkweed. Enjoy a fine view of the North Yolla Bollys. The trail leaves the glade, crossing a gully to descend gradually west. Your path begins a winding, steepening descent.

The track levels briefly at 3⅛ miles. Resuming your descent, you almost regain the ridgetop, but switchback right to descend north. Drop steeply by three more switchbacks, then continue a winding descent through pleasant oak and pine forest with a grassy floor liberally sprinkled with lupine.

Your trail approaches the edge of a steep, deep canyon at 3⅞ miles. Descend gradually south across a steep slope, then switchback right, dropping steeply into the canyon. Indian pink and paintbrush grow on the fourth switchback. After the sixth switchback, vegetation turns lush. Descend by shorter switchbacks past trillium and snowberry to ford tiny Long Gulch Creek at 4⅜ miles, lined with luxuriant vegetation. On the west side, steep Long Ridge Trail climbs north.

Your trail traverses the steep west wall of the canyon, heading southwest. Descend to South Fork Cottonwood Creek at 4½ miles, where poison oak, bleeding heart, meadow and red larkspur, miners lettuce and lupine line the creek.

Ford to Hawk Camp on the west bank. The camp sits on a rocky flat above the creek, a lovely spot in a deep, wooded canyon. The camp is home to scorpions, skinks and western fence lizards. Hawk Camp's primary problem is also its charm; it sits extremely close to the creek. If you camp here, you must use care with waste and biodegradable soap. Be sure to go at least 100 feet up the steep trail—beyond the first bend—for your toilet and washing. Throw waste water on the big rocks uphill, feeding the mosses and lichens instead of polluting the creek. Biodegradable soap takes up to ten years to break down in water, too long in a pristine environment.

The trail climbs steeply, switchbacking left and right to South Fork Cottonwood Trail (Trail #34—offers day hike and overnight trips north and south). Our described hike forks right, climbing four switchbacks. Enter the bottom of Sulphur Springs Glade, cross a seep and reach the junction of South Fork Cottonwood and Lazyman Trails at 4⅞ miles.

The described hike turns left to climb Lazyman Ridge Trail (signed "LAZYMAN MEADOW, THE KNOB"). The tread is vague at first, climbing south across the top of the large glade. The path bends right to strong-smelling Sulphur Spring on your left. A camp sits north of the spring in a sunny clearing where yellow ground iris grows. The trail winds, climbing gradually past a less sulphurous spring at the top of the glade. A shady camp is on the edge of the forest to the east.

Your trail climbs gently through patchy forest, then bends right on a moderate climb up the ridge. Pass rock outcrops and climb over a large fallen log as the habitat becomes drier, with sugar pine, manzanita and mountain mahogany in mixed forest.

Ascend steadily, switchbacking left, then right to overlook South Fork Cottonwood Canyon. Climb past the first of many tiny wild onions. The trail switchbacks left at 5¾ miles, passing Purdy's sedum. Climb steeply through open pine forest by long switchbacks.

Your switchbacking climb turns gradual beyond 6 miles. Pass little prince's pine and Piper's lomatium. The tread turns rocky around 6½ miles, climbing steadily. Then return to duff tread, climbing with expanding views. Ascend vague tread briefly where the path bends right to head west. Pass paintbrush as you switchback left to climb east.

Ascend three sharp switchbacks where incense cedars join the forest, then make a winding, gentle climb. The trail climbs southwest at 7⅜ miles as views expand to include the South Yolla Bollys. Descend briefly on lupine-lined tread to a gully crossing where Douglas wallflowers grow. If the ford is dry, you can reliably find water 150 feet downstream.

Begin a steep winding climb. The ascent eases as squaw carpet covers the ground. Climb moderately, then steeply west at 7⅞ miles. Veer left across the head of a gully, ascending steadily southwest through pine forest with pinemat manzanita.

Crest a hill around 8½ miles and descend gently to the lush, verdant swath of Lazyman Meadow, an oasis of tall green grass in a gently sloping gulch spattered with blue irises and purple swamp onions. A forest of large pines and firs surrounds the meadow. A metal sign at a sharp bend in the trail points toward "LAZYMAN MEADOW." A campsite is 50 feet south of the sign. A spring lies 250 feet west of the campsite.

The trail becomes extremely vague as it climbs from Lazyman Meadow. Look for blazed pines indicating the route west, then northwest, quickly resuming a steady climb. If you are continuing up Lazyman Ridge, be certain you find the trail before proceeding into this isolated, steeply rugged corner of the wilderness. The tread becomes easy to follow again by 8¾ miles, climbing steeply northwest through stately pine forest.

The path turns north briefly as the climb eases around 9 miles. Come to a broad flat on the ridgetop where the trail winds west on a gentle climb. The climb steepens to moderate, winding up the ridge. You can soon see South Yolla Bolly, Solomon and Hammerhorn Peaks on your left. Continue a steady climb as Jeffrey pines and incense cedars join the forest.

Your climb steepens before 9⅜ miles as the path is lined with lupine, paintbrush, showy phlox and yarrow. Then contour past

hairy star tulip, phacelia, blue spreading phlox, gilia and meadow larkspur. Resume climbing through a burned area with sporadically scorched forest. The track becomes vague around 9⅝ miles. Stay south of the ridge, winding through burned, fallen timber until the tread improves.

Return to the ridgetop at 9¾ miles, where red-leaved dwarf miners lettuce spans the trail. The trail winds to the north face of the ridge, then climbs gradually to the ridgetop. Climb steeply through a gravelly, eroded area. Returning to the north side of the ridge, climb steeply through white fir forest. As you return to the ridgetop, an amazing pyramid-shaped rock on the left supports curl-leaved mountain mahogany. The South Yolla Bollys rise beyond the chasm of Buck Creek Canyon.

You will probably be relieved to know you are nearing the summit of 6541-foot Lazyman Butte. The trail returns to the ridge's north face, climbing one more hill. Contour around Lazyman Butte to 10⅜ miles, about 60 feet below its rocky top.

The tread turns rocky across steep slopes as you begin a gradual descent. Then a very steep descent begins suddenly. The path becomes vague and splits in two; take the steeper right fork and proceed slowly on a severe descent of loose, often vague tread in scorched forest.

At 10¾ miles the plunge ends at a saddle. Pass a dry camp, then veer left to the ridge's south face for a moderate descent on vague tread. Descend the ridgetop to a saddle, where bright sunflower faces of deltoid balsam root line the path.

Climb gradually, then steeply to a crest. Your path contours the ridge's north face, then returns to the ridgetop, climbing

past whitethorn, rabbitbrush, buck brush, manzanita, live oak and penstemon. The trail bends left, traversing the ridge's steep south face at 11⅜ miles. Cross a barren slope of large loose talus. Then duff tread contours through pleasant small hollows south of the ridge. Climb steeply to the ridgetop, then traverse bare rocky slopes with expansive views. Climb gradually on open ridgetop, then through forest to a 6180-foot summit.

Return to barren, rocky slopes with curl-leaved mountain mahogany. Descend into mixed forest where extensive carpets of pinemat manzanita line the sheltered south face of the ridge. Descend steeply, then contour. Regain the ridgetop around 12¼ miles, climbing gradually. Contour across the ridge's north face, with grand views of Devils Hole Ridge and the North Yolla Bollys. The trail bends left, descending south to a view of The Knob less than a mile away. Then descend southwest on the ridgetop to a saddle where blue field gilia, lupine and paintbrush grow sheltered by manzanita and whitethorn.

Climb gradually from the saddle. Soon, in one of the most barren spots on the ridgetop, you may spot the stunning light pink flowers of bitterroot Lewisia, a low-growing, multiple flowered beauty whose blossoms close up in the evening. Lupine and three-bracted onion also grow here. Climb to a small knob, then descend slightly to a saddle. Ascend gradually, then steeply before contouring on level ridgetop. Descend to Devils Hole Ridge Trail at 13 miles.

Devils Hole Ridge Trail is described in Trail #30; you can follow it in reverse for points north. For Frying Pan Meadow, turn left and follow Devils Hole Ridge Trail 1¼ miles, reaching the meadow 14¼ miles from Tomhead Trailhead.

36

IDES COVE LOOP

HIGH COUNTRY OF SOUTH YOLLA BOLLYS

This trailhead, at 6900 feet elevation, is the highest in Yolla Bolly Wilderness. The 11⅛-mile loop, a National Recreation Trail, explores glaciated subalpine slopes generally buried in snow from October to early June. Even the access road may not open before Memorial Day.

This steep terrain was the territory of the Nomlaki Wintun people. They had villages to the east along Elder Creek and southeast along Thomes Creek. The Nomlaki would come to the high country in summer to hunt and forage in a land of abundance, ranging several days walk from their home village. They stayed close to home during the harsh winters. You might think of the Nomlaki Wintun people's indelible ties to the natural world as you walk this area they knew so well. Peter Knudtson states it concisely in his book on the Wintun:

> *Every feature of the landscape came to hold spiritual meaning and to be intimately known by each of them. Each animal and plant was endowed with name, aura, and practical usefulness; each was addressed with humility in deference to its place in the unbounded reality of which [people were] only one small part.*

It was about a two-day hike from the nearest Wintun village, Tlopom, on the banks of Elder Creek to the slopes of South Yolla Bolly Mountain where the trail begins.

Sign in at the trail register on the west end of the parking area and primitive campground (two tables and fire pits, no toilet or water) at road's end. Climb west on an old road to the wilderness boundary sign where the trail climbs northwest through red fir forest. Descend slightly to a spectacular view of Tomhead Peak and Sacramento Valley, with snowy Mount Shasta, the Trinity Alps and Lassen Peak rising beyond.

The trail turns west, climbing through fir forest and sunny clearings with pussy paws and gooseberry. Cross a small, spring-fed stream lined with corn lily and alder. Stock up on water here, especially if you hike the lower loop first. Contour north across several seasonal drainages, passing mountain and Shelton's violets, waterleaf, phacelia, shooting star, bitter cherry and whitethorn. Meet the junction with the lower loop at ½ mile. Our described hike forks left, returning on the right.

Climb west, zigzagging up a steep slope. Contour as views open to a glacially carved basin ahead, then descend through small gullies and along a gulch. The trail crosses two spring-fed creeks, then undulates across more gullies to one mile.

IDES COVE LOOP:

7400
7200
7000
6800
6600
6400
6200
6000

0 ½ 1   2   3   4   5   6   7   8   9   10   11¼

DISTANCE: **11⅛ miles for full loop**; 1⅜ miles to Square Lake, 1⅝ miles to Burnt Camp Cut-off (5⅝ miles for short loop), 2¼ miles to Long Lake, 2⅞ miles to South Yolla Bolly Trail, 4¾ miles to D Camp Trail, 7 miles to Cedar Basin Camp, 8 miles to Burnt Camp, 9¾ miles to South Fork Cottonwood Trail, 10¼ miles to Brown Camp Trail.

TIME: Day hike for Square or Long Lake or short loop, overnight for full loop.

TERRAIN: Climbs gradually on rocky north slope to Square Lake basin; climbs wooded slope past Long Lake to ridgetop; descends steeply, then undulates along crest to D Camp Trail; descends north slope by switchbacks; long traverse to Cedar Basin; ups and downs on wooded north slope, until steady descent to Burnt Camp; ups and downs along north slope until steep climb to South Fork Trail; climbs gradually to Brown Camp Trail, followed by very steep climb to complete loop.

TRAILS INTERSECTED: Lower Loop, Square Lake, Burnt Camp Cut-off, Long Lake, South Yolla Bolly, Thomes Pocket Ridge, D Camp, South Fork Cottonwood, Brown Camp/Horsepacker.

BEST TIME: July and August. May be accessible late June and September.

WARNINGS: Road often blocked by snow until late May. Lakes may not thaw until mid-June.

DIRECTIONS TO TRAILHEAD: From Corning exit on Interstate 5 (M.9.2 - Tehama County), go west on Corning Road (.5 mile to Corning Ranger District office—information and fire permits) 20 miles to fork on left side of Paskenta Store (last gas, supplies). Take right fork—Toomes Camp Road. About 38 miles from I-5, go right on Road 23N01 (pavement ends). In 6 miles at Cold Springs "Y", go right on Road M22 (25N01). Go 9 more miles (53 miles from I-5), then left on Road 25N27 for 2 miles to Horsepacker Trailhead. In 100 yards, go right on Road 25N29 for .5 mile (rough) to trailhead.

FURTHER INFO: Corning Ranger District, Mendocino National Forest (916) 824-5196.

OTHER SUGGESTION: BURNT CAMP CUT-OFF 1⅝ miles from trailhead, shortens loop to 5⅝ miles.

Climb to a small ridge with pinemat manzanita where the trail bends left into Mount Linn's cirque basin. Meet the unmarked spur to Square Lake beyond 1¼ miles. (The spur winds southwest to the lake shore in 200 feet, where footpaths branch in both directions to round the lake. The squarish lake sits in a grassy clearing, Mount Linn's craggy face towering to the south. The two best camps are on a rise northwest of the lake, beneath red firs and western white pines. You might see the rare, aptly named, ¾-inch-long pink flower called steer's head in the lush lakeside vegetation.)

From the unmarked junction, Ides Loop heads across Square Lake's outlet stream, then turns northwest on a winding climb of a dry slope with paintbrush. Climb over a small, then a larger ridge to meet Burnt Camp Cut-off at 1⅝ miles. (The right fork, signed "BURNT CAMP," switchbacks steeply down a ridge, dropping 800 feet to the lower loop at Burnt Camp in ⅞ mile. It provides the choice of a rigorous 5⅝-mile loop.)

For the full loop, bear left and descend, with views west across the breadth of Yolla Bolly Wilderness. Your trail soon climbs across a steep slope where snow may linger into June, then descends gently west with campsites on the left and right. Pass a wet meadow known as Boulder Lake, once a glacial tarn before erosion filled it. Descend across a seasonal creek at 2 miles, then climb gently along the edge of a meadow.

Veer right to climb steeply on indistinct, switchbacking tread, coming to a saddle on a small, rugged ridge before 2⅛ miles. Several camps around a junction provide flatter terrain than the steep, wooded slopes around Long Lake to the north. (A spur forks right, descending steeply to the wooded lake, following its east shore to the outlet at ¼ mile. The outlet, the start of Slides Creek, tumbles 800 feet down a glaciated cliff to the meadows around Burnt Camp.)

Ides Loop climbs southwest across a stream and along the edge of a wet meadow with swamp onions—last chance for water in the next 3¼ miles. Make a mostly gradual climb through red fir forest to 2¾ miles. Contour across a gentle scree slope to crest the western ridge of the South Yolla Bollys at 2⅞ miles, meeting South Yolla Bolly Trail (Trail #37) where it climbs southeast up the ridge. Gnarled Jeffrey pines and grand views surround the junction.

Ides Cove Loop (signed "D CAMP") makes a zigzagging descent southwest, then west on rocky tread along a mostly bare ridge. Red firs shelter pinemat manzanita and whitethorn. Little else grows here but wind-shaped Jeffrey pines and scattered silver lupine and succulents. Drop to a saddle before 3½ miles, then climb along the ridge's south face past western white and Jeffrey pines, mountain mahogany, mountain violet, three-bracted onion and tiny purple dwarf monkeyflower.

The trail contours south, winding around a 7100-foot knob,

kav.92

then climbs briefly to the ridgetop. Veer south of another ridgetop knob, contouring to a saddle at 4 miles. Climb gradually, then moderately to another saddle, then ascend steeply, veering left of a 7200-foot knob on the ridge. Ascend to 4½ miles, then descend briefly through shady forest to Thomes Pocket Ridge Trail, which forks left (descends one mile to a jeep road at wilderness boundary).

Descend northwest past a saddle, then climb along the south side of the ridge to an unsigned junction at a saddle before 4¾ miles. Faint D Camp Trail (Trail #38) follows the ridge northwest beyond Harvey Peak, the summit of which is ⅜ mile from here.

Descend north on Ides Cove Loop, leaving the ridge. You soon switchback right to drop east through fir forest. Switchback left and descend with views of the Trinity Alps and Mount Shasta. After a small glade, your descent steepens as the trail turns north, then bends right. Climb briefly into a small glade with corn lilies, willows and wild onions at 5¼ miles. The trail contours, then descends before ascending a small ridge.

Contour past a spring on the left at 5½ miles, then one on the right before descending briefly. Climb moderately over a ridge, then descend through red fir forest into a small grassy basin at 5⅞ miles. The trail climbs briefly, descends, then ascends to a ridge. Descend through fir forest with pinemat manzanita and lupine. After a seasonal stream you contour to 6¼ miles.

Make a winding descent into Cedar Basin, your arrival marked by several big cedars. Shooting star, Shelton's violet, phacelia and waterleaf also grow here. Drop past an alder thicket and small glades with corn lilies. The trail levels at 6⅜ miles, a six-foot-wide cedar on your right.

Cross a small creek and climb to a rock outcrop. Descend through a bare gravel opening where two cairns are the only sign of your trail. Rocky tread drops to ford a creek with alders and stream violets at 6⅝ miles, then follows it downstream. Ford two more seasonal streams where mugwort, white Macloskey's violet and blue Jessica's stickseed grow.

The trail contours north, then climbs to a ridge. A gradual winding descent meets a spur trail at 7 miles. (The spur descends left to a pleasant glade surrounded by large cedars, Cedar Basin Camp.)

Ides Cove Loop contours to a seasonal drainage, climbs to ford a creek, then contours again. Climb fitfully to top Slides Ridge at 7⅝ miles in mixed forest with a carpet of pinemat manzanita. Descend gradually, then moderately, switchbacking left for views of the immense meadow along Slides Creek, Mount Linn towering behind it. Your descent ends at the edge of the meadow. Ford Slides Creek at 8 miles and veer right to Burnt Camp and the junction with Burnt Camp Cut-off.

The Cut-off is signed "IDES COVE." (If you go right, the return to the trailhead is 2½ miles, ⅝ mile shorter than the left fork. Both routes gain 1200 feet elevation, with some descents as well. Both have steep climbs. The left fork is recommended unless you are in a big hurry to leave.)

The left fork (signed "BROWN CAMP") climbs southeast, then switchbacks left to climb northeast moderately. Your path soon bends left on a steep climb over rocky slopes in mixed forest. Top a ridge and veer right to ascend gently, then descend to a seasonal creek beyond 8⅜ miles. Climb over another ridge, then contour through a dry gully at 8¾ miles. Ascend moderately, then gradually, then contour to 9 miles. Climb across a seasonal drainage, then ascend steeply before contouring south to ford the fork of Slides Creek flowing from Square Lake.

Climb to another ford, then pass a seasonal, moss-lined pond. Contour east through two small basins, then switch left to climb north, a huge Douglas fir on the left. Switchback to the right at 9½ miles, climbing by two more switchbacks to a large rock outcrop with a grand view north to the Trinity Alps and Mount Shasta and south to Mount Linn.

Climb to South Fork Cottonwood Trail (Trail #34) at 9¾ miles. Ides Loop continues southeast, gaining 200 feet by 10 miles, then descending and contouring to 10⅜ miles, where Brown Camp/Horsepacker Trail continues south. You want to make a sharp right on faint tread, climbing steeply northwest for 300 feet, then bending left to wind steeply up a hellish hill (especially at the end of a long day), the steepest on the loop.

Climb west through young red fir forest. Your climb steepens before meeting the upper loop at 10⅝ miles. Go left, descending ½ mile to Ides Cove Trailhead at 11⅛ miles.

37

SOUTH YOLLA BOLLY

NEW TRAIL ON PEAK'S SOUTH FACE

This recently constructed trail provides access to the high country on the south face of South Yolla Bolly Mountain. The trail was completed in 1987, finally signed in 1991. Our map is the only printed mapping of the trail.

The new trail expands choices for those hiking the traditional Ides Cove Loop (Trail #36). You can combine South Yolla Bolly Trail with the first 2⅞ miles of Trail #36 for a 7-mile loop through some of the highest terrain in the wilderness. More adventurous explorers might consider launching a cross-country climb of 8092-foot Mount Linn, the highest peak in the Northern California Coast Range, from the South Yolla Bolly Trail. This trail, not the loop that borrowed its name, passes through Ides Cove, an old sheep camp in a verdant subalpine basin of meadows and springs on the first portion of trail.

South Yolla Bolly Trail leaves from the same trailhead as Ides Cove Loop. At 6900 feet, it offers the highest starting point in Yolla Bolly Wilderness. Where the Ides Cove Loop goes right, you go southwest on an old jeep road closed to vehicle traffic. The road climbs through fir forest with dense shrubs of bitter cherry and whitethorn in the understory. Gooseberry, water-leaf, mountain and Shelton's violets, mountain pennyroyal and pussy paws also grow here. The road contours beyond ⅛ mile, with views south to Snow Mountain on the horizon.

After a brief climb, the route contours toward the South Yolla Bollys. After a bend left, you climb moderately, then gently past paintbrush, yarrow, mullein and creeping snowberry. Descend gradually around ⅝ mile. After crossing a gully, the road descends steadily into Ides Cove.

Cross the headwaters of Fish Creek, lined with willow, alder, buttercup and gooseberry, at 1⅛ miles. The road bends left into the lush green pastures of Ides Cove where corn lilies abound. The grassy track climbs, swinging left to cross a seasonal tributary and passing several camps in the south end of this pleasant basin. Beyond the remains of a gate, the road levels briefly, then climbs moderately west.

Just before 1½ miles the road levels and bends left. South Yolla Bolly Trail forks right to climb northwest. In 100 feet the trail bends left, climbing west over a bare slope. Pass a wilderness boundary sign and enter forest. Your trail descends, bending right to cross a double gully. Climb gradually, then descend to cross another gully at 1¾ miles, where the trail becomes vague briefly. It climbs south, then west. After another gully, climb gradually, making a slow bend right.

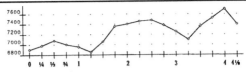

DISTANCE: 4⅛ miles to Ides Cove Loop (8¼ miles round trip), 7-mile loop with upper portion of Ides Loop.

TIME: Full day hike or overnight.

TERRAIN: Follows old road along south slope to Ides Cove; trail climbs gradually through forest, crossing several drainages; descends steeply to creek crossing, then climbs steeply through rugged terrain up barren south face of South Yolla Bolly Mountains, then descends ridge to Ides Cove Loop.

TRAILS INTERSECTED: Ides Cove Loop.

BEST TIME: July and August. May be good late May, June, September and October (depending on spring thaw and first big autumn storm).

WARNINGS: Trail is not blazed and may be difficult to locate in spots on second half.

DIRECTIONS TO TRAILHEAD: Same as Trail #36.

FURTHER INFO: Corning Ranger District, Mendocino National Forest (916) 824-5196.

Around 2 miles your path levels atop a ridge on the south flank of Mount Linn. (Its summit is ⅝ mile north, a 700-foot climb up the ridge from here.) Your trail makes a slow bend right, soon climbing gradually through red fir/pine forest. As the gentle climb turns north, you have views of Hammerhorn, Solomon, Sugarloaf and Harvey Peaks. Then ascend through dense fir forest with some level stretches to 2½ miles.

Beyond a gully crossing, the trail climbs northwest gradually. The climb steepens, turning northeast briefly, then bends left. Descend briefly, then climb, descend and level before dropping to a wooded seasonal creek crossing at 2⅞ miles, with bare rocky slopes above the ford.

The trail turns west on a gradual descent. You soon switchback left and descend steeply by four more switchbacks to ford the only year-round creek on this side of the mountain, a headwater of Thomes Creek. The trail descends rough tread on a brushy, rocky slope. Switchback left and right, descending steeply, then moderately on uneven tread to 3¼ miles.

Your trail turns west, traversing a steep slope on a winding gentle climb. After a short steep climb, ascend gently along a bare, rocky slope with Jeffrey pines. Pass evidence of a lightning-strike fire and continue the gentle ascent to 3½ miles.

The trail switchbacks to the right, climbing steeply up a ridge with ground cover of whitethorn, pinemat manzanita and curl-leaved mountain mahogany. You may see flowering plants as well: pussy paws, mountain violet, pennyroyal, three-bracted onion and spotted mountain bells, green flowers with burgundy and yellow spots. Switchback left to ascend steeply, then switchback right and left on a moderate ascent of the ridge as grand views unfold.

Your trail climbs steeply north through a rock outcrop, switchbacking four times. The only vegetation is gooseberry, phacelia, mountain mahogany and a few rock-clinging succulents. Level briefly atop the outcrop, then climb along the crest of the ridge.

At 3⅞ miles the trail bends left to climb steeply, then climbs back to the ridgetop at 7600 feet elevation. The only places higher than this in Yolla Bolly Wilderness are three peaks in the North Yolla Bollys and the two South Yolla Bolly peaks north and east.

The trail descends west, then northwest following the west ridge of the South Yolla Bollys, where the yellow flowers of western bladder pod are abundant. Drop to the junction with Ides Cove Loop at 4⅛ miles. You can return the way you came for an 8¼-mile round trip. Or turn right on Ides Cove Loop for a 7-mile loop. (Trail #36 describes Ides Cove Loop.)

38.
D CAMP/KINGSLEY LAKE LOOP
SUBLIME HEIGHTS TO RIDICULOUS DEPTHS

This short, rugged loop connects Ides Cove Loop with Summit and Soldier Ridge Trails to the west, offering pleasant possibilities to extend trips on Trails #36, 37, 39 or 40. Be warned that the last 3 miles, descending from Kingsley Lake to Thomes Creek and climbing to complete the loop, offer some of the steepest hills in Yolla Bolly Wilderness. Only the most fit hikers should attempt it. This section is difficult but not unbearable for a day hike, but backpackers might consider returning on D Camp Trail rather than crossing the abyss.

At the west end of Ides Loop, a sign points west along the ridge for "KINGSLEY LAKE." This is D Camp Trail. It climbs gently

D CAMP/KINGSLEY LAKE LOOP:

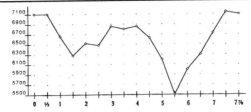

DISTANCE: **7⅞ miles for full loop**; 3⅛ miles to Summit Trail (7⅞ miles from Ides Trailhead via Ides Loop, 7¼ miles via South Yolla Bolly Trail), 4¾ miles to Kingsley Lake.

TIME: One or two nights.

TERRAIN: Undulates on ridgetop to D Camp, then climbs ridge to Summit Trail; down and up on Summit Trail to Kingsley Lake Trail; descends moderately to lake, steeply to Thomes Creek; climbs extremely steeply to complete loop.

TRAILS INTERSECTED: Ides Cove Loop, Summit, Soldier Ridge.

BEST TIME: June and July. Good in August and September.

WARNINGS: Watch for rattlesnakes at lower elevations. Loop beyond Kingsley Lake is extremely steep and difficult.

DIRECTIONS TO TRAILHEAD: Inside wilderness at west end of Ides Cove Loop (Trail #36). You can also join loop via Trails #39 or 40.

FURTHER INFO: Corning Ranger District, Mendocino National Forest (916) 824-5196.

northwest for the first ¼ mile, staying mostly on the south side of the ridge. The sparsely vegetated ridge has wind-gnarled Jeffrey pines and red firs, with scattered ground cover of bitter cherry, whitethorn and gooseberry, and a sprinkling of lupine, bleeding heart and pussy paws. You have fine views south to Anthony Peak, Black Butte and Snow Mountain in the distance, and west across Thomes Creek Canyon to Solomon Peak and Hammerhorn Mountain near Summit Trail.

The trail contours to ½ mile, traversing a steep scree slope on Harvey Peak's south flank. You nearly regain the ridge, but descend gradually on its south face instead. The descent turns steep, soon returning to the ridgetop and dropping 400 feet to ⅞ mile.

Descend gently to a junction at one mile, where a sign on the left warns "STEEP TRAIL." This is Kingsley Lake Trail, your return route if you complete this loop. Continue along the ridgetop on the path marked "D CAMP," descending gradually and steadily along the ridge's south face. The descent steepens as you switchback left and right at 1¼ miles. Reach a saddle, then climb, descend and level as incense cedar, white fir and sugar pine join mixed forest. Descend moderately along the south side of the ridge, then gradually to regain the ridgetop, reaching another saddle at 1⅞ miles.

Your trail climbs along the manzanita-covered south face, rising gradually, then moderately turning southwest. A tangle of whitethorn and bitter cherry shelters purple spreading larkspur. The trail levels at 2¼ miles, the ridgetop now on your left. Descend from pines into patchy fir forest.

The trail levels at 2⅜ miles with a glade on your right. D Camp nestles in a grove of firs, then D Camp Spring burbles to the right of the path. White Macloskey's violets grow in the spring, deltoid balsam root nearby. Glades roll down the steep north slope to Buck Creek's heavily wooded headwaters.

D Camp Trail climbs gently southwest, then turns south as the ascent steepens. The climb eases, returning to the ridgetop, but turns steep as you ascend the south face of a barren ridge. Climb steeply switching right and left past the purplish leaves of frosted miners lettuce and a few scraggly pines. Ascent and trail end beyond 3 miles at Summit Trail (Trail #39).

The described loop turns left, following Summit Trail south for 1⅛ miles. Descend switchbacks and a rocky gully, then contour through seasonal drainages to 3½ miles. The trail undulates to 3⅞ miles, then ascends through a glade. Climb gently to a small ridge at 4⅛ miles. Reach an unmarked junction in 250 feet where Trail #40 forks right toward Minnie Lake.

Take the left fork on a moderate descent south-southwest. Before 4⅜ miles you meet another spur to Minnie Lake. Bear left toward "LAST CAMP." In 250 feet bear left again for "KINGSLEY LAKE" (right for Last Camp). Head east briefly, then make a winding descent northeast, passing pinemat manzanita, pennyroyal, houndstongue hawkweed and buttercup. Descend steeply through red fir forest.

As you turn east on a gradual descent into a large glade, a fine camp nestles amidst small red firs 100 feet to the right. The trail continues across the top of the glade, then descends through forest north of the lush lower glade. Reach a clearing at 4¾ miles. A small cairn marks a faint spur that heads south 250 feet to Kingsley Lake.

The tiny, shallow lake, perhaps the smallest in Yolla Bolly Wilderness, lies in a large meadow. The ancient pond is slowly disappearing, being replaced by meadow as erosion fills it. Ridge-tailed salamanders and frogs live here, but no fish.

The shortest way back to Ides Cove Loop is NOT the easiest.

The trail east from Kingsley Lake descends 1000 feet in a mile, then climbs 1100 feet in 1⅛ miles. To return the way you came takes 1⅝ miles longer, but saves 500 feet of elevation change.

If you insist on doing it the hard way, the faint trail into the abyss leaves from the camp on the north shore of the lake, heading east to cross the outlet stream above its confluence with the main creek. Then better tread descends gradually northeast, angling away from the creek. Descend east on loose, rocky tread, crossing a gully at 5 miles.

Begin a winding descent along a ridge, passing large sugar and Jeffrey pines. Watch for rattlesnakes on a steep descent by ten switchbacks, coming to Thomes Creek at 5¾ miles.

A sign on the east bank points northeast for Harvey Peak. Your trail heads 100 feet up a side creek, then climbs steeply east, switchbacking up a bare slope. The tread is extremely vague but you can see a distinct blaze on a pine at the top of the bare slope. Continue steeply northeast to a ridge, which you ascend moderately.

The trail soon bends right, dips through a gully, and climbs steeply south to a broader ridgetop at 6 miles. Make a winding, steep climb along this ridge. All you can do on a climb like this is put it in low gear, taking short breaks when heart and lungs insist. When you pause, turn around for grand views of Hammerhorn and Solomon Peaks.

The climb eases around 6⅜ miles, but quickly turns steep again. The trail becomes extremely vague around 6¾ miles. Look east for blazes as the path bends right on a gradual climb, then resumes the steep ascent, switchbacking twice to meet the D Camp Trail at 6⅞ miles. Retrace your steps east, ascending D Camp Trail to Ides Cove Loop at 7⅞ miles.

39.

SUMMIT VIA GREEN SPRINGS
ALONG THE SPINE OF THE WILDERNESS

If the Pacific Crest Trail had a western loop, these summit-seeking 11 miles would be among its highlights. This trip, when hiked with Trails #27 and 30, traverses the entire spine of Yolla Bolly Wilderness in 24 miles. The distance is not great but the trip entails a grandeur beyond its length. The route is easy to follow (unless buried in snow), but recommended only for the fit.

If you want to car camp and take spectacular day hikes, this trail offers exciting opportunities, including moderately easy chances to bag two of the five 7500-foot peaks in the wilderness. English Camp offers one of the most pleasant primitive

SUMMIT VIA GREEN SPRINGS:

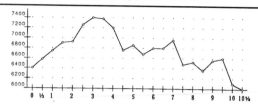

DISTANCE: **10⅝ miles to Frying Pan**; 2 miles to Bauer Spring
Trail, 2¾ miles to Hammerhorn Ridge, 3⅜ miles to Solomon
Peak Trail, 4 miles to Last Camp, 5¾ miles to Soldier Ridge
Trail or Kingsley Lake, 6¾ miles to D Camp Trail, 9½ miles
to Wrights Ridge Trail.

TIME: Two days to Frying Pan.

TERRAIN: Climbs bare ridgetop, with a few descents, to
Hammerhorn Ridge; contours Hammerhorn Peak's west face;
descends Solomon Peak's east face to Kingsley Lake junction;
climbs Sugarloaf Peak's east face; contours on ridgetop;
beyond Wrights Ridge Trail, mostly descends ridgetop;
descends through forest to Frying Pan Meadow.

TRAILS INTERSECTED: Bauer Spring, Hammerhorn Ridge,
Solomon, Kingsley Lake, Soldier Ridge, Sugarloaf, D Camp,
Wrights Ridge, Knob Cut-off, Devils Hole Ridge, Long Ridge.

BEST TIME: July and August. May be good in June and
September—inquire about snow level.

WARNINGS: Trail may be obscured by snow early and late
season. Water limited by August.

DIRECTIONS TO TRAILHEAD: FROM WEST: Follow directions
for Trail #40 to Indian Dick Road. Go 19 miles, then right on
Road M21 (23N01). Pass Hammerhorn Campground at .9
mile, Smokehouse Ridge Trailhead at 4.9 miles. At 8.6 miles
go left on Road M2 (23N01) 2.2 miles, then left on Road
23N01H .6 mile to trailhead.

FROM EAST: Follow directions for Trail #36 to Cold Springs
"Y". Go left on Road M2 (23N01) 20 miles, then right on Road
23N01H .6 miles to trailhead.

FURTHER INFO: Corning Ranger District, MNF (916) 824-5196.
Covelo Ranger District, MNF (707) 983-6118.

OTHER SUGGESTION: PONY RIDGE TRAIL heads west from
English Camp, then descends ridge to spur road above
Smokehouse Creek. FRENCH COVE (problem bears!) can be
reached via BAUER SPRING TRAIL at 2 miles or
HAMMERHORN RIDGE TRAIL at 2¾ miles. SOLOMON PEAK
TRAIL leaves Summit Trail at 3⅜ miles, climbing Solomon
Peak in ½ mile, descending to Soldier Ridge Trail in 2 miles.

campgrounds in the Yolla Bollys, with four sites, a pit toilet, two corrals and sweet abundant spring water.

The trail climbs steeply north from the upper corral on eroded tread, winding up the steep face of the ridge. The mixed forest includes red and white firs, ponderosa and sugar pines and cedars, with manzanita and whitethorn in the understory.

The climb eases to moderate as red firs become the dominant tree, with a carpet of pinemat manzanita. Your eroded path continues a steady climb north. Beyond ⅜ mile the trail descends slightly to the signed wilderness boundary. You may see grazing cattle in the area. Just beyond the boundary, an unmarked trail forks left.

By ½ mile you resume a moderate climb on open ridgetop. Pass blue penstemon, yarrow, pennyroyal and naked stem buckwheat, abundant plants along the rest of the trail. Your ascent winds, as bitter cherry tangles with whitethorn. Climb a double track past wind-sculpted Jeffrey pines as views expand in all directions. Two more plants common on this route join the mix: sulphur flower and rabbitbrush.

At ¾ mile the path forks. Take the right fork, less steep and eroded, climbing along the east side of the ridge. The paths join again, climbing the ridgetop to the trail register at one mile.

The climb turns steep along the east side of the ridge. Switchback left to climb past California mountain mahogany. The path regains the ridgetop, climbing gently through a stand of red firs, then steeply along the ridgetop as the South Yolla Bollys rise above the horizon to the northeast. Pass patches of lupine and narrow-leaved mule ears.

The ascent eases beyond 1⅜ miles as a view of Hammerhorn Mountain and Ridge unfolds. Your path descends slightly or contours on the ridgetop to 1⅞ miles. Climb gently to the Bauer Spring Trail at 2 miles. (Signed "HAMMERHORN RIDGE," forks left to contour 1¼ miles to Hammerhorn Ridge Trail.)

Summit Trail climbs north and northwest on the ridge, passing dwarf monkeyflowers tucked among the rocks. Mount Shasta graces the horizon to the north. The trail turns southwest to climb through dense red fir forest, then along the ridgetop. Look for purple snapdragon skullcap growing beside purple penstemon and pink showy phlox. Your path climbs steeply and steadily on rocky tread, passing tiny lupine, scarlet gilia, western mugwort and northern buckwheat with multiple white flowers.

Ascend to a junction before 2¾ miles, at 7387 feet. (The trail on the left heads southwest along Hammerhorn Ridge, another route to French Cove.) Summit Trail contours north on the ridge then into red fir forest on the peak's west slope. The trail bends right, returning to the ridgetop briefly, then contours or climbs slightly on the ridge's west face. You have views into French Cove and out to the ocean on the clearest days.

ian. 92

Your trail climbs briefly on rough, faint tread as views open to the northwest: Soldier and Wrights ridges with Shell Mountain beyond. The tread improves, contouring through forest. Return to the ridgetop for views east to much bare rock. Many stunted and dead red firs line the route. Climb gradually along the west side of one knob, then the east side of another to Solomon Peak Trail at 3⅜ miles.

On the right Summit Trail follows the ridgetop past heavily folded rock. You soon descend gently. Switchback right to descend moderately, then steeply just east of the crest. The descent turns gradual through a stand of red firs, coming to an unmarked fork at 3⅝ miles. (The spur on the right climbs roughly east to a rocky summit with foxtail and Jeffrey pines.)

Summit Trail descends steeply north. Snow may cover this north slope even in early July, although blazed trees indicate the route. The trail switchbacks left, descending moderately west through forest at the base of an alpine meadow. Descend gradually northwest and north to a wet meadow. Ford its outlet stream and contour west, then descend north to the area called Last Camp, 4 miles from Green Springs.

Several diverse and pristine camps are scattered around lush meadows, springs and twisted rock outcrops in the area, the closest thing to alpine habitat in the Yolla Bollys. Though you are not above timberline, the bare flanks of Solomon Peak towering to the northwest and the precipitous plunge to Thomes Creek make Last Camp seem higher than its 7200 feet. Corn lily and wild onion abound in the meadows and wildflowers linger all summer. Mountain lions have been seen in the area, but are extremely reclusive.

Beyond Last Camp Spring, above the pond in the meadow, Summit Trail heads north, then climbs west. The trail bends right and passes one more Last Camp, this one signed. Descend northwest to ford two creeks before climbing and dipping past two more small creeks.

Descend steeply across mostly bare slopes with grand views, soon switchbacking right and left. At 4⅝ miles your path levels in a stand of firs with a large gravel clearing on the right and jagged Solomon Peak on the left. Climb moderately, then steeply. At 4¾ miles rough tread bends left, climbing up a rocky gully. Cross the gully and climb past California and curl-leaved mountain mahogany, then through a stand of Jeffrey pines.

Your path bends left for a gentle descent and a short steep drop. Pass giant frasera, then climb gently through a carpet of pinemat manzanita where sugar pines mix with red firs. The path contours, then descends gradually. Descend moderately around 5⅜ miles, soon meeting the first of two trails that branch right to tiny Kingsley Lake. (This one descends northeast ⅜ mile to the lake.) Summit Trail descends north to a small wet meadow, then climbs gently, coming to the second Kingsley Lake junction (see Trail #38).

Climb northwest to a third junction at 5½ miles. (The trail on the left climbs steeply to the ridgetop, then descends to Minnie Lake.) Summit Trail, on the right, climbs northwest to an unmarked junction with Trail #40 (descends to Minnie Lake) before 5¾ miles. Your trail heads north, then quickly bends left to descend west. Just beyond the bend, faint Sugarloaf Trail branches left. (This low-maintenance trail goes over the top of Sugarloaf Mountain rather than traversing its east slope.)

Your trail turns north again, descending slightly to a sparse

---

HAMMERHORN MOUNTAIN/SOLOMON PEAK

A spur trail forks right 300 feet beyond the junction at 2 ¾ miles. The spur ascends steeply northeast to reach the 7567-foot top of Hammerhorn Mountain in ¼ mile. The craggy top, where a fire *lookout once stood, offers stunning views over the wilderness and beyond.*

For another peak climb, take Solomon Peak Trail at 3⅜ miles. The trail ascends ½ mile to pass within 100 feet of Solomon's 7581-foot summit. Saunter to the top for a glimpse into the depths of Minnie Creek Basin and surrounding precipitous terrain. The trail then descends steeply to Soldier Ridge Trail at 2 miles.

glade lined with corn lilies. The descent steepens briefly, followed by a gradual rocky descent through whitethorn, with meadow larkspur and tiny purple and white flowers called Torrey's blue-eyed Mary. Soon a spring on the left has white Macloskey's violets, purple western dog violets and buttercups.

The trail contours past delicate bleeding hearts shaded by whitethorn. A series of short ups and downs passes white oak brush and scarlet fritillaries. A short steep descent ends at a spring with willows, yellow stream violets and monkeyflowers. Tank up on water, scarce along the trail beyond this point.

Summit Trail climbs steeply, then moderately, crossing another seasonal stream around 6¼ miles. After a steep climb, contour through fir forest. Start a steady ascent with some rough tread through a rocky gully. Then climb three switchbacks to D Camp Trail (Trail #38) atop a ridge at 6¾ miles.

Summit Trail climbs up the ridge, then across an east facing slope. Reach a summit and the north end of Sugarloaf Trail at 6⅞ miles. This junction offers a good rest stop with a view of the entire north half of the wilderness. From left to right you can see Wrights Ridge, Vinegar Peak, The Knob, Devils Hole Ridge, the North Yolla Bolly Mountains, Opium Glade Ridge, Lazyman Butte and Mount Shasta. If you need water, a spring lies ⅛ mile west, 300 feet below in Hopkins Hollow.

Summit Trail follows a descending ridgetop northwest, dropping moderately steeply to a saddle. Make a brief gentle ascent, then descend along the barren, windswept ridgetop, where only tiny plants like pussy paws and phacelia grow.

Descend moderately, then gradually along the rocky ridgetop where curl-leaved mountain mahogany trees grow from stone. Soon incense cedars join scattered pockets of red firs and Jeffrey pines, with an understory of manzanita.

Reach another saddle at 7⅜ miles. Short, gentle ups and downs alternate with level stretches along the ridgetop. Descend moderately, then gradually to a lupine-lined saddle at 7⅞ miles. The trail again undulates along the ridgetop.

At 8⅛ miles you begin a moderate descent, coming to a wooded saddle. Contour to 8⅜ miles, then begin a gradual ascent of Vinegar Peak. Around 8⅝ miles your trail switches to the east side of the peak, ascending moderately. Pass the summit and descend gradually through fir forest with scattered sugar pines. Curl-leaved and California mountain mahogany and waterleaf serve as patchy ground covers. Your descent soon steepens, a steady, switchbacking plunge to another saddle at 9 miles.

The trail immediately begins a steady ascent through mixed forest. Your climb eases briefly, then switches left and right to climb steeply. Meet Wrights Ridge Trail (Trail #42) at 9½ miles, signed "INDIAN DICK."

For Frying Pan and points north, Summit Trail (signed "THE

KNOB") continues north up a short hill. Descend steeply by three switchbacks through an area of charred red firs, then gently along the ridgetop. Descend steeply by four switchbacks around 9¾ miles, where the terrain on your right plunges steeply to Buck Creek. Your trail straightens as the descent eases. The ridgetop supports whitethorn, pinemat manzanita, mountain violet, scarlet fritillary, paintbrush and wild onion.

Summit Trail meets The Knob Cut-off at 9⅞ miles. (This short trail follows the ridgetop to Devils Hole Ridge Trail, a time saver if you are heading north and have sufficient water to bypass Frying Pan.) Summit Trail bends left, leaving the ridge to descend by big S curves and switchbacks into the basin of which Frying Pan is the centerpiece. Your descent eases at a small glade where several seasonal creeks meet. After a slight climb, descend two switchbacks to ford a tiny creek at 10⅜ miles. The trail contours to meet Devils Hole Ridge Trail (signed "THE KNOB," Trail #30), which forks right.

Continue northwest on a short climb. As Frying Pan Meadow appears ahead, a camp is on your right where an unmarked spur forks left. (The spur heads south around the big meadow to a wooded camp at the base of the cirque wall. A spring trickles from a white pipe just above the camp.) The main trail descends, crossing the stream at the foot of the meadow, coming to a sunny camp, 10⅝ miles from Green Springs Trailhead.

Frying Pan Meadow is the physical center of Yolla Bolly-Middle Eel Wilderness, perhaps some kind of spiritual center as well. The Middle Fork Eel River originates at Frying Pan, dropping counter-clockwise in a big loop to bisect the wilderness flowing south. The big meadow nestles in a cirque basin, carved by a glacier from the north wall of Wrights Ridge. When the Yolla Bollys were young, a lake must have filled the basin. Then eons of erosion filled the lake, creating the lush meadow you see now. If you explore around the meadow, you will discover a wonderland of diverse plant species, the remains of a gateway on the eastern edge and the site of an old cabin southwest of the lower camp.

40.

SOLDIER RIDGE

TO THE SPINE OF THE WILDERNESS

This route provides the easiest access to the heart of the Yolla Bolla high country. The 9 miles to Frying Pan Meadow offer grand wilderness views without difficult route finding. It can be done in a long day's backpack, but is more enjoyable as a two-day hike-in. The trailhead lies at the end of Indian Dick Road, 31 steep winding miles from Mendocino Pass Road. The beautiful

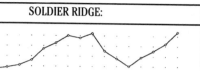

DISTANCE: **4¼ miles to Summit Trail** (4¾ miles to Kingsley Lake, 9¼ miles to Frying Pan); 2⅛ miles to Johnson Headquarters, 3⅜ miles to Minnie Lake.

TIME: Full day hike to Minnie or Kingsley Lake, two or more nights to Frying Pan.

TERRAIN: Climbs ridgetop to Minnie Lake Trail, descends north slope to Minnie Creek, then climbs to ridge and Summit Trail.

TRAILS INTERSECTED: Hole-in-the-Ground, French Cove, Solomon Peak, Summit, Kingsley Lake.

BEST TIME: Mid-June through August.

WARNINGS: Water may be scarce in late season.

DIRECTIONS TO TRAILHEAD: Leave Highway 101 at Longvale (M.59.35) and go east 31 miles on Highway 162. One mile beyond Covelo (last supplies), Highway 162 turns east. Go 10 miles to cross Middle Fork Eel River bridge. Go left on Indian Dick Road (M1). This steep, winding scenic route is paved, then dirt. In 27 miles, Indian Dick Ranger Station is on right. Go 4 more miles on deteriorating road to trailhead.

FURTHER INFO: Covelo Ranger District, Mendocino National Forest (707) 983-6118.

OTHER SUGGESTION: Unmaintained HOLE-IN-THE-GROUND TRAIL drops steeply to Balm of Gilead Creek, climbs steeply to Wrights Ridge. FRENCH COVE TRAIL descends to Rattlesnake Creek, then climbs through French Cove (problem bears!) to Hammerhorn Ridge at 3¼ miles. SOLOMON PEAK TRAIL ascends 1½ miles to peak, turns north to Summit Trail. For KINGSLEY LAKE TRAIL, see Trail #38.

ridgetop forest at trailhead is marred by logging, a last reminder of civilization before you enter pristine backcountry.

The trail heads east-northeast past a bulletin board, then a sign indicating Soldier Ridge Trail. Please sign in at the trail register beside Sunflower Glade. The trail circles north of the glade, starting a steady climb east. For the first ¼ mile a clearcut scars the south side of the ridge. Ascend through forest of white fir, Jeffrey pine and incense cedar, with whitethorn in the understory.

The trail winds to the north side of the ridge and climbs through pinemat manzanita. The climb eases with a view of Solomon Peak. Continue ascending the ridgetop as greenleaf manzanita, hairy star tulip and scrubby white oak join the understory. The ascent steepens beyond ⅝ mile. After contouring briefly, the path winds to the south side of the ridge, then climbs back to the ridgetop. Climb steeply as the trail winds left through dense timber where red firs join the forest.

The trail climbs along the south side of the ridge beyond 1⅜ miles, with views of Hammerhorn Ridge and Rattlesnake Creek Canyon. Level briefly, then resume a gentle climb past large red firs and pines, soon regaining the ridgetop. In early season a pond on the left supports aquatic buttercups. By mid-season it becomes a grassy clearing. Then a tiny glade dense with yarrow is on your right.

Climb past a sign welcoming you to the wilderness—this is the old boundary; you entered wilderness at the trail register. The trail ascends through a clearing with sparse grasses, spreading phlox and scattered pines.

The path levels to meet Hole-in-the-Ground Trail at 1⅞ miles. (The vague, unmaintained trail climbs north, then descends 1600 feet to Balm of Gilead Creek in about 2 miles, recommended only to hardy souls handy with map and compass.) The junction offers a view of Solomon and Hammerhorn Peaks.

Soldier Ridge Trail continues east on the south side of the ridge. Descend briefly to a saddle with small glades on the left and right. Jessica's and pink stickseeds grow at the edge of the forest. Climb gradually through forest of mostly red firs.

Descend gradually to the meadow known as Johnson Headquarters at 2⅛ miles, where a spring flows year round. Two camps provide views of meadow and surrounding highlands. (French Cove Trail heads south vaguely, then improves to descend through pretty country.) Soldier Ridge Trail climbs northeast through sparse fir forest, soon topping the ridge.

At 2⅜ miles a sign on the right points left for Minnie Lake Trail. (Solomon Peak Trail continues along the ridge.) Bear left on faint Minnie Lake Trail, passing left of a scraggly Jeffrey pine to descend northeast through a stand of young red firs. In early season you may encounter snow drifts as you leave the ridgetop for north-facing slopes; be careful not to lose the trail. It soon bends right, heading east-northeast on a sidehill descent of a moderately steep north slope, staying not far below the ridgetop. You have views over sparse glades to the North Yolla Bollys' high peaks.

The trail soon contours past broad leaved lupine, gooseberry, phacelia, waterleaf and yarrow. Climb briefly over a spur ridge, passing bitter cherry, pennyroyal and scattered sugar pines.

Your trail descends moderately steeply by three switchbacks.

ian 92

Pass a large ponderosa pine, then several venerable cedars, with young seedlings all around and a ground cover of squaw carpet. Your descent steepens on tread of loose rock at 2⅞ miles as paintbrush and meadow larkspur border the path. The winding descent soon eases. Pass a seasonal creek, then a glade with corn lilies. The trail descends generally northeast. You may see glacier lilies in June.

At 3¼ miles the trail descends into the rocky gulch cut by Minnie Creek. Turn north to ford the creek, then climb steeply on winding duff tread. The ascent eases, coming to tiny (¼-acre) Minnie Lake at 3⅜ miles. The icy, shallow lake is hazardous for swimming. The mud bottom hides sharp branches. Willows, azaleas, white firs, cedars and sugar pines border the lake. Flat ground nearby (unlike the very steep and broken surrounding terrain) supports two nice camps. The camps lie between the lake and the rocky gorge of Minnie Creek. North of the creek, jagged cliffs rise abruptly toward Solomon Peak. A dependable year-round spring flows from beneath an immense fallen cedar east of the pond. Wild onions grow in the murmuring stream.

From the lake the trail heads east to the edge of Minnie Creek's cutbank, then makes a winding climb northeast, gaining 500 feet in ¾ mile. Ascend through a glade with a seasonal spring, then climb steeply, switchbacking through red fir forest to top the north-south running ridgetop, spine of the Yolla Bolly high country, at 4⅛ miles. The ridgetop offers a view east to the South Yolla Bolly Mountains. To their left Lassen Peak rises beyond the Sacramento Valley.

You meet a junction at the ridgetop. (The trail straight ahead descends to meet Summit Trail from the south, reaching Kingsley Lake in ⅝ mile—see Trails #38 and 39.) For points north, take the connector trail on the left to join Summit Trail in about ¼ mile. The sometimes vague connector follows the contours, saving ¼ mile and some climbing for all points north. It traverses the east face of the ridge on a gentle climb.

Top a spur ridge with Jeffrey pines at 4¼ miles, soon coming to an unmarked junction with Summit Trail. (See Trail #39 for 5 miles north to Frying Pan).

41.
INDIAN DICK TO HAYNES DELIGHT
POPULAR ROUTE THROUGH GLADES AND FOREST TO EEL

This may be the most popular trail in Yolla Bolly Wilderness. If you backpacked in the Yolla Bollys before, chances are about even you have been on this trail. It offers fine, diverse scenery on a moderately steep, not particularly long trail. Avoid it on holiday weekends. Haynes Delight is a small area; it can feel as crowded as Yosemite Valley when several parties converge there.

The starting point is sometimes referred to as Georges Valley, although that geographical feature is farther to the northwest than Indian Dick Guard Station is to the southwest. The station's name refers to an Indian man who came from Nevada to homestead here in the 1890s. When Richard died without an heir, the land reverted to federal ownership. The Forest Service Guard Station was built in the 1930s.

Haynes Delight Trail descends east from the signed trailhead. Wildflowers around the trailhead include harvest and elegant brodiaeas, Ithuriel's spear, verbena, Indian pink, lupine and yarrow. Please sign in at the trail register in 300 feet.

Your trail bends left on a gradual descent north, passing purple penstemon, Sierra cliff brake, whitethorn, California mountain mahogany, manzanita and white oak brush beneath Douglas fir/ponderosa pine forest. Various lilies flower in May and June. Views encompass the wooded canyon of Balm of Gilead Creek, with Lower Glade beyond.

Descend a cooler slope beyond ⅜ mile, where sugar pines and white firs join the forest, with squaw carpet, pipsissewa, wood rose, sticky currant, creeping snowberry and white-veined shinleaf on the forest floor. Pass purple milkweed and Fremont silktassel as your descent offers views up Balm of Gilead Creek to Sugarloaf Mountain (7367').

The decline steepens as you enter designated wilderness, passing coral root orchid and the tiny blue flowers of California harebell. Descend moderately at ¾ mile. Cross a rocky slope

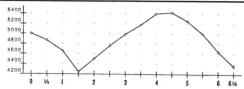

INDIAN DICK TO HAYNES DELIGHT:

DISTANCE: **6¼ miles to Haynes Delight and Eel River**
  (12½ miles round trip); 1½ miles to Balm of Gilead Creek,
  2⅝ miles to Lower Glade Camp, 3⅝ miles to Upper Glade
  Camp, 3¾ miles to Wrights Ridge junction.

TIME: Full day hike to glades, overnight to Haynes Delight.

TERRAIN: Descends to Balm of Gilead Creek; climbs through
  Lower and Upper Glades to Wrights Ridge Trail; contours,
  then descends through forest to river.

TRAILS INTERSECTED: Wrights Valley, Wrights Ridge,
  Yellowjacket.

BEST TIME: June and July; August and September also good.

WARNINGS: Haynes Delight ford may be dangerous in early
  season. Bear bag food at camps on this trail. Watch for
  rattlesnakes.

DIRECTIONS TO TRAILHEAD: Same as Trail #40 to Indian Dick
  Station. Then go one mile, then left on Road 25N15B .6 mile
  to trailhead.

FURTHER INFO: Covelo Ranger District, Mendocino National
  Forest (707) 983-6118.

OTHER SUGGESTION: WRIGHTS VALLEY TRAIL heads
  northwest from Upper Glade, dropping to river (may be
  underground by August) at 1⅝ miles, climbing to Buck Ridge
  Trail at 2¾ miles (vague in spots, very steep beyond river).

where prickly currant grows, then drop past bitter cherry
bushes. Switchback right to descend gradually past trail plant,
honeysuckle, paintbrush and hazel.

Begin a steep winding descent at 1¼ miles, dropping by six
switchbacks to Balm of Gilead Creek at 1½ miles. Pleasant camps
are on both sides of the creek, where alders, willows and
Oregon ash grow. Bear bag your food if you camp here.

Beyond the easy ford your trail turns right and climbs past a
large sugar pine, heading upstream. Ascend moderately past
blue field gilia, wild cucumber vine, mule ears and much naked

184

stem buckwheat. You have views of the creek as the climb eases past dense California mountain mahogany and silktassel.

After the ascent steepens at 1¾ miles, head away from the creek. Climb north past soap plant, narrow-leaved collomia and Indian pink beneath large Douglas firs. Take one last view up Balm of Gilead Creek as the trail switchbacks left, climbing to the bottom of Lower Glade at 2⅛ miles. Ascend north through the glade, where narrow-leaved mule ears, brodiaea and a purple penstemon grow with scattered pines and cedars.

Your path bends left beyond 2¼ mile, climbing northwest along a bleached, fallen snag. A spur forks right, but disappears before climbing to Lower Glade Spring; use the spur ¼ mile beyond. The main path climbs through glade and forest, then skirts the western end of the glade, where verbena thrives in summer. A spur on the right at 2½ miles is signed "LOWER GLADE SPRING." (It climbs to the spring and a camp above the glade in 500 feet.)

The main trail leaves the glade, dipping through two gullies, the second with white brodiaea and California skullcap. Climb gently west through forest alternating with pockets of grassland. Dip through a third gully, then begin a steady climb. The ascent steepens as your path bends right to climb northwest.

Wind through a barren, rocky clearing around 3 miles, then ascend along a sparsely brushy ridge with views west to the confluences of Balm of Gilead Creek, Middle Fork Eel and its North Fork, with Bull Ridge and Castle Peak beyond. Climb steadily along the south-facing ridge.

Wind in and out of a small glade around 3½ miles, where the trail has been rerouted. Climb for another 300 feet to the junction with Wrights Valley Trail. (Bear left for Upper Glade Camp and Spring [⅛ mile], Wrights Valley [1⅝ miles] and Buck Ridge [2¾ miles].)

Haynes Delight Trail ascends moderately north through large Upper Glade to meet Wrights Ridge Trail (Trail #42) at 3¾ miles. (Signed "FRYING PAN," it forks right, climbing northeast.) Junipers grow at the junction.

Stay left on Haynes Delight Trail, descending gradually north through young forest. Climb a short hill with medium-sized ponderosa pines where white oak brush is the dominant ground cover, with squaw carpet and other ceanothus species.

Your trail dips through a gully, with a (usually) dry rocky falls on the left. Wind through several short ups and downs, then contour along the base of Wrights Ridge past much native bunch grass and three-bracted onion.

A rock outcrop left of the trail at 4⅜ miles offers a view of Eel River Canyon and wooded peaks beyond. Descend to traverse the base of an immense rock outcrop where the path is lined with silktassel and Sierra cliff brake. Resume a gradual winding descent with glimpses of Wrights Valley in the Eel Canyon.

The path contours, meandering through more bunch grass. Pass alternately through forest of young trees and large ponderosas. Just beyond 4¾ miles you pass the nearly indistinguishable junction with the old Wrights Ridge connector trail (see 1954 topo map). The faint, unmaintained trail is marked by a blaze on a large cedar 25 feet east of your path.

The route to Haynes Delight descends gently, winding through forest of large ponderosa pines, Douglas and white firs with a dense understory of young trees. Wind left at a large sugar pine and descend moderately as black oaks mix with the forest. Your winding descent continues, varying from gentle to moderate. After a dry gully, drop through pristine tall forest with ground covers of whitethorn, squaw carpet, creeping snowberry, lupine, pipsissewa, trail plant and wood rose.

The descent steepens beyond 5½ miles, except for a gradual drop along a ridge. Make a winding plunge through mixed forest, with Buck Ridge visible beyond the river.

The forest thins as the terrain turns rocky and jumbled. Your path winds, dropping past Oregon grape, pennyroyal and manzanita to the river at 6¼ miles. The rocky river channel is lined with alder, willow and bigleaf maple trees, along with umbrella plant, sneezeweed, Douglas spiraea, paintbrush, verbena, Indian pink and gooseberry. The best camps surround the glade above the west bank, but do not attempt a crossing when the ford runs high and fast. In that case, you must settle for the rocky camps along the east bank. When the ford is safe, you can extend your trip by looping back on the trail northwest and Buck Ridge Trail (Trails #23 and 44). Eel River is closed to

fishing at Haynes Delight; you can fish above the confluence with Uhl Creek to the northeast.

42.

WRIGHTS RIDGE

DRY AND SCENIC RIDGETOP CONNECTOR

This trail provides unobstructed views of the heart of the wilderness on a waterless route to Frying Pan Meadow and Summit Trail. This is the way to reach Frying Pan from Haynes Delight or Wrights Valley. Wrights Ridge Trail offers loop choices with Summit Trail and other challenging, less traveled routes, as well as access to 7081-foot Windy Mountain.

From its junction with Haynes Delight Trail, Wrights Ridge Trail ascends east on a grassy ridge where junipers, ponderosa pines and oaks struggle in sparse soil. Views quickly open up south to Soldier and Hammerhorn Ridges, with Anthony Peak beyond. The climb soon steepens heading northeast, the prevalent direction of this route. The ridge alternates sparse, rocky terrain with white oak and squaw carpet brushiness.

Soon views expand northwest to Buck Ridge and Shell Mountain. The path levels briefly as oak brush crowds your ankles, with brodiaeas and Indian pinks in summer. Climb gently to ¾ mile, where the wooded ridgetop is rich with the sweet scent of Jeffrey pine.

Descend briefly, then climb steeply to a knob. A short descent looks north to the North Yolla Bollys. Climb gently, then moderately on the rocky ridge as patches of pinemat manzanita join the other brush species. Descend moderately steeply to a saddle at 1⅜ miles, passing sugar pine, red fir and incense cedar. Ascend moderately, then gradually, passing many woolly, white-leaved alpine buckwheat plants.

After a short steep climb, your trail ascends moderately through fields of squaw carpet and manzanita to 2 miles. Contour along the ridge's north face through patchy whitethorn, then along the ridgetop. After a moderate ascent, contour along the ridgetop to 2⅜ miles.

Climb moderately with views southeast over the deep canyon of Balm of Gilead Creek to Solomon Peak. A great diversity of plants here include penstemon, pussy paws, rabbitbrush, bitter cherry and two buckwheats: naked stem and sulphur flower. Climb steeply around the right side of a rock outcrop, then through a stand of Jeffrey pines on the ridge's south face, where mountain shieldleaf grows among the rocks.

Your path climbs back to the ridgetop, where the first curl-leaved mountain mahogany bushes on the route grow low and

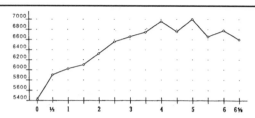

WRIGHTS RIDGE:

DISTANCE: 6⅝ **miles to Summit Trail** (10 miles from Indian
   Dick Trailhead); 3½ miles to Hole-in-the-Ground Trail, 5⅛
   miles to Willow Basin Cut-off.
TIME: One or two nights.
TERRAIN: Climbs steadily, with a few descents, along dry, view-
   rich ridge to spine of wilderness.
TRAILS INTERSECTED: Haynes Delight, Hole-in-the-Ground,
   Willow Basin Cut-off, Summit.
BEST TIME: June and July. August and September also good.
WARNINGS: Steep dry climb; must carry all your water.
DIRECTIONS TO TRAILHEAD: Leaves Haynes Delight Trail
   (Trail #41) beyond 3¼ miles.
FURTHER INFO: Covelo Ranger District, Mendocino National
   Forest (707) 983-6118.
OTHER SUGGESTION: WILLOW BASIN CUT-OFF leaves Wrights
   Ridge beyond 5⅛ miles, descending ½ mile to Long Ridge
   Trail, where right turn leads to Frying Pan at 10⅝ miles.

scrubby. Climb steeply again on the ridge's south face, then
regain the ridgetop at 3 miles, where a fire ring on the left offers
a dry camp with views in all directions. Look for the showy white
to light pink blossoms of dwarf Lewisia for the next ⅛ mile.

The trail contours east along the sparsely wooded, rocky
ridgetop, with large cairns marking occasionally vague tread.
Descend briefly to a saddle, then climb moderately, although
intermittently, to meet Hole-in-the-Ground Trail at 3½ miles.
You have climbed to 6700 feet. Views of Lassen Peak, Mount
Linn and the surrounding wilderness reward your efforts. (The
steep, unmaintained side trail descends southeast.)

Our route, signed "WILLOW BASIN," climbs briefly, then
contours along the ridge's south face before ascending to a
level ridgetop. In early summer this high ridgetop supports

diverse annuals and tuberous plants including purple larkspur and penstemon, pussy paws, mountain violet, hairy star tulip, three-bracted onion, waterleaf, Jessica's stickseed, yarrow and white and purple phlox. Perennials include paintbrush, whitethorn, sedum, squaw carpet, gooseberry, bitter cherry, California and curl-leaved mountain mahogany and manzanita.

After a short steep ascent, your path switches to the ridge's north face for an undulating traverse of several rocky knobs supporting Sierra cliff brake. Descend to a saddle before climbing steeply by four switchbacks to a massive red rocky top (6949') around 4 miles. After passing south of the summit, descend rough tread along the ridge's south face. The tread improves, contouring, then descending to a saddle.

Climb to the right of another top, passing a 3-foot-diameter red fir. Descend gradually to a saddle, then contour south of a small ridgetop knob before dropping to another saddle at 4½ miles. Your trail undulates for ⅛ mile to another saddle.

The track turns north, ascending steeply until you pass just south of the southernmost of Windy Mountain's three 7000-foot summits. Contour along the south face of the ridge.

Meet Willow Basin Cut-off beyond 5⅛ miles. (Turn left for the shortest route to Willow Basin and Frying Pan Meadow, dropping 500 feet in a steep ½ mile to Long Ridge Trail—Trail #25—where a right turn leads to Frying Pan in another 1⅝ miles [10⅝ miles from Indian Dick Trailhead].)

WINDY MOUNTAIN

From the junction beyond 5⅛ miles, you can make an easy ascent of Windy Mountain's highest (7081') peak, a ⅞-mile round trip. Climb northwest cross country to the ridgetop, then follow the knobby ridge west, then northwest to its highest summit. It is easier than it looks from the junction, with just one short steep climb beyond the saddle between the two peaks. The rocky top offers unhampered views. On the clearest days, like the summer solstice day I visited, you have a 75 degree sweep of the glistening Pacific on the western horizon beyond the King Range!

This description follows Wrights Ridge Trail east to its terminus at Summit Trail. Take the right fork, signed "VINEGAR PEAK," on a sidehill traverse. Then descend to the ridgetop, where Jeffrey pines dominate, with red firs favoring its north face. Continue a winding descent along the ridgetop to a saddle at the head of Willow Basin around 5½ miles.

Climb along the ridge's south face before resuming your descent, returning to the ridgetop where junipers mix with pines and firs. Descend to a saddle, then climb moderately for ⅛ mile. The trail bends right to contour a wooded south slope. Drop briefly to the 6-mile point, then contour past bleeding hearts and dwarf monkeyflower sheltered by whitethorn.

Level stretches alternate with short climbs until you descend slightly to a saddle. As you climb along the ridgetop, you might glimpse Frying Pan Meadow due north. Descend to a saddle, contour along the ridge's south face, then climb to the ridgetop around 6⅜ miles. Descend moderately, traversing the north face of the ridge through red fir forest, then wind right on a gradual descent to Summit Trail before 6⅝ miles. Turn left for Frying Pan (⅝ mile longer than via Willow Basin), Devils Hole Ridge and other points north. A right turn would follow Summit Trail (Trail #39) south to Vinegar Peak and beyond.

43.
ROCK CABIN TO RIVER
UPS AND DOWNS ALONG WOODED RIVER CANYON

This trail explores middle-elevation country along river canyons where the best hiking is early or late season. In spring the first portion of trail opens when the snow level rises to 5000 feet. Then the question is whether River Camp ford is safe, although you can camp before the ford. In autumn the trail provides chances to see steelhead in river pools and splashes of color in the deciduous species prevalent in river canyons. You may also see large gatherings of ladybird beetles along the bank. They meet to winter and reproduce on shrubs beside the stream.

At the trailhead beside a rustic, pretty campsite, the sign points the way to "FERN POINT, RIVER TRAIL, BUCK RIDGE." Your trail descends west, then northwest through forest of ponderosa and sugar pines, white and Douglas firs, incense cedars and black oaks. Pass through small glades in the majestic forest.

Cross the year-round trickle of Rock Cabin Creek, then sign in at the trail register. The trail descends gradually west through an understory of manzanita, buck brush, deer brush and scrubby white oak. Soon more small glades offer views southwest to Red Rock, then south to Castle Peak and Leech Lake Mountain. As your winding trail descends moderately south then west, look for barren Ant Point rising west-northwest.

Wind north, dropping through a shady gully where bigleaf maples mingle with large Douglas firs and sugar pines. Watch for poison oak, raspberry, gooseberry and snowberry in the understory. Descend moderately northwest, then southwest.

Merge with a vague old jeep track at ⅞ mile and descend to a junction. (Unmaintained Hoxie Trail on the left descends to private property.) River Trail veers right between two large ponderosa pines, then descends gently and contours through

ROCK CABIN TO RIVER:

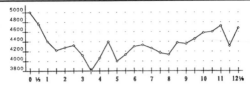

DISTANCE: **12⅛ miles to Yellowjacket Trail (24¼ miles round trip); 3⅝ miles to River Camp, 4¼ miles to Buck Ridge Trail; 5⅝ miles to Police Camp, 8⅛ miles to Rock Creek Camp, 9¾ miles to Four Corners Rock Trail.**

TIME: Day hike or overnight to River Camp, two nights to end.

TERRAIN: Descends through forest to River Camp; climbs steeply to Buck Ridge Trail; undulates along steep slopes above North Fork Middle Fork Eel River, descending to river only at Rock Creek and Yellowjacket Creek.

TRAILS INTERSECTED: Hoxie, Fern Point, Buck Ridge, Morrison, Four Corners Rock, Yellowjacket, Waterspout.

BEST TIME: May and June. May be accessible into October.

WARNINGS: Watch for rattlesnakes and poison oak. Many ups and downs; harder than it looks. River Camp ford may be impassable in early season.

DIRECTIONS TO TRAILHEAD: Same as Trail #40 to Indian Dick Station. Then in .5 mile turn left on Road 25N15C (signed Lucky Lake). Go .75 mile, then left toward Rock Cabin Camp to trailhead on left in .25 mile.

FURTHER INFO: Covelo Ranger District, Mendocino National Forest (707) 983-6118.

OTHER SUGGESTION: FOSTER GLADES TRAIL leaves Indian Dick Road one mile above Rattlesnake Creek; descends to ford Middle Fork, then climbs to ASA BEAN TRAIL (Trail #45).

the forest. The path climbs steadily for 300 feet, then undulates past squaw carpet, wood rose, trail plant, white-veined shinleaf and live oak brush beneath tall forest. Descend gently north on an old river terrace, dipping through a rocky gully with dogwood and Oregon grape.

Climb steeply through a scree clearing, then gradually on rocky tread to 1⅞ miles. Contour across a steep, shady north slope, then descend past pipsissewa and Oregon grape beneath fir forest. After crossing an old road, the trail continues a moderate descent.

191

Meet the old Fern Point Trail at 2¼ miles. (This dead-end left fork once crossed the river on a swinging bridge.) Stay right to contour along a steep slope. Your trail soon turns northeast on a gentle descent past serviceberry. Wind through a gully, climbing to switchback sharply right for a view of rocky Fern Point above the confluence of North Fork Middle Fork with Middle Fork Eel River. Ascend past the end of an old logging spur road amidst many dogwoods. The climb continues to 2⅞ miles, where you have a view up the Middle Fork Canyon.

Your ¾-mile descent to the river begins gradually, then switchbacks left to descend moderately. After three more switchbacks, pass a seat cut from a stump. As you descend to switchback left at a scree slope, the sound of tumbling water rises from the canyon. Drop past two more switchbacks to a level traverse of a steep cutbank 150 feet above the river.

Make a final descent to the river, switchbacking right for a winding, steep drop to the canyon floor at 3⅝ miles. Head north through alders, willows and Oregon ash to the ford (unsafe at high water). Umbrella plant and bear grass line the river.

Look northwest for the trail up the north bank. A gravelly climb immediately turns east to pleasant River Camp, beneath conifers and maples overlooking the Eel. Just upstream from the camp, steelhead and ladybird beetles gather in autumn, awaiting the onset of winter. Watch for poison oak around camp.

The trail continues east up the river terrace for ⅛ mile, then switchbacks left to climb moderately. Switchback right to ascend into mixed forest on a sunny south-facing slope. After switchbacking left, the trail climbs through deer brush, then winds north to an old river terrace. Climb gradually past a year-round spring near a camp on your right. Ascend to Buck Ridge Trail (Trail #44) at 4¼ miles at the old wilderness boundary.

River Trail forks left, contouring through forest where hawkweed grows. Climb gently until the trail levels rounding the bare, rocky ridge of Fern Point, with views into the rugged gorge below. Descend across a talus slope into forest.

Your path crosses another talus slope beyond 4⅝ miles, bending right to climb moderately across the scree, then through a stand of live oaks. Red penstemon grows beside the trail. Round another rocky point where the terrain on your left drops steeply to the river. Climb gradually, enjoying fine views along North Fork Middle Fork Canyon.

Pass through a patch of forest and descend gradually across a bare rocky slope with naked stem buckwheat. Climb gently over mostly bare slopes with knots of live oak, manzanita, sugar pine and Douglas fir.

Pass a rock outcrop at 5 miles where juniper grows with sedum, serviceberry, Fremont silktassel, saxifrage and sword fern. The trail descends through a shady gully then undulates through the forest, crossing three more gullies.

At 5½ miles you climb gradually into a glade where vague tread is marked by cairns. Police Camp sits at the top of the glade. Your path bends left, descending gently across a corner of the glade to Police Camp Spring. Its flow is just a trickle by fall, but the water always tastes sweet, unlike the tart fruit of Klamath plum which grows 100 feet beyond, offering splashes of bright red color in summer and fall. Morning glory vines twine through the grass.

Climb past a dry gully, then descend through forest before resuming a moderate ascent. Your trail descends to cross a gully then undulates through mature mixed forest. Climb moderately until you cross a rocky side ridge, then dip through another gully. Your path levels near two huge Douglas firs, then descends moderately to 6⅜ miles.

The trail bends right and levels at Brown Camp. You will find level ground nearby but no camp worth mention. The spring is poor and mosquitoes abound. After a brief climb, contour past large firs and sugar pines.

Descend gradually, then steeply through dense forest. Wind through a gully at 6¾ miles where twisted stalk, gooseberry and whitethorn grow. After a short climb your trail contours, then winds through another drainage, passing coral root orchid.

The trail descends to cross a seasonal stream around 7 miles. This moist, pretty pocket provides habitat for thimbleberry, serviceberry, solomon's seal, bedstraw and Oregon grape. Climb steeply to meet Morrison Trail. (It forks left and descends steeply to the river to climb west.)

River Trail continues its undulating course up the rugged canyon. Bear right of a deadfall tree before 7½ miles and top a hill. The trail descends moderately to ford two seasonal streams at their confluence. Climb steeply, then gradually before an easy winding descent. Dip through a small gully, then climb before contouring through deep forest.

Descend moderately to the deep canyon of Rock Creek at 8⅛ miles. Where the trail bends right to follow Rock Creek upstream, a spur forks left to a roomy, pleasant camp at the confluence of Rock Creek and North Fork Middle Fork Eel River. Cottonwoods and willows line the river, with the tiny to large leaves of umbrella plants rising from the stream course.

Leaving Rock Creek Camp, the trail descends east to ford Rock Creek, then ascends, soon switchbacking right to pass mossy outcrops and traverse a slide area. Contour, then climb gradually along the steep sidewall overlooking a deep, narrow portion of the river canyon. Beyond 8¾ miles your path winds, contouring through several gullies.

Dip across a seasonal tributary, then contour along the main canyon before descending to ford a creek at the south end of a glade at 9⅛ miles. River Trail ascends through the steeply

van. 92

rolling grassland, then descends slightly.

After climbing into another small glade, your winding path contours, with one short climb and a steep, short descent. Contour across a very steep slope that plunges 200 feet to the river. Descend gradually, then steeply to cross a small creek, climb to 9¾ miles, then descend briefly, coming to the lower end of a large rolling glade.

On your left a rotted signpost points southwest for vague Four Corners Rock Trail (see Trail #22—the trail is not recommended, although you might follow the route marked with white plastic flags. It descends southwest through the glade to the top of the river's cutbank, then heads northwest to the ford above a nice pool. The brushy, often invisible path climbs west along a creek canyon, then northwest past Washington Rock.)

You might consider the pleasant campsite in a small glade southwest of the junction on a big bend of the river. It has another fine pool to wash off the trail dust (and ample feed if you are traveling with stock).

River Trail climbs north through the large glade, a vague track marked by rock cairns. The grassland has abundant flowers in spring, including checker lily, yarrow, wood strawberry and the purple blooms of meadow larkspur and dog violet. The tread improves as it contours through a dry clearing, then through the forest. Make a gradual winding descent to cross a tiny drainage and climb gradually.

After offering several glimpses into the steep river canyon, the trail descends to cross a creek and its small tributary at 10⅜ miles. Climb steeply to a saddle, then descend to a small creek, which you follow upstream for ⅛ mile.

River Trail leaves the seasonal creek at 10¾ miles, climbing gradually, then moderately through forest. Contour across a dry, south slope brushy with manzanita and white oak, with a dusting of violets and soap plant. The clearing has views west to Washington Rock, Four Corners Rock behind it on the right, and southwest to wooded Bull Ridge.

The trail descends gradually, then moderately, passing abundant cream lilies and shooting stars in spring, and Oregon grape year round. Descend steadily through a rocky clearing with stonecrop and across a small tributary to bisect a glade overlooking the river. Beyond the grassland your trail climbs gradually. Calypso orchids and trilliums thrive here in spring. Your trail levels 100 feet above the river, then descends north.

River Trail skirts a lovely campsite near the ruins of a cabin above the confluence of Yellowjacket Creek with North Fork Middle Fork Eel River. The trail fords the creek at the confluence. After 150 feet of vague tread beside the river, the trail turns right at an old sign pointing northeast for "BUCK RIDGE, SHELL MOUNTAIN" and west for "WILDERNESS BOUNDARY." The latter refers to an unmaintained trail shown on the 1954 topo map. When I first visited this spot in 1975, an even older sign said "CALIFORNIA NATIONAL FOREST, RUTH 29." (California National Forest became Mendocino National Forest in 1932.) I could not find, let alone recommend, the trail west.

River Trail climbs northeast, soon following a small ridge. Ascend steeply, then gradually past many shooting stars. The path levels briefly, then climbs the ridge to trail's end at a junction before 12⅛ miles. Waterspout Trail goes left to continue north along North Fork Middle Fork Canyon, while Yellowjacket Trail bears right to head east to Sulphur Glade (⅜ mile), Buck Ridge and Haynes Delight. See Trail #23 for more information.

44.

BUCK RIDGE
REMOTE RIDGETOP ROUTE TO SHELL MOUNTAIN

This seldom traveled trail is brushy in spots but generally not difficult to follow. It traverses the ridge between the forks of Middle Fork Eel River, dry country with expansive views. You are not likely to see many people on this route, but you must carry water, especially on overnight trips. The trail offers opportunities for loop trips in combination with adjoining trails.

Buck Ridge Trail climbs north from River Trail. Your winding ascent begins gradually, but soon turns moderate in forest of Douglas fir, ponderosa and sugar pines, incense cedar and live oak. The trail turns east briefly, lined with squaw carpet and manzanita. Then switchback left to climb northwest. Switchback twice more, soon ascending on the ridgetop briefly with views of the wooded river canyon to the east. Then climb along the west face of the ridge. Switch to the ridge's east face before ½ mile, climbing with views up Balm of Gilead Creek.

The trail switchbacks left to meet Wrights Valley Trail. (It climbs steeply north before plunging to the Middle Fork in 1⅛ miles, then ascends east.) Your trail veers left, climbing steeply southwest. After a six-foot-wide Douglas fir, the trail makes a slow bend right. Ascend steeply as views expand southwest to Red Rock and south to Leech Lake Mountain.

Climb gradually, then moderately, winding along the ridgetop. After leveling briefly, the trail ascends moderately on the ridge's east face. Regain the ridgetop at one mile for a moderate, then gradual climb. Wind east of the crest, ascending through forest, then a small glade of native bunch grasses.

The trail returns to the ridgetop at 1½ miles, climbing north past thickets of whitethorn beneath large ponderosa pines and medium cedars with scattered sugar pines, white and Douglas firs. The climb turns gentle through a stand of black oaks on the ridge's west face. Snowberry, white-veined shinleaf and conifer seedlings grow sparsely beneath mature forest.

Your trail climbs gradually east to return to the ridgetop, following the crest past little prince's pine. Then ascend along Buck Ridge's west face to top the ridgetop at 5400 feet, 2 miles from River Trail. The trail descends gently, east of the ridgetop. You soon see Shell Mountain and Upper Buck Ridge to the north and the North Yolla Bolly Peaks northeast. Then the terrain drops steeply on the right of the path, now a narrow though well blazed track.

By 2⅜ miles you contour north across the steep east-facing

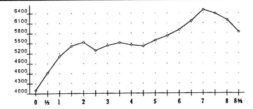

BUCK RIDGE:

DISTANCE: 8⅜ miles to Long Ridge Trail; 4⅞ miles to
Haynes Delight Trail, 5⅛ miles to Yellowjacket Trail, 7¼
miles to Cherry Camp, 8 miles to Shell Mountain, 8¼ miles
to Doe Ridge and Dead Puppy Ridge Trails (12½ miles from
Rock Cabin Trailhead).

TIME: Day hike from River Camp or overnight.

TERRAIN: Climbs steeply, then moderately along ridge; gentle
climbs alternate with short descents on middle portion;
climbs steeply along ridgetop beyond Yellowjacket Trail, then
descends through forest to Doe Ridge/Dead Puppy junction,
then to Long Ridge junction.

TRAILS INTERSECTED: River, Wrights Valley, Haynes Delight,
Yellowjacket, Dead Puppy Ridge, Doe Ridge, Long Ridge.

BEST TIME: June and July. Lower portion may be open early as
May or late as October.

WARNINGS: Water extremely scarce, may only be available at
Cherry Camp. Brushy in spots.

DIRECTIONS TO TRAILHEAD: Inside wilderness at junction
with River Trail, 4¼ miles from Rock Cabin Trailhead.

FURTHER INFO: Covelo Ranger District, Mendocino National
Forest (707) 983-6118.

slope. The trail climbs left around a deadfall fir and suddenly
regains the ridgetop. Descend gradually on the narrow, wooded
crest, passing pinedrops, snowberry and shinleaf.

After the descent ends at a saddle, climb gradually along the
narrow ridgetop, crossing several deadfalls as the tread
deteriorates. Your trail climbs moderately along the west face
of the ridge, then slowly bends right to ascend the ridgetop,
angling northeast on occasionally faint tread.

Cross more deadfalls, then contour before descending
gradually, then moderately to a saddle at 3¼ miles. The trail
ascends gradually along wooded ridgetop, then makes a winding,

moderate climb to expansive views: east to Wrights Ridge and Windy Mountain, southeast to Solomon Peak, and west to Jones Ridge and barren Ant Point, with the King Range near the coast often visible beyond.

Contour on the ridgetop, then along its brushy east face where dense brush crowds the trail in spots. Tiny drought-tolerant Sierra cliff brake abounds here, as do silktassel and live oak brush. After a quick descent to a saddle, climb gently on the ridgetop, then moderately on its west face, where more chaparral crowds the trail. Contour on or near the brushy ridgetop, descending briefly to a wooded saddle at 3⅞ miles.

A short climb brings you to a twisted old incense cedar atop a rock outcrop above a rocky slope that drops toward the Middle Fork. This is an excellent spot to pull up a rock and enjoy the stunning views spreading from Schoolmarm Ridge to the northeast all the way south to Anthony Peak and Black Butte outside the wilderness. The rugged Middle Fork canyon cuts a deep swath through the panorama. Juniper and buck brush grow along with cedar in the sparse vegetation. In spring you may see scarlet fritillary, shooting star and hairy star tulip.

Your trail descends north along the brushy ridgetop, then undulates through brush to another view-studded clearing at 4⅛ miles. Your faint trail contours along the crest through dense forest before descending along a large deadfall pine. After the trail bends right, you must hop over or detour around three more deadfalls. Walk a level, open trail through mature forest, then pick your way through more blowdown.

Your trail climbs, winding to the right around 4½ miles. Drop to a saddle and ascend through fir forest with dense squaw carpet, then through a stand of pines where shooting stars litter the ground. Descend briefly to another saddle before climbing gradually, winding along the now broad ridgetop.

Brush again crowds the trail, but at 4⅞ miles your vague,

winding path meets Haynes Delight Trail (Trail #23) at an unmarked junction beside a one-foot-wide white oak with a rock cairn at its base. Turn left to continue up Buck Ridge, ascending Haynes Delight Trail for ¼ mile, with one sharp switchback to the right. You meet Yellowjacket Trail at 5⅛ miles. (It forks left to descend northeast.)

Buck Ridge Trail forks right, climbing east on the ridgetop through dense young forest of white fir and scattered cedars. An understory of manzanita, whitethorn and white oak brush crowds the trail. The path veers to the right side of the ridgetop for a view of the North Yolla Bollys and Devils Hole Ridge.

Ascend the ridgetop through dense squaw carpet. The trail swings left for views of Shell Mountain and the rising ridgetop ahead. Dip to the right of the crest for a brief respite from the steady ascent, then climb again, turning to the ridge's west side. The ridgetop turns rocky and barren as junipers become the dominant tree. Ascend the ridgetop as the tread gets vague through intermittent brushy patches.

Reach a bare knob on the ridge at 5½ miles, where a clear day affords a view west to the King Range on Humboldt County's Lost Coast. Drop along the east side of the ridge, then return to the ridgetop to climb steadily. Wind around the right side of a knob, descending gently before climbing steeply along the crest, passing large windblown Jeffrey pines.

Your trail switches to the ridgetop's right edge around 6 miles to make the steepest climb so far on Buck Ridge Trail. After a brief descent, climb through forest of white firs, cedars and Jeffrey pines. Climb steeply to 6½ miles, then pass to the right of a 6234-foot knob. Descend steeply to a saddle, only to climb steeply again through weather-beaten forest of ancient scraggly Jeffrey pines, twisted cedars and junipers. Take a break as trail and ridgetop level with views left and right.

Head north up a hellishly steep hill at 6¾ miles. It soon steepens (if possible), continuing to strain your muscles all the way to 7⅛ miles. The climb ends suddenly as you top a subtle divide and descend gently into young fir forest where snow banks may hide the trail into June. Red firs grow to four

SHELL MOUNTAIN

Where the trail turns northeast beyond 7⅜ miles, the top of Shell Mountain is an easy scramble— 1⅛ miles round trip—if you want to bag a peak. Head north-northwest, climbing for 400 feet, then descending to a saddle. Ascend northwest to the next obvious high knob on the ridgetop, then descend to another saddle. Climb moderately, then steeply on the ridgetop. The climb eases ½ mile from where you left the trail, coming to the 6700-foot top of Shell Mountain in another 300 feet, where on a clear day you can see most of northwestern California.

feet in diameter on your right.

The path levels in a small clearing 250 feet from the divide. A sign on your left points west to Cherry Spring, about ⅛ mile down slope. Your mostly level trail bends right, then left. Climb gradually, then steeply but briefly to the first of several immense cairns marking the vague track ahead. Follow the gentle, barren ridge of dark gravel (erosion pavement) from cairn to cairn. Reach the summit at 7⅜ miles, 6560 feet above sea level. Walk 200 feet north to the next cairn, where an old rotted signpost lies northwest of the rock pile. Your trail turns northeast to descend Dead Puppy Ridge.

Buck Ridge Trail descends northeast, entering dense fir forest 300 feet from the junction, where a blaze on a snag marks the faint tread. Contour until the trail descends along the left side of the wooded ridge.

The descent steepens on a well blazed route with much blowdown. As the ridge becomes distinct, the trail descends the ridgetop, then its right edge. By 7⅞ miles the path bends left to descend along the ridge's west edge with a view of the steep, glaciated north face of Shell Mountain. Descend moderately, then gradually on the crest through forest with a carpet of pinemat manzanita. Then descend along the west face of the ridge with views of the Trinity Alps and North Yolla Bollys.

The descent becomes steep, first through fir forest, then along open ridgetop to 8¼ miles. As the ridge nearly levels, Buck Ridge Trail ends. Watch for Doe Ridge Trail (Trail #24) on the left, a faint track descending west-southwest. Take Dead Puppy Ridge Trail, descending northeast to leave the ridge.

Your trail switchbacks right, then bends left, descending moderately through chaparral on faint but clear tread. The descent eases at 8⅜ miles, meeting Trail #25. A sign bolted to a fir snag on your left points right for "FLOURNOY" and "FRYING PAN" (Long Ridge Trail) and straight ahead for "WILDERNESS BOUNDARY" (Dead Puppy Ridge Trail to Hopkins Camp). So many choices! In this neck of the wilderness, all of them are seldom traveled.

45.
ASA BEAN/HOTEL CAMP
RUGGED ROUTE THROUGH REMOTE COUNTRY

This route explores diverse terrain in the southernmost corner of Yolla Bolly Wilderness. This remote region, the only part of the wilderness area within Mendocino County, was added to the wilderness in 1984. The first 3¼ miles of the route were constructed several years ago but have not yet been properly signed. The rest of the route follows Asa Bean and Hotel Camp

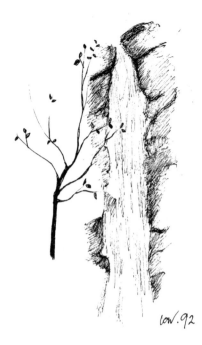

low.92

Trails, much older paths traditionally reached via Foster Glades Trail from Indian Dick Road. Although the new trail drops 800 feet before climbing to Asa Bean Flat and Hotel Camp, it is still much easier than the traditional route across the Eel River. The 5-mile round trip to the stunning waterfalls on Stick Lake Creek make a wonderful day hike.

From the unmarked trailhead where the road ends at a landslide, follow a distinct trail northwest across the slide. In 250 feet the trail continues on the closed road, ascending through a partially logged area. Veer left to cross a creek, then resume climbing on the roadbed. The road levels briefly, then climbs gradually.

Pass the splintered remnant of a wooden sign beyond ⅝ mile. It denoted the wilderness boundary before a bear rearranged it. Go ⅛ mile to a tiny sign on the left side of the road pointing north for the "NATIONAL RECREATION TRAIL." In 150 feet a second sign points northeast as the road bends west.

Take the footpath northeast, soon following an old spur road on a gentle descent north. The partially logged forest has Douglas fir, incense cedar, sugar and ponderosa pines and black oak with an understory of buck brush, manzanita and grass. The trail follows the old road as it dips through a washout at one mile, then continues a gentle descent along a ridge.

The road bends sharply left, turns south briefly, then climbs gently west as the roadbed deteriorates. Pass a level glade on the left, then continue west 200 feet. Where the road bends left, blocked by a wood pile, your footpath heads west past a blazed

ASA BEAN/HOTEL CAMP:

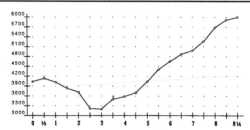

DISTANCE: **8¾ miles to Red Rock**; 2½ miles to Stick Lake Creek, 3 miles to Line Gulch Creek, 3¼ miles to Hotel Camp Trail (¼ mile west of river), 4½ miles to Asa Bean Flat, 5¾ miles to Hotel Camp.

TIME: Full day to creeks, river or flat; overnight to Hotel Camp.

TERRAIN: Climbs old road, descends skid road; trail descends through forest to brushy promontory; descends through scrub oak forest by switchbacks; fords creek below waterfalls, traverses wooded slopes to another ford; climbs to Hotel Camp and Foster Glades Trails; climbs moderately to Asa Bean Flat, then steeply to Hotel Camp and ford, then Red Rock.

TRAILS INTERSECTED: Hotel Camp, Foster Glades, Henthorne, Leech Lake Mountain.

BEST TIME: May and June. May be nice mid-September to November.

WARNINGS: Low elevation hot in summer. Fords may be dangerous in spring runoff. Watch for rattlesnakes and poison oak.

DIRECTIONS TO TRAILHEAD: Leave Highway 101 at Longvale (M.59.35) and go east 31 miles on Highway 162. One mile beyond Covelo (last supplies), Highway 162 turns east. Go 9.25 miles to Ham Pass Road (24N21). Go left 20.5 miles to end of road. (Trailhead unmarked—follow closed road ⅞ mile to vaguely marked trail.)

FURTHER INFO: Covelo Ranger District, Mendocino National Forest (707) 983-6118.

OTHER SUGGESTION: LEECH LAKE MOUNTAIN ROAD & TRAIL leaves left side of Ham Pass Road at 8.8 miles. Also known as 11W12, this old road climbs from locked gate north on Pine Ridge, coming within 300 feet of Leech Lake Mountain (6637') at 3 miles, then heads northwest over Red Rock (6239') at 4½ miles, entering wilderness, then descends to HOTEL CAMP TRAIL around 5⅛ miles. First 4½ miles open to mountain bikes.

black oak into the forest. The trail crosses a skid road, bends left, then switchbacks to the right at a large downed fir. The path soon bends left, descending south through forest.

Your path bends right to cross a gully, soon descending northwest past cedars. You have views across the deep Eel River Canyon to the high country beyond. Switchback right and left to descend west through open virgin forest. After crossing a gully where Sierra cliff brake grows, the trail switches right on a winding descent northwest. Pass a sparse, level glade on the right, then descend gently along a wooded ridge.

Reach a brush-covered, gravelly promontory beyond 1¾ miles. It offers views north across the Eel Canyon to Foster Glades and east toward Hammerhorn Ridge. The trail switchbacks right to descend southeast, becoming vague in 150 feet at a clearing above a seasonal creek. Continue southeast briefly on vague but ducked tread. Switchback left and descend through brush to a ford, then climb northeast.

Your still vague trail forks before 1⅞ miles. Take the left fork to descend north. The tread improves on a gentle descent northeast through forest of scrubby white oaks. The descent steepens as the trail switchbacks left to head west briefly. Seven more short switchbacks descend through oak forest to 2¼ miles, where the path levels briefly.

Your path continues a switchbacking descent through scrub oak forest, becoming faint in rough terrain. Orange plastic flags indicate the vague track. Seven more switchbacks descend past two dark rock outcrops into conifer forest, soon fording the rocky gully you have been paralleling.

Climb west to a rocky clearing above the steep rugged canyon of Stick Lake Creek. The trail descends northwest to wind into the canyon, but look left up the canyon for a view of three waterfalls (8, 40 and 15 feet) in a spectacular setting. The cascades are beautiful year round, but really thunder in spring.

The trail descends steeply to ford the creek, then climbs north out of Stick Lake Canyon. Continue generally north traversing the steep slopes of Eel River Canyon through five short ups and downs to 3 miles. Dogwood, honeysuckle, wood rose and moss grow beneath live oak and Douglas fir.

Make a winding descent to ford Line Gulch Creek, then climb briefly. A flat above the creek on the right offers a pleasant camp not far from the confluence with the Eel River. The trail climbs gradually, then moderately, winding north through buck brush, redbud and California mountain mahogany, with scattered mule ears and Oregon grape.

A mostly gradual climb heads northwest to an unsigned "T" junction around 3¼ miles. This is Asa Bean Trail. (On the right it descends ¼ mile to Middle Fork Eel River. From there one must follow the river canyon nearly ⅛ mile upstream to find the trail climbing northwest and north into Foster Glades, then continuing steeply 1300 feet up to Indian Dick Road, 2¼ miles from this junction.)

Our described route turns left at the junction. Climb moderately along a ridge, then wind right and left to ascend steeply on rocky tread. The climb turns gradual, winding along a ridgetop through mixed fir forest. Ascend moderately through brushy terrain to 3⅞ miles, then gently through forest.

Around 4⅜ miles you may hear the sound of a creek on the left. Your path soon bends right and becomes vague, if not completely obscure in the large glade at Asa Bean Flat. The mapped route climbs gradually northwest along the eastern edge of the glade to meet the Henthorne Trail at the north end of the clearing. This route is indistinct, however, and the junction is unmarked, while the trail north is not maintained.

An unmapped, faint but easy-to-follow route heads west into the glade from the bend near 4⅜ miles, passing near a spring around 4½ miles, with pleasant camps in the area. Continue west through the glade to the distinct Hotel Camp Trail in the southwestern corner of the clearing before 4⅝ miles.

From the glade Hotel Camp Trail climbs south and southwest through brush and forest, gaining a ridge around 5¼ miles. After ascending along the ridge, the trail bends left to climb southeast. The path bends right to descend to Hotel Camp on Line Gulch Creek at 5¾ miles.

Beyond Hotel Camp the trail is not recommended for backpacking. It climbs unevenly, gaining almost 2000 feet elevation in 3 miles to Red Rock. The trail leaves the designated wilderness area just before Red Rock. Designated or not, the sparsely vegetated high ridges offers spectacular country. Just before Red Rock, Hotel Camp Trail ends at a junction. The left fork climbs the ridge east, then southeast to join Leech Lake Mountain Trail (see OTHER SUGGESTION). The right fork descends southwest along Asa Bean Ridge.

46.

TRAVELERS HOME

CREEKS, GLADES AND CHAPARRAL ALONG EEL CANYON

This National Recreation Trail offers a fitting end to the Yolla Bolly portion of the book. Travelers Home Trail provides nearly year-round access to middle elevation country outside the wilderness. The closest trail to civilization (and accommodations) in the wilderness section of the book, it is nevertheless one of the least traveled trails in the Yolla Bollys. The trail offers varied opportunities: day or overnight hiking, mountain biking, horseback riding, perhaps even cross-country skiing for

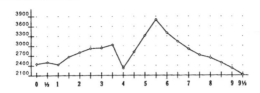

TRAVELERS HOME:

DISTANCE: **9½ miles to river, one way** (19 miles round trip);
2¼ miles to first creek with camp, 4 miles to West Fork
Travelers Home Creek, 4¾ to next creek, 5½ miles to upper
trailhead on Road 24N13, 7¼ miles to Devils Den Spring.

TIME: Day hike or overnight.

TERRAIN: Descends road; contours steep slopes before steep
descent to creeks and glades around Travelers Home; climbs
steeply to upper trailhead; descends steeply east to Middle
Fork Eel River.

BEST TIME: April and May. Late September to mid-November
also nice. May be accessible year round, when snow level
above 3500 feet.

WARNINGS: Watch for rattlesnakes and extensive poison oak.
Hot country in summer.

DIRECTIONS TO TRAILHEAD: Leave Highway 101 at Longvale
(M.59.35). Go east on Highway 162 for 31 miles to Covelo
(last supplies). In one mile, Highway 162 turns east. Go 9.25
miles to Ham Pass Road (24N21). Turn left and go 2.8 miles
to locked gate/trailhead on right. FOR UPPER TRAILHEAD: Go
9.1 miles farther, turn right on Road 24N13. Go 1.5 miles.
Trailhead on right as road makes big bend left.

FURTHER INFO: Covelo Ranger District, Mendocino National
Forest (707) 983-6118.

intermediate skiers when the snow falls low enough. This trail
was here before 1900, used by settlers to reach the rugged country
to the north.

The first 3½ miles offer easy hiking. Then the trail plummets
700 feet in ½ mile to Travelers Home, where a series of creeks
and a vast, steep glade offer the prettiest scenery on the route.
The trail climbs 1500 feet in the next 1½ miles to a drivable road,
then dives 1700 feet in 2¾ miles to Middle Fork Eel River. This
last third of the hike is not recommended because of steepness,
several large clearcuts and unstable landslide crossings.

From the gate, your trail follows a road on a steep descent east. In 120 feet a sign says "PRIVATE PROPERTY—FOOT & HORSE TRAIL ACCESS ONLY." Descend through oak forest with scattered Douglas fir and plenty of poison oak. The road bends left at ¼ mile to a logging landing with invasive star thistle. The road descends north from the landing.

At ⅜ mile you fork left to climb north on a faint trail marked by a sign. The tread soon improves through partially logged mixed forest with poison oak, manzanita, deer brush and live oak in the understory. Angle northeast on a gentle climb at ½ mile. In 200 feet a section marker indicates the National Forest boundary. The trail levels in forest of Douglas fir, ponderosa pine, black oak and madrone. Climb briefly, then descend

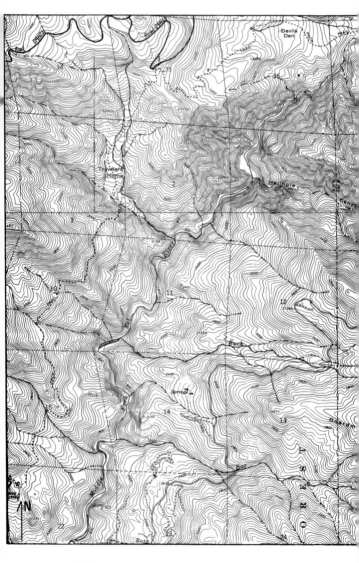

across a steep sidehill, winding through broken country.

Cross a dry gully, then climb briefly up a rocky hillside. Make a winding descent to cross a seasonal creek beneath six-foot-wide Douglas firs before ⅞ mile. Honeysuckle vine and wood rose carpet the forest floor. Your path contours through forest, then a rolling glade. Return to forest and descend north into a small glade. Climb briefly, then drop to ford a seasonal creek where elk clover grows beneath bigleaf maple.

The trail bends right on a winding moderate climb into a dry forest of oaks, the Eel River Canyon visible below. The path levels beyond 1⅜ miles, returning to conifer forest. Climb gradually, then moderately through two small glades and into forest. The ascent soon turns gentle across a steep slope. You can hear the Eel River murmuring in its deep canyon.

Climb moderately across a steep, partially logged hillside. Your path contours, crossing a gully. Descend gradually to traverse the bottom of a glade where the trail becomes vague. It heads north through forest on the east side of the glade, then descends gradually to ford a creek lined with dogwoods and lady ferns around 2¼ miles. A camp lies just upstream.

The trail veers right to climb steeply east, then bends left for a steep winding ascent north. The terrain turns brushy as your climb eases. The chaparral includes chamise, manzanita, California mountain mahogany, live and black oaks and redbud. The winding path contours with views across the river canyon. Return to forest, then descend to a seasonal creek at 2⅝ miles.

Travelers Home Trail contours through a small glade with redbud, then climbs gradually through a gully. Contour east across a steep rocky slope in a forest of live oaks. Pass through a rocky, brush-filled clearing where yerba santa and Fremont silktassel grow, with views south across the canyon to Etsel Ridge, then east to the river twisting in its rugged canyon.

At 3 miles the trail bends left, contouring through the forest, with views up the canyon into the designated wilderness. Your trail soon bends left on a steep winding descent across an old landslide. The rocky, uneven terrain continues as you climb across a talus slope where many snags stand.

Ascend steeply through forest on a steep rocky slope. The tread is vague as you continue a steady, winding climb. The path bends right, then climbs gradually to a rocky outcrop with good views. Then your trail undulates across steep rocky slopes.

Some people say the National Recreation Trail ends at 3½ miles. In fact it continues, but you might think the fun is over as the path descends steeply, losing 700 feet elevation in ½ mile. The climb out is certain to be arduous! Your descent starts moderately, but turns steep, descending by six switchbacks and down a small ridge. The trail bends left to leave the ridge, continuing its steep drop past Oregon grape, sword fern, gooseberry and saxifrage.

Reach the first fork of Travelers Home Creek at 4 miles, where dogwood, maple, Douglas fir, madrone, live oak and Oregon ash line the banks. Your vague trail heads north briefly, then bends right to climb steeply for 250 feet. Enter the large rolling glade called Travelers Home as the path becomes faint, climbing northwest past two rock cairns, then a large white oak. A pleasant hillside camp on your right overlooks the glade.

Continue a steady climb northwest past another large blazed oak where the route becomes extremely vague. Look north for a cairn and more faint blazes on white oaks. Climb north through the heart of the glade, where you must watch for poison oak. The tread soon improves, ascending past iris and silver lupine. It bends right and left before 4¼ miles, continuing to climb northwest past more cairns and blazed oaks.

The tread soon becomes vague again. Look for a bend to the right where the trail climbs steeply east, returning to distinct tread. You soon turn north again, climbing through forest with poison oak, honeysuckle and grass in the understory. The winding, steady climb continues north on a small wooded ridge, the sound of a tumbling creek on the right.

Your trail descends briefly, heading east to a ford around 4¾ miles. Level terraces beneath huge madrones before the ford offer pristine camping. Be very careful with fire and dismantle any fire ring before you leave. Elk clover, alder and maple line the creek in this pleasant spot, especially nice in autumn when colorful leaves carpet the forest floor.

The trail climbs steeply up the cutbank and heads east to more level spots. Then climb northeast along a ridge, soon winding steeply up a rocky area with willows, California buckeye and phacelia. Ford another fork of the creek, where woodwardia ferns grow, beyond 4⅞ miles.

The trail heads southeast briefly, then resumes the climb northeast. Follow a wooded ridge, then climb along the east edge of a glade. Climb into a larger glade at 5⅛ miles, where the tread becomes indistinct. Look north-northeast for a large cairn in a gully. Reach the rock pile in 200 feet, then climb steeply, winding northeast and north on a vague ducked route.

Climb steeply through Douglas fir/black oak forest. The climb turns moderate, then comes to an unmarked "T" junction at 5½ miles. The left fork comes to Road 24N13 in 100 feet, where a tiny sign indicates the National Recreation Trail. If you take the right fork, Travelers Home Trail descends 1700 feet in 2¾ miles to end at Middle Fork Eel River. This last section is recommended only for fit people with orienteering experience.

BOOKWINKLE'S

CHILDREN'S BOOKS

Kasten & Albion Streets
Post Office Box 270
Mendocino CA 95460
(707) 937-KIDS (5437)

Special Orders Welcome
Open Every Day 10 to 6

Tony Miksak, Owner
Linda Pack, Manager
Bob Lorentzen
Carol Goodwin Blick
Lenora Shepard
Celeste Bautista
Liz Petersen
Katy Tahja
Donna Bettencourt
Jennifer Benorden
Dan Kozloff

Gallery Bookshop

319 Kasten Street
Post Office Box 270
Mendocino CA 95460

(707) 937-BOOK (2665)

Special Orders Welcome
Open Every Day 10 to 6
Open til 9, Fri. & Sat.

Tony Miksak, Owner
Linda Pack, Manager
Bob Lorentzen
Carol Goodwin Blick
Lenora Shepard
Celeste Bautista
Liz Petersen
Katy Tahja
Donna Bettencourt
Jennifer Benorden
Dan Kozloff

SNOW MOUNTAIN WILDERNESS

As you drive north on Interstate 5 beyond Sacramento on a clear day, the Coast Range rises subtly on your left. A high peninsula of rounded peaks protrudes east into the great valley ahead. The mountains appear unsubstantial at first, but by Williams (60 miles from Sacramento, 120 from San Francisco) one can see they rise dramatically and precipitously above the surrounding Coast Range. Snow Mountain and Saint John Mountain, 7056 and 6743 feet respectively, are twice the height of most Coast Range peaks to the south. They announce the start of the high country that sprawls north until the Coast Range meets the Klamath Mountain province, encompassing some of the least inhabited and explored areas of California.

Snow Mountain is a moist sky island in otherwise dry lands, geologically and botanically distinct from surrounding country. Rocks at the base of the range, primarily sandstone, shale and chert, are related geologically to the adjacent terrain, formed about 200 million years ago during the Mesozoic geologic era. The upper mountain is a volcanic sea-mount no more than 150 million years old. It formed as a volcano on the ocean floor, then was scraped off the descending oceanic plate and emplaced along the edge of the continent. Uplifted by the folding of the continental plate, the volcano rose more or less intact to its present position.

The upper parts of the mountain consist of metamorphosed pillow lava called greenstone, which was erupted beneath an ancient ocean. A thrust fault, demarcating the volcanic rock above and the sedimentary rock below, wraps around Snow Mountain, roughly following the wilderness boundary. The volcanic rock above the fault stands high because it is more resistant to erosion than the surrounding rock. Precipitation and the glaciers of the Ice Age eroded Snow Mountain into the weathered forms we see today.

The native cultures that inhabited Snow Mountain were isolated from the surrounding peoples by rugged terrain. The Northeastern Pomo lived along Stony Creek, claiming the country east of Snow Mountain divide. They were isolated from the main body of Pomo and had a culture less elaborate than that of their kin. They controlled valuable salt deposits. The Northeastern Pomo generally got along well with their neighbors from the western slopes of Snow Mountain, the Onkolukomno'm group of the Yuki people. The rich and diverse flora and fauna on the varied elevations of Snow Mountain, while not as bountiful as the Clear Lake region, offered abundant resources.

Today Snow Mountain Wilderness Area encompasses 37,000 acres. About three hours from the Bay Area, this wilderness is little known and generally overlooked by people seeking a high country destination. Yet the subalpine terrain above 6000 feet offers solitude and grand scenery in a compact, diverse area explored by the two described loop trails. The two other trails presented here, Bearwallow and Bathhouse, offer virtually year-round hiking. They are best for exhilarating winter treks with views of the high country and surrounding rugged canyons. In case you missed them, two other trails earlier in the book explore pristine country adjacent to Snow Mountain Wilderness, Bloody Rock/Cold Creek and Deafy Glade Trails.

Year-round access to Snow Mountain is best from the Sacramento Valley side via the tiny towns of Maxwell, Stonyford and Elk Creek. Winter access may only be possible from there.

In summer the vast, little traveled southern portion of Mendocino National Forest offers exciting, diverse terrain for exploring back roads by car and many locales by foot, horse or mountain bike. You can reach the Snow Mountain area in summer on scenic, winding dirt roads originating near Ukiah or Upper Lake. These roads generally offer quicker summer routes from Mendocino, Humboldt or Lake Counties. (If you are closer to Sacramento than to Ukiah, the quickest route to Snow Mountain is from the east.)

The quickest summer route from the west leaves Highway 20 at Upper Lake. Go north on paved M1 for 16.5 miles, then go right on unpaved M10, crossing at least two fords of Bear Creek in 7 miles to the junction with M3. Left on M3 leads to North Ridge Trailhead in 21 miles. If you go straight 1.2 miles on M1, then right on Road 17N16 for 5.7 miles, then left on Road 17N29, you climb to Summit Springs Trailhead.

In case you might be inclined to take the back way in late autumn, winter or spring, the following tale of one May journey that might have been disastrous should discourage you.

The road looked good on the map, a solid line connecting two points, with only two creek crossings. The day had been partly cloudy, but the weather seemed to be clearing. So we took one more back road, extending a journey that had explored wonderful, flower-spangled corners in seemingly forgotten parts of the National Forest. The road started well, then narrowed slightly. We climbed briefly, then descended through a gentle valley as the first cloudburst hit. In the next hour it hailed and rained twice each, but the sun shone brightly in between.

The first ford was not even on the map. It looked minor and the road looked good on the other side. I slipped our compact wagon into four-wheel mode (just in case) and stepped on the gas. We plunged into the ford as the surging creek swallowed the front wheels, then broke over hood, windshield and roof in one graceful motion. (Never hesitate after you have entered a ford in a vehicle!) We emerged beyond the creek with water pouring from the car as if we had left a high pressure car wash.

Our hearts raced as we got out to check for damage (OK!) and *pondered our fate. The map showed only one creek crossing ahead, then a climb over a ridge. It seemed better to continue than to risk another crossing of the ford that nearly swallowed the car. In fact, we crossed four more fords before the ridge. Fortunately none of them were as deep as the first, but if the cloudburst had continued . . . who knows? We got out in one piece and laughed hard between the heart-thumping crossings. But I always get out and scout fords meticulously now. And I would never recommend that route to anyone without a jeep, at least not in spring.*

47.

WATERFALL/CROOKED TREE/ NORTH RIDGE LOOP

DIVERSE LOOP THROUGH CANYONS & MEADOWS & OVER RIDGES

The trails ascending Snow Mountain from the north side have changed since the Forest Service printed its Wilderness Map in 1988. The old Crooked Tree Trail was closed to prevent vehicle intrusion into the wilderness. The new Waterfall Trail offers a moderate route to Milk Ranch, easier than the steep North Ridge Trail. This description follows the new trail and the outer portion of Crooked Tree Trail to the vast meadow at Milk Ranch, returning via North Ridge Trail. The loop is arduous, but offers opportunities to break the trip into manageable portions, unlike the unrelentingly steep North Ridge Trail. Or you can car camp at the trailhead and explore the wilderness on day hikes.

Waterfall Trail is dedicated to Tom Maloney, "tireless worker for wilderness," who spent many years exploring Snow Mountain even when no trails offered easy access. The Audubon Society member encouraged protection of Snow Mountain as a Wilderness Area and development of its trails.

Crockett Peak's rocky 6172-foot crag towers over the trailhead. Sign in at the trail register and head west on North Ridge/ Waterfall Trail. Cross a gully and turn south on a gentle descent. Willows crowd the gully on your left. The surrounding mixed forest includes incense cedar, ponderosa, Jeffrey and sugar pines, Douglas and white firs. A sign declares "NORTH RIDGE TRAIL - 8W20."

Climb gently through an understory of live oak brush, manzanita and creeping snowberry. Before ¼ mile your path descends as the gully you have been following becomes a gurgling creek. Continue your gentle descent along the creek as twisted stalk and naked stem buckwheat join the understory.

Your trail turns south, passing rabbitbrush, white-veined

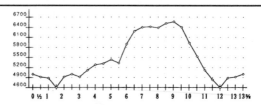

DISTANCE: **13⅜-mile loop** (14 miles with waterfall spur); 1⅜ miles to first camp, 2⅛ miles to first junction, 2⅝ miles to waterfall, 2⅞ miles to upper ford, 5 miles to Crooked Tree Trail, 7¾ miles to Milk Ranch, 8¾ miles to North Ridge.

TIME: Day hike to waterfall, one or two nights to Milk Ranch.

TERRAIN: Descends gently down canyon to creek, then ascends to junction; contours through forest to ford; ascends moderately to ridge, then steeply until descent to Milk Ranch; ascends to, then contours along North Ridge; long descent completes loop, returning to creek; climbs to trailhead.

TRAILS INTERSECTED: North Ridge, Summit Springs.

BEST TIME: Late May, June and July. August and September may be good.

WARNINGS: Watch for rattlesnakes. Use caution at fords during spring run-off. Popular for deer hunting in October. Stay off ridges in thunderstorms. Water scarce late season.

DIRECTIONS TO TRAILHEAD: Exit Interstate 5 at Willows. Take Highway 162 west 21 miles, then go left through Elk Creek (food, gas). Go right 5.2 miles on Road 308, then right on Road 20N01 (Ivory Mill Road) 9.5 miles to Road M3/24N02. Go left on M3 for 15 miles. Turn left on Road 18N66 (signed "WEST CROCKETT CAMP/NORTH RIDGE") and go .4 mile to trailhead.

FURTHER INFO: Stonyford Ranger District, Mendocino National Forest (916) 963-3128.

shinleaf, pipsissewa, mule ears, houndstongue hawkweed, trail plant and coral root orchid, with leopard lilies among willows along the creek. Wind through a drainage where meadow lotus, twinberry and bedstraw grow beneath willows and alders, then resume your course down the main creek.

Descend along a rocky canyon at ¾ mile, passing curl-leaved mountain mahogany, Fremont silktassel, gooseberry, saxifrage and sword fern as the descent turns moderate on loose gravelly

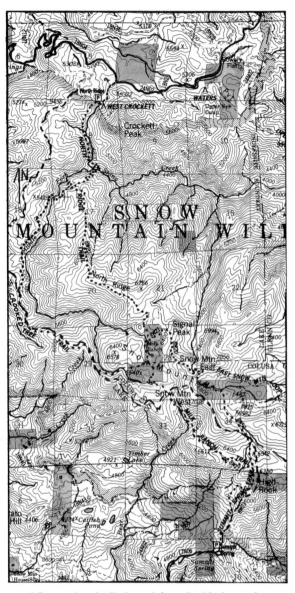

tread. Descend gradually through forest beside the creek at one
mile, passing angelica and bracken fern. Soon thimbleberry
grows in a lush green tangle beside the creek. Ford the creek
and climb south.

Your path turns east, descending through forest of western
white and sugar pines, white and Douglas firs where silver
lupines carpet the ground. Switchback right and left, descending
to ford Middle Fork Stony Creek, where scouring rush and cow
parsnip grow beneath bigleaf maples and conifers. A pleasant
campsite is on the left beyond the ford.

The trail follows the creek downstream to 1⅜ miles, then

van. 92

climbs away from the creek. Switchback to the right, ascending steeply. Climb by three more switchbacks, passing rosy sedum. Then ascend steeply with expanding views north to Crockett Peak and east down Stony Creek Gorge. Climb moderately, switchbacking right and left, then zigzagging up a rocky slope. The climb eases at 1⅞ miles as the trail turns south. The steep ascent soon resumes as you switchback twice more.

Climb to an unmarked junction at 2⅛ miles. The described loop returns by North Ridge Trail on the left. Take Waterfall/ Crooked Tree Trail on the right, contouring west through gentle terrain. Dip through short downs and ups, then descend gradually past serviceberry.

Meet an unmarked spur on the right at 2⅜ miles. (It descends by five switchbacks to overlook a graceful waterfall on Middle Fork Stony Creek, ⅝ mile round trip. The falls plunge 40 feet into a pool. The spur ends before making the steep drop to the falls.)

The main trail continues west, contouring across a steep slope. The path bends left, passing the bright red blossoms of California fuchsia, then many Indian pinks. Climb gently, with views of the creek and the ridge beyond. Cross a rocky gully, then make a winding climb through whitethorn and rabbitbrush to top a spur ridge. A winding descent with two long switchbacks ends at a ford of Middle Fork Stony Creek at 2⅞ miles.

A pleasant campsite sits on the far bank, where serviceberry grows ten feet tall with creek dogwood, meadow lotus, wood rose and bedstraw. Bear grass and willows line the creek.

Good tread climbs north briefly, then switchbacks left for a winding, mostly gradual ascent southwest. Climb steadily through sparse mixed forest on rocky slopes where fuchsia abounds. Dip through a small gully, then ascend moderately. Switchback right and left on a brief steep climb, then ascend moderately with views up the canyon. Descend briefly, then ascend gently to top a ridge before 3⅞ miles.

The track meanders west on the broad pine-covered ridgetop. Descend from the ridge by two switchbacks. Your track switchbacks left at a gully and climbs moderately across a slope to a spur ridge with much creeping snowberry. Dip through a gully at 4⅜ miles, then make a gentle winding ascent to another gully. Climb moderately, then gradually to another spur ridge.

Ascend steadily to gain the main ridgetop at 5 miles, meeting the jeep-worn double track of Crooked Tree Trail at a 5440-foot saddle. The old trail has not been recently worked like Waterfall Trail, but it is easy to follow as it climbs gently south along the ridgetop. Soon a sign indicates "MILK RANCH - 3, SNOW MTN. SUMMIT - 4½." Actual distances are slightly less.

Your trail bends right and traverses the ridge's west face, avoiding the steeply rising ridgetop. The tread is vague in places, but the route is well blazed. You have views west to Lake Pillsbury and the mountains beyond. After short ups and downs, your path turns southeast at 5¼ miles. A sign on a large ponderosa indicates Trail #8W21. Silver lupine grows nearby. Contour across a steep side hill, then dip through a gully.

Climb south through dense fir forest. The ascent soon turns extremely steep. Your path switches to the ridge's east face, climbing steeply through a grassy, rocky area with sulphur flower, bitter cherry, rabbitbrush, pussy paws, whitethorn and cream bush, passing in and out of fir forest.

Your steep climb eases briefly at 5¾ miles, then resumes as the trail turns east on the ridgetop. Pause at the next clearing to enjoy the view north to the Yolla Bollys, with Middle Fork Stony Creek Canyon in the foreground. Continue a moderate, then steep climb along the crest.

The ascent eases as gnarled, crooked Jeffrey pines mix with fir forest, with pennyroyal the dominant ground cover. You soon resume a steep ascent along the wooded ridgetop, with a rocky floor where white-veined shinleaf grows. Your climb eases beyond 6¼ miles at a bare rocky clearing on the ridgetop. Pass a large cairn on your left as the path ascends gently, then contours along the winding ridgetop.

The ridgetop narrows at 6⅝ miles. A steep drop on the left provides a view across upper Middle Fork Stony Creek Canyon to North Ridge. Contour south along red-fir-covered ridgetop where the yellow flowers of goldenbush grow. Climb once again along the crest, passing purple penstemon. Ascend south with grand alpine views of various Snow Mountain peaks.

The trail turns southeast to descend into upper Middle Fork
Stony Creek Canyon at 7 miles. Contour across a steep slope
and into red fir forest. Descend northeast to ford the seasonal
Middle Fork at 7⅜ miles, where checker mallow and corn lilies
grow. Your trail heads east, climbing fitfully through open red
fir forest with phacelia and pussy paws scattered on mostly bare
ground.

Turn northeast around 7⅝ miles. Your route crosses private
property for the next ¾ mile. In the wilderness this primarily
means you should treat the land with love and respect, as you
always do. It may also mean that if you camp at Milk Ranch, your
friendly neighbors might own the 40 surrounding acres. Milk
Ranch was a dairy ranch for many years, supplying old Fouts
Springs Resort with dairy products. Pack trains hauled the
dairy goods down Milk Ranch and Trout Creek Trails to the
resort twice a week. Such a rough journey might turn the cream
to butter without coaxing.

Your trail climbs to a saddle, then descends gently. Crooked
Tree Trail ends at Milk Ranch Trail at 7¾ miles. (The trail south
from the junction is described in Trail #50.)

Our described loop turns left to descend north to the popular
campsite beside large Milk Ranch Meadow. Not far beyond, at
7⅞ miles, is the junction of North Ridge Trail and East Snow
Mountain Loop. (See Trail #50 for the trail on the right.)

The described loop stays left on North Ridge Trail. Descend
gently north along the creek, following the edge of the meadow
and forest. The descent turns moderate past a sign, "NORTH
RIDGE TRAIL, WEST CROCKETT - 4." (Actual distance: 5½
miles). The path draws alongside the creek at 8 miles. Where
a camp sits on the left, the trail fords the creek. Brooklime
grows in the water at the ford.

A row of cairns marks the vague tread heading north-northeast
across a gravel bed. Follow it past mountain aster, yarrow,
phacelia, pussy paws, pennyroyal and sulphur flower. As you
cross a neck of the lower meadow, you have a view east to 6684-
foot Signal Peak.

Leave the meadow on a moderate ascent northwest through
fir forest with cedars. The path bends right to climb steeply,
then eases before topping a spur ridge. Dip north through a
gully, then ascend moderately. Climb gently until a brief, steep
ascent gains the top of North Ridge at 8¾ miles.

Your path contours through whitethorn and bitter cherry
along the west side of the ridgetop. Here at 6560 feet, you have
a fine panorama of Snow Mountain's summits from southeast
to southwest. From left to right these include unnamed (6994'),
Signal Peak (foreground - 6684'), Snow Mountain East (7056'),
Snow Mountain West (7038'), unnamed beyond Milk Ranch
(6773', 6540' and 6578') and Crooked Tree Ridge (6800').

Climb briefly around the 9-mile point to one last 6560-foot knob with grand vistas west. Descend gradually along the sparsely wooded, broad ridgetop. Soon nothing but a tiny club moss grows on the crest, although low red firs hunker with bitter cherry and whitethorn on the lee (east) face.

Your path contours along the ridgetop, interspersed with short, easy descents. The vegetation becomes more diverse, with pinemat manzanita, beautiful Christmas-tree-shaped red firs, scattered cedars, western white and Jeffrey pines. As you continue a gentle descent, look north for the Yolla Bollys. On clear days you see Mount Shasta on their right, 140 miles away.

The trail descends constantly from 9⅝ miles, dropping 1000 feet in the next mile. You soon descend north through fir forest. Drop steeply beyond 10 miles along open ridgetop alternating with dense fir forest. The descent eases briefly, winding through a whitethorn thicket, then turns steep again for a winding plunge down the ridgetop.

Leave North Ridge at 10¾ miles, veering left to descend west through pine forest. Your path soon bends right, descending moderately north along a gully filled with bracken ferns and grasses, then abundant California fuchsia.

The trail turns right and descends to Waterfall Trail beyond 11¼ miles. Bear right and retrace your route from the start of this trip, dropping to the ford at 12 miles, then making the easy climb to West Crockett Trailhead to complete the journey.

48.

BEARWALLOW

BETWEEN SAINT JOHN MOUNTAIN AND THE GORGE

This trail bisects remarkably steep country, traversing the middle of a slope rising 3600 feet from Stony Creek Gorge to Saint John Mountain in only 1¼ miles. It offers a three-season route into Snow Mountain Wilderness, with fine views of gorge and high country. You can day-hike the 6-mile round trip to Bear Wallow Basin, or backpack in for a short overnight or weekend. Bearwallow Trail does not link with other trails in the wilderness. The trail shown on the Forest Service Wilderness Map climbing to Milk Ranch does not exist. You can go left on Upper Nye Trail above Bear Wallow, but it is unmaintained and impossible to follow past Bear Wallow Creek.

Gray pines and interior live oaks shade your trailhead, which has views east over foothills to East Park Reservoir. Sign in at the trail register and climb southwest into forest where knobcone pines mix with live oaks. The forest soon thins as brush

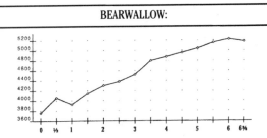

DISTANCE: **6⅜ miles to Windy Point** (12¾ miles round trip);
   2⅝ miles to Bearwallow, 4⅛ miles to upper (seasonal) creek.

TIME: Full day hike or overnight.

TERRAIN: Climbs from knobcone pine forest through chaparral,
   crossing steep talus slopes on St. John Mountain's south face;
   climbs through lush, wooded basin; traverses brushy ridge,
   then contours through forest.

BEST TIME: April through June, before summer heat. Good most
   of year if snow level is above 5000 feet and access road open.

WARNINGS: Watch for rattlesnakes. Deer hunting in October.

DIRECTIONS TO TRAILHEAD: From Interstate 5, take Maxwell
   Road exit (M.26.5 from south, M.27.0 from north, Colusa
   County). Go west 32 miles to Stonyford. Go left at general
   store (gas and supplies). In .2 mile, go left 8 miles on Fouts
   Springs Road (M10). Pass Mill Creek Campground, then turn
   sharply right on Road 18N03. After 2.4 miles, go left on Road
   18N06 for 4.3 miles to signed trailhead on left, beyond big
   bend. UPPER TRAILHEAD: Same as Trail #47, but reach
   signed Windy Point Trailhead 3 miles before Road 18N66.

FURTHER INFO: Stonyford Ranger District, Mendocino National
   Forest (916) 963-3128.

OTHER SUGGESTION: You can hike to the old BRITTAIN
   RANCH on a path that leaves Road 18N06 .8 mile from Road
   18N03. This 2-mile, low-elevation (2200-2400') hike loops
   through meadows to ranch site. In summer, you can drive to
   WINDY POINT TRAILHEAD at the top end of BEARWALLOW
   TRAIL and hike east.

includes bay laurel, white oak, manzanita and Fremont
silktassel. Ascend steadily on rocky tread, switchbacking right
and left. A view opens southwest to the Snow Mountain high
country. Scarlet fritillary grows on a bare hillside on your right.

    You crest a ridge and overlook rugged Middle Fork Stony
Creek Gorge. Your trail parallels the gorge for the next 2 miles.

The steep, brushy south slope of Saint John Mountain rises to the north as the trail descends gradually, soon passing the first ponderosa pine. Cross a large scree slope around ⅝ mile. Live oak, redbud and gooseberry grow low and brushy, struggling in sparse soil. You may also spot small silver-gray ferns peeking from beneath rocks, Sierra cliff brake.

Descend to an intermittent stream. Even when the ford is dry, the creek may surface 100 yards uphill. A huge bay laurel, young bays and California buckeyes thrive on the underground moisture. Your rocky trail climbs steeply to one mile, then gradually. Chamise, silktassel and manzanita cover the slope, with scattered gray and knobcone pines.

You soon cross another seasonal stream, then climb gradually across brushy slopes as views of the high country unfold. Cross more loose scree slopes around 1¾ miles, then pass the first big sugar pines on the route. Your path contours, then resumes its gradual ascent.

The trail turns north at 2¼ miles, angling away from Middle Fork Gorge and into the steep basin of Bear Wallow Creek where Douglas firs mix with ponderosa pines and oaks. The path levels, then descends into a grove of big trees. You might find a patch of level ground, the first spot suitable for an overnight camp. (Better camping lies ahead.) Your trail crosses a seasonal fork of Bear Wallow Creek at 2½ miles. A second creek 400 feet beyond flows year round. Bay laurels, Oregon ashes and large oaks overhang this pretty ford.

Your trail ascends to ford a third stream. Its flow is small, but ash trees three feet in diameter and other moisture-loving plants indicate water is found here most of the year. Gentle, rolling terrain offers good choices for camping.

Climb gently past an immense ponderosa pine, then through two small clearings with gooseberry vines and other moist-habitat plants. Turn north, climbing into live oak forest.

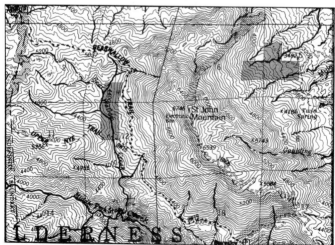

von · 92

At a small stand of black oaks at 2⅞ miles, one oak holds a sign pointing west. Upper Nye Trail descends ¼ mile to Bear Wallow Creek, then fades out beyond the creek.

Bearwallow Trail continues north, climbing gradually through forest of ponderosa and sugar pines, Douglas fir and black oak. You can soon see the metal towers atop Saint John Mountain. After a seasonal creek your trail bends left, then turns north again past abundant whitethorn. Leave the forest for low-growing chaparral. You have excellent views of Bear Wallow Basin. The trail fords another tributary, then returns to forest.

Climb to ford a seasonal creek at 3⅜ miles. The trail is hard to spot on the far side; it lies 20 feet uphill from the crossing. Lupine, pinemat manzanita and yarrow line the path. Your trail contours, then descends through chaparral. Climb gradually in stately pine and oak forest with young white firs.

Ford the main trunk of Bear Wallow Creek at 4⅛ miles. It cascades down Saint John Mountain's steep northwest slope. The creek is seasonal here, dry as a bone by late season. Near the creek a moisture-loving wildflower garden includes three-bracted onion, saxifrage, sulphur flower, purple penstemon and several varieties of succulents. Bird's foot and sword ferns and poison oak also grow here.

The terrain changes abruptly beyond the ford. The trail turns northwest on a dry, rocky south-facing slope with gray and Jeffrey pines, western juniper, bay laurel, California mountain mahogany, live oak brush and Sierra cliff brake. Climb gradually along the bare, sunny slope, passing phacelia and naked stem buckwheat. Jeffrey pines below the path support dense

220

wild grape vines and poison oak. At 4¼ miles climb across dry talus slopes and into a dense stand of gray pines.

Climb along a dry, rocky gully through an understory of white and live oak brush. The path becomes vague, turning north and climbing steeply to a ridgetop beyond 4½ miles. Scraggly junipers share the ridge with gray pines and chaparral.

The trail climbs gently west along the ridgetop, with views north to Sheetiron Mountain (6503') and south to Snow Mountain high country. You might see Mount Lassen to the northeast on a clear day. Climb moderately steeply, then gently to one last knob on the brushy ridgetop beyond 4⅞ miles. Make a gradual winding descent on the ridgetop to a saddle.

Your trail climbs gradually, soon bending right to leave the ridgetop and enter north-slope Jeffrey pine forest. Continue a gentle climb, winding west through pleasant shady forest. Black oaks and white firs mingle with the pines by 5¼ miles. The trail climbs northwest as Douglas fir joins the mixed forest, with serviceberry in the understory.

Your trail makes a big bend left around 5⅝ miles to cross the head of a dry gully. Climb north, then wind left through a willow-filled gully. Climb gently north, then drop briefly to a third gully crossing at 5⅞ miles.

Climb moderately, then make a gradual winding ascent through brushy forest until silver lupines cluster in a clearing. Contour through a small gully, then a larger one. Head north on a level traverse of a steep brushy slope. Your path winds through one more gully, then contours on a shady last stretch, reaching Windy Point Trailhead on Road M3 at 6⅜ miles.

49.

BATHHOUSE

SOUTH SLOPE TRAVERSE IDEAL FOR WINTER HIKE

This trail, starting at the lowest elevation of all our wilderness routes, affords off-season access to Snow Mountain's steep slopes and rugged canyons. It follows the edge of the area burned in the 1987 Fouts Fire. The hike is easy to Welton Glade, except for the steep ¼-mile ascent to the expansive grassland. The trail continues, often steeply, on a dip and rise course, ending at tree-lined Deafy Glade. (Trail #20 offers an easier route to the glade, except when rampaging runoff blocks it in spring.) Bathhouse Trail can offer T-shirt weather and wildflowers in January, but be prepared for bad weather too.

Campgrounds near the trailhead are popular with motor-bike riders, so expect whining engines, especially on weekends October to May. On weekdays the camps often offer solitude. The hike

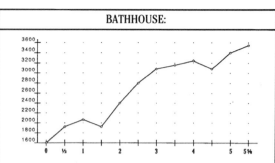

BATHHOUSE:

DISTANCE: 5⅝ **miles to Deafy Glade**—see map on page 94 (11¼ miles round trip); 1½ miles to Trout Creek, 2⅝ miles to Welton Glade, 3¾ miles to West Welton Glade.

TERRAIN: Follows closed road to footpath; traverses steep south slope through chaparral, glades and forest, ascents alternating with short descents.

TRAILS INTERSECTED: Trout Creek, Deafy Glade.

BEST TIME: November through May, when creeks are not running high; too hot in summer.

WARNINGS: Watch for rattlesnakes in warm season. Fords dangerous at high water.

DIRECTIONS TO TRAILHEAD: From Interstate 5, take Maxwell Road exit (M.26.5 from south, M.27.0 from north, Colusa County). Go west 32 miles to Stonyford. Turn left at general store (gas and supplies). In .2 mile, go left 8 miles on Fouts Springs Road (M10). In .1 mile past Mill Creek Campground, turn right on Road 18N03. In .4 mile, go left to trailhead.

FURTHER INFO: Stonyford Ranger District, Mendocino National Forest (916) 963-3128.

starts with a 1 ½-mile road walk beyond a fence that discourages ORV's from breaching the wilderness.

Sign in at the register and climb past the gate (signed "AUTHO-RIZED PERSONNEL ONLY"—don't be dissuaded). Ascend moderately west on the road through patchy grassland and chaparral with gray pines, manzanita and live oak brush. Buck brush, yerba santa and chamise soon join the chaparral.

Views expand to Fouts Springs Valley and its Boys' Ranch beyond ¼ mile. Climb steadily past much star thistle. Your ascent eases where white oaks line the road. From ¾ mile the

222

road contours through dense chaparral with toyon, club moss and mullein. The track soon turns south through a glade. Unmaintained, unmarked Trout Creek Trail forks right to climb west beyond 1⅛ miles.

Follow the road on a winding descent to its end at 1½ miles. The real trail starts here, descending to an easy ford of Trout Creek and entering the wilderness. Alder, bay laurel, maple and buckeye line the stream, with lush understory of saxifrage, sheep sorrel, berry vines, maidenhair and other ferns.

Your path climbs steeply from the ford, bending left to head south. A sign says "TRAIL #7W15, WELTON GLADE - 1, DEAFY GLADE - 3." (The latter is 1⅛ miles farther than the sign indicates.) The ascent eases to moderate, passing California mountain mahogany between white oaks. Switchback right and ascend a ridge between Trout Creek and deep South Fork Stony Creek Canyon.

The trail bends right and left, climbing around a slide at 1¾ miles. Leave the ridge to traverse a steep south-facing slope. Ascend moderately past toyon, live oak brush, desert cliff brake and naked stem buckwheat. You may have to maneuver around some deadfall as you ascend steadily above roaring Stony Creek, passing gray pine, buckeye, redbud and soap plant on the steep slope.

The path alternates between gentle and steep climbs. Paintbrush grows here year round, even flowering in January. Cross a gully and ascend steeply, then pass beneath a charred gray pine. Descend briefly, then contour before ascending gradually past large live oaks, through a glade and into oak/gray pine forest.

The trail forks before 2⅜ miles. Take the steep right fork; the left is washed out. Ascend very steeply, passing a blazed white oak. Wind left and right, alternating between gentle and steep ascent as you enter the vast grassland called Welton Glade.

Pass the first flat spot and potential camp on your right, then ascend gradually through the expansive glade dotted with white oaks. Ford a small seasonal creek, then climb past a water trough at 2⅝ miles. Pass the sign for Welton Glade, then ascend along the boundary between glade and white oak woodlands.

Pass a little used fire ring and meet a junction. (The vague, unmaintained trail on the right climbs steeply north to Rattlesnake Glade.) Stay left (signed "DEAFY GLADE"), descending to ford the largest, most dependable stream since Trout Creek. It may be dry in summer or early fall.

Bathhouse Trail ascends steeply south from the seasonal creek, then contours through a brushy burned area with ceanothus and coffeeberry. Look northwest up the steep slope for a view of Rattlesnake Glade 1000 feet above.

Dip through a deep gully, then climb briefly before descending to a small glade around 3 miles. A spring there supports

watercress, although eating it would not be advisable due to cattle in the area. Redbud grows nearby.

Your path climbs through chaparral, then descends moderately south past the bottom of the glade. Descend west to a gully crossing, then south through a small glade with white oaks, where cow paths may be mistaken for the real trail. The correct route ascends south-southwest at 3⅛ miles, then descends into a deep wooded gully where Douglas fir, gray and knobcone pines mix with live oaks.

The trail climbs steeply by short switchbacks, quickly entering chaparral as you return to the burn zone. You soon descend steeply, traversing a declivitous slope with many soap plants. Contour across two scree slopes then ascend to contour across another rocky slope. After a short up and down, you climb steeply on a slope of fine gravel, then contour in fir/oak forest.

Ascend gradually into a glade at 3¾ miles. The path becomes vague, following the upper edge of the clearing to a spring burbling from a plastic pipe beside a cattle trough. A sign on a nearby fire-fallen pine says "WEST WELTON GLADE."

The trail heads southwest out of the glade and climbs gradually through chaparral with bay laurel, coffeeberry, Fremont silktassel, California mountain mahogany, chamise and live oak. Your path makes a sharp bend right as the dark outcrop called Deafy Rock comes into view up the canyon. Climb gently before you dip through a rocky gully, then a brushy one.

Your trail continues its winding, up-down ways, angling southwest across brushy slopes with charred trees and tall ghosts of brush crowded by healthy regenerating chaparral. Beyond 4⅜ miles your path mostly descends, interspersed with two short climbs.

Ford a small year-round creek at 4⅝ miles where maple leaves carpet the ground. Contour south briefly, then ascend southwest to cross another fork of the creek and return to chaparral. Deafy Rock rises to the west as you ascend steeply. Douglas fir, sugar pine and incense cedar soon replace oak forest.

224

Top a ridge not far above Deafy Rock around 5¼ miles. The trail bends right to contour northwest. Descend briefly to ford a creek around 5⅝ miles, the largest stream since Trout Creek. Climb southwest briefly into Deafy Glade, a pleasant, rolling grassland with towering pines. Many fine campsites lie under ponderosas, maples and Douglas firs surrounding the glade. Bathhouse Trail angles southwest through the grasslands, ending at Deafy Glade Trail at the glade's west end, 5¾ miles from the trailhead.

50.
SUMMIT SPRINGS/MILK RANCH/ EAST PEAK LOOP
POPULAR LOOP THROUGH BURN TO HIGH RIDGES AND GLADES

This trail, the most popular route on Snow Mountain, was charred by the massive Fouts Fire of 1987. You will see charred forests and healthy regeneration on both access road and trail. This area's steep slopes and dense brush are highly susceptible to fires. This loop offers the shortest, easiest hike to Snow Mountain and Milk Ranch. Above the fire zone, you will see vast forests, large glades and meadows and high, exposed ridges.

Your trail climbs north from road's end, entering Snow Mountain Wilderness Area. Sign in at the register in 75 feet. The path bends right on a moderate, winding ascent northeast through forest of Jeffrey and sugar pines, white fir, black and white oaks. Enter a grassy, oak-brush-filled opening which offers fine views west and south. Ascend a ridge through patches of burned forest. Silver lupine, gooseberry and Fremont silktassel thrive in the sunny understory.

The path levels on the ridgetop around ¼ mile, with views east to East Park Reservoir and Sutter Buttes, the world's smallest mountain range. Climb gradually along the rocky, burned ridgetop, passing manzanita, oak brush, Oregon grape, mule ears and penstemon. Your trail bends left at ⅝ mile, leaving the ridgetop to head north, alternating between gradual and moderate ascent. Elderberry, bitter cherry, phacelia, rabbitbrush and snowberry join the oak and other brush species.

The path bends right, winding through a canyon with living white fir forest. Cross two seasonal tributaries around one mile where willows grow. Begin a switchbacking, winding ascent, recrossing one of the drainages and climbing back onto the ridgetop by 1½ miles.

Ascend along the crest through a partially burned zone where many short, stout Jeffrey pines survived the fire. Whitethorn

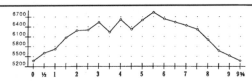

DISTANCE: **9⅜-mile loop**; 2 miles to Cedar Camp, 3½ miles to Bear Creek, 4½ miles to Milk Ranch, 5¾ miles (long way) to ridgetop junction.

TIME: Full day hike or overnight.

TERRAIN: Climbs ridge through burn to live forest; descends to meadow at Cedar Camp, then climbs through forest to headwaters of Bear Creek and over pass; descends gently to Milk Ranch; climbs to saddle of Snow Mountain, then descends east of ridge, completing loop at Cedar Camp.

TRAILS INTERSECTED: Box Springs South, Crooked Tree, North Ridge, East Snow Mountain, West Snow Mountain, Box Springs North.

BEST TIME: Late May, June or July. August and September OK. October possible.

WARNINGS: Stay off ridges in thunderstorms.

DIRECTIONS TO TRAILHEAD: Exit Interstate 5 onto Maxwell Road (M.26.5 from south, M27.0 from north, Colusa County). Go west 32 miles to Stonyford. Turn left at general store (gas and supplies). In .2 mile, go left on Fouts Springs Road (M10) for 24.5 miles. Go right 1.5 miles on Road 24N02, then right 1 mile on Road 17N29 to end, trailhead and dry camp.

FURTHER INFO: Stonyford Ranger District, Mendocino National Forest (916) 963-3128.

OTHER SUGGESTION: TO CLIMB SNOW MOUNTAIN (West or East Peak), the shortest route turns right at Cedar Camp, about 4 miles to either peak from trailhead. EAST SNOW MOUNTAIN LOOP (8W25) is a 2½-mile loop east of the desribed loop near Snow Mountain East; you can extend Trail #50 by 1¾ miles by adding 8W25 to your hike.

crowds the trail in spots. Soon prickly poppy, mullein, gooseberry and thistles grow where no trees have survived. The path ducks in and out of forest, veering west of the ridgetop. Climb past a gnarled four-foot-wide Jeffrey pine, then an outcrop of dark, brooding rock on the left, with light colored rocks on your right.

Your trail levels in a grove of red and white firs, reaching a junction at 1⅞ miles. The abandoned Box Springs Loop, signed "FOUTCH CAMP," is on the right. (It is difficult to follow and very steep, dropping 1700 feet to Box Springs.)

Go straight on Summit Springs Trail, signed "SNOW MTN SUMMIT - 2." Contour through forest of large firs, then descend to another junction on the edge of a level meadow at 2 miles. East Peak Trail is on the right. If you follow the described loop, you will return via that trail. (Go right for the shortest route to Snow Mountain's East or West Peaks, about 2 miles from here—see PEAK box below.) The pleasant campsite at the junction is Cedar Camp, although no cedars can be seen in the surrounding fir forest.

Turn left at the junction and descend on Milk Ranch Trail. Its vague tread improves as you skirt the left edge of the meadow. After crossing the outlet stream, pass a camp and ascend gradually northwest through forest with five-foot-wide red firs. Descend slightly to 2⅜ miles, then resume climbing. A camp sits on the left near a burned area. Maps show a spring above the trail at its low point, but none was in evidence in September.

Ascend past verbena, mullein, Douglas wallflower and the showy scarlet blooms of California fuchsia in rocky terrain. Climb moderately from 2½ miles through healthy forest. The incline eases, skirting the burn zone. Ascend moderately through skeleton forest at 2¾ miles. Bleeding heart, gooseberry, whitethorn, phacelia and elderberry provide a little greenery. Your path levels, turning northwest through the burn, with views of barren peaks all around.

Descend steeply north, switchbacking left and right, then descend gradually into live forest. Switchback four more times on a steady decline. Your trail levels to cross a small drainage at 3¼ miles. A healthy raspberry patch is above the crossing, with white skullcap, pennyroyal and bleeding heart.

Ascend moderately through cedar and red fir forest. The burbling year-round creek below on your left is upper Bear Creek. Look for purple penstemon and the red penstemon called mountain pride along the path. The climb eases, becoming gradual around 3½ miles as you skirt the edge of the burn. If you need water, descend to Bear Creek here; the path does not cross it ahead.

Plunge through a willow thicket crowding the trail and continue your ascent. Cross a dry gully, then climb moderately to a saddle at 3⅞ miles. This ridge is a major divide; you are leaving Eel River watershed for the Sacramento River drainage.

Your trail descends gradually through dense fir forest. After a sparse meadow with a camp on the right, contour before descending gradually past a lush green meadow below on the left. Turn north on a moderate descent until the path levels at a meadow before 4¼ miles. You cross the private property of Milk Ranch for the next ⅝ mile. Continue north over a slight rise, then descend gradually through forest. Then descend moderately with a deep gully on your right.

Soon you skirt the left side of Milk Ranch Meadow. At a bare gravelly clearing, the nearly invisible Crooked Tree Trail (Trail #47) enters on the left. To confirm this, look back up the trail you descended for a sign, "FOUTCH CAMP - 2." Another sign 50 feet on your left points to "CROOKED TREE."

Milk Ranch Trail descends north, passing through Milk Ranch Camp beyond 4½ miles. Descend gently past a second camp on your left and immediately meet another junction. (North Ridge Trail [#47] goes straight, descending ⅛ mile to another camp at the lower meadow.)

Our described loop turns right, descending vaguely east 150 feet to cross a tiny creek. The path becomes distinct, climbing northeast away from the meadow. Ascend along a barren ridge, the route marked by large red-rock cairns. Pussy paws litter the rocky ground, with scattered cedars and red firs. Ascend moderately with the meadow on your right.

Climb gradually in dense forest, then moderately through patchy forest with views north. The understory is mostly bare, with occasional clumps of pinemat manzanita and whitethorn. Switchback right and climb south. By 5 miles the trail ascends gradually along a ridgetop with rabbitbrush and pennyroyal. Turn around for the best view of the 6684-foot knob of Signal Peak. Rugged, rocky Snow Mountain East rises to the east.

Ascend moderately, not far from the exposed ridgetop. Crest the ridge at 5¼ miles, passing a giant cairn where you have a sweeping view north over Stony Creek Gorge to the Yolla Bollys. Snow Mountain West rises to the south. Descend gradually

across a wooded north slope. Drop to a saddle, then contour to a small seep and meadow where swamp onion and corn lily thrive. Climb east through patchy red fir forest.

The path bends right and meets a vague junction marked by a cairn at 5⅝ miles. An old trail climbs northeast. The path you want ascends south on a steep incline to a ridgetop junction in 300 feet. At 6840 feet, this is our loop's highest point.

SNOW MOUNTAIN PEAKS

You can expand your trip by turning left or right on short ascents of Snow Mountain East (7056') or West (7038'). The right fork ends at West Peak. The left fork is 2½-mile East Snow Mountain Loop (8W25). It climbs ⅛ mile, where a spur forks left ascending ⅛ mile to the highest point in the wilderness. The right fork, Trail 8W25, makes a nice loop descending east to Apple Tree Camp (6040 feet) where it meets Trail 8W20. Trail 8W25 climbs west past Angel Springs, returning to the main loop after 2½ miles.

Our route descends south from the ridgetop junction on Trail 8W50. Views expand east over sparse slopes to Stonyford and the Sacramento Valley. Descend southeast through red fir forest with pinemat manzanita. Wind around a green swath with small seeps below the path. Your descent continues with great views of Snow Mountain East, soon following an oddly uniform row of large red firs, with a glade on your left. Your winding trail descends along the edge of the glade.

A seasonal creek replaces the glade by 6 miles. Bright patches of mountain pride line the stream. Pass a venerable cedar where jagged rocks rise on the right. Your path veers south, leaving the creek. Descend gradually through a bare gravel clearing, views of Snow Mountain West on your right. Drop through forest, another gravelly clearing, then a small glade.

Climb briefly, then contour to Angel Springs Trail at 6½ miles. (Signed "DARK HOLLOW CREEK, BOX SPRINGS, BONNIE VIEW," the side trail, 8W25, heads north then descends east. This is where East Snow Mountain Loop returns to our loop.)

Continue south on 8W50, climbing gradually to a ridge where a camp is on your right. Descend moderately through dense red fir forest. Beyond 6⅞ miles, the fir forest includes sugar and Jeffrey pines. Descend gradually through deep forest, passing a camp on the left where the path bends right. You soon cross the meadow, returning to Cedar Camp at 7⅜ miles.

Stay left, retracing your steps on the climb southeast to Box Springs junction, then descending south to return to the trailhead at 9⅜ miles.

CROSS REFERENCE LISTING

TRAILS SUITABLE FOR A PARTICULAR ACTIVITY

TRAILS FOR HANDICAPPED ACCESS

2. Willits Creek/Gooseberry Loop—see OTHER
   SUGGESTION: Fawn Lily first ½ mile
6. Kaweyo Horse—across dam
7. Low Gap Park Loop—first ¼ mile
11. Fetzer Valley Oaks Garden
13. Dorn Nature Loop—see OTHER SUGGESTION
See also INTRODUCTION for Mendocino National Forest

Portions of the following may be passable under best
   conditions or with assistance:
4. Shakota—picnic area
5. East Shore—campground and picnic area roads
14. Anderson Marsh—to Pomo village
15. Boggs Lake Preserve—first portion

TRAILS FOR MOUNTAIN BIKES

2. Willits Creek/Gooseberry Loop
3. Little Darby Loop—see OTHER SUGGESTION
4. Shakota
5. East Shore
6. Kaweyo Horse
7. Low Gap Park Loop—see OTHER SUGGESTION
9. Upper Mayacmas—trail & OTHER SUGGESTION
10. Upper Glen Eden
11. Fetzer Valley Oaks Garden—see OTHER
    SUGGESTION
16. Hoberg Loop
17. Ball Cap/Road 600/John's Loop
18. Cache Creek Wildlife Area
19. Bloody Rock/Cold Creek
46. Travelers Home—trail & OTHER SUGGESTION
48. Bearwallow—see OTHER SUGGESTION

TRAILS FOR EQUESTRIANS

2. Willits Creek/Gooseberry Loop—trail & OTHER
   SUGGESTION
5. East Shore
6. Kaweyo Horse
8. Mayacmas from Willow Creek—see OTHER
   SUGGESTION
9. Upper Mayacmas
10. Upper Glen Eden
12. Glen Eden from Scotts Valley
16. Hoberg Loop
17. Ball Cap/Road 600/John's Loop
18. Cache Creek Wildlife Area
19. Bloody Rock/Cold Creek
20. Deafy Glade

21-50. All wilderness trails open to horses but hazardous
sections exist on following trails:

29. Black Rock Mountain
31. North Yolla Bolly Lake
34. South Fork Cottonwood Creek

TRAILS FOR BACKPACKING

2. Willits Creek/Gooseberry Loop—see OTHER
SUGGESTION
5. East Shore
6. Kaweyo Horse—combined with #5 to Miti
Campground
10. Upper Glen Eden
12. Glen Eden from Scotts Valley
18. Cache Creek Wildlife Area
19. Bloody Rock/Cold Creek
20. Deafy Glade
21-50. All wilderness trails open to backpacking

COMMON & SCIENTIFIC NAMES
OF PLANTS ALONG THE TRAILS

adobe lily, *Fritillaria pluriflora*

alder, *Alnus spp.*

alpine buckwheat, *Eriogonum ovalifolium*

alpine Lewisia, *Lewisia pygmaea*

alum root, *Heuchera micrantha*

angelica, *Angelica arguta*

aquatic buttercup, *Ranunculus aquatilis*

arnica, *Arnica spp.*

aspen, *Populus tremuloides*

azalea, *Rhododendron occidentale*

azure penstemon, *Penstemon azureus*

baby blue eyes, *Nemophila menziesii*

bay laurel, *Umbellularia californica*

bear grass, *Xerophyllum tenax*

bedstraw, *Galium spp.*

bigleaf maple, *Acer macrophyllum*

bindweed, *Convolvulus spp.*

bitter cherry, *Prunus emarginata*

bitterroot, *Lewisia rediviva*

black oak, *Quercus kelloggii*

bleeding heart, *Dicentra formosa*

blueblossom, *Ceanothus thyrsiflorus*

blue elderberry, *Sambucus caerulea*

blue-eyed grass, *Sisyrinchium bellum*

blue field gilia, *Gilia capitata*

blue oak, *Quercus douglasii*

bracken fern, *Pteridium aquilinum*

brewer oak, *Quercus garryana var. breweri*

Bridge's cliff brake, *Pellaea bridgesii*

broad leaved lupine, *Lupinus latifolius*

brodiaea, *Brodiaea spp.*

brooklime, *Veronica americana*

buck brush, *Ceanothus cuneatus*

bulrush, *Scirpus spp.*

bunch grass, *Sitanion spp., Agropyron spp.*

buttercup, *Ranunculus spp.*

California buckeye, *Aesculus californica*

California harebell, *Campanula prenanthoides*

California hazel, *Corylus cornuta var. californica*

California juniper, *Juniperus californica*

California lilac, *Ceanothus thyrsiflorus*

California mountain mahogany, *Cercocarpus betuloides*

California skullcap, *Scutellaria californica*

California poppy, *Eschscholtzia californica*

California stickseed, *Hackelia californica*

California waterleaf (squaw lettuce), *Hydrophullum occidentale*

calypso orchid, *Calypso bulbosa*

canyon gooseberry, *Ribes menziesii*

canyon live oak, *Quercus chrysolepis*

celery-leaved lovage, *Ligusticum apiifolium*

chamise, *Adenostoma fasciculatum*

chaparral honeysuckle, *Lonicera interrupta*

checker lily, *Fritillaria lanceolata*

checker mallow, *Sidalcea oregana*

chinese houses, *Collinsia heterophylla*

chocolate lily, *Fritillaria biflora*

cinquefoil, *Potentilla spp.*

clintonia, *Clintonia andrewsiana*

clover, *Trifolium spp.*

club moss, *Lycopodium spp.*

coffee fern, *Pellaea andromedaefolia*

coffeeberry, *Rhamnus californica*

columbine, *Aquilegia formosa*

coral root orchid, *Corallorhiza spp.*

corn lily, *Veratrum californicum*

cottonwood, *Populus spp.*

cow parsnip, *Heracleum lanatum*

coyote brush, *Baccharis pilularis*

cream bush, *Holodiscus microphyllus*

cream lily, *Erythronium purpurascens*

creek dogwood, *Cornus stolonifera*

creeping snowberry, *Symphoricarpos mollis*

curl-leaved mountain mahogany, *Cercocarpus ledifolius*

currant, *Ribes spp.*

cypress, *Cupressus spp.*

dagger pod, *Phoenicaulis cheiranthoides*

deer brush, *Ceanothus integerrimus*

deer fern, *Blechnum spicant*

deltoid balsam root, *Balsamorrhiza deltoida*

desert cliff brake, *Pellaea compacta*

desert elderberry, *Sambucus mexicana*

Douglas fir, *Pseudotsuga menziesii*

Douglas mugwort, *Artemisia douglasii*

Douglas spiraea, *Spiraea douglasii*

Douglas wallflower, *Erysimum capitatum*

downingia, *Downingia bella, D. pulchella, D. bicornuta, D. cuspidata*

dwarf miners lettuce, *Montia perfoliata var. depressa*

dwarf monkeyflower, *Mimulus nanus*

elderberry, *Sambucus spp.*

elegant brodiaea, *Brodiaea elegans*

elk clover, *Aralia californica*

fairy bells, *Disporum hookeri*

fascicled broom-rape, *Orobanche fasciculata*

fat solomon's seal, *Smilacina racemosa*

fawn lily, *Erythronium californicum*

fescue, *Festuca spp.*

few-flowered navarretia, *Navarretia pauciflora*

fiddleneck, *Amsinckia intermedia*

filaree (storksbill), *Erodium cicutarium*

five-finger fern, *Adiantum pedatum*

forktooth ookow, *Dichelostemma congestum*

foxtail pine, *Pinus balfouriana*

Fremont lily, *Zygadenus fremontii*

Fremont silktassel, *Garrya fremontii*

frosted miners lettuce, *Montia perfoliata forma glauca*

giant frasera, *Frasera speciosa*

giant trillium, *Trillium chloropetalum*

gilia, *Gilia spp.*

glacier lily, *Erythronium grandiflorum var. parviflorum*

globe lily, *Calochortus amabilis*

godetia, *Clarkia spp.*

goldenback fern, *Pityrogramma triangularis*

goldenbush, *Haplopappus bloomeri*

golden chinquapin, *Castanopsis chrysophylla*

gooseberry, *Ribes spp.*

gray (digger) pine, *Pinus sabiniana*

great basin violet, *Viola beckwithii*

green gentian, *Frasera speciosa*

greenleaf manzanita, *Arctostaphylos patula*

green spleenwort, *Asplenium viride*

ground cone, *Boschniakia strobilacea*

ground iris, *Iris purdyi*

hairy honeysuckle, *Lonicera hispidula*

hairy star tulip, *Calochortus tolmiei*

harvest brodiaea, *Brodiaea coronaria*

hawkweed, *Hieracium spp.*

hedge hyssop, *Gratiola heterosepala*

hedge nettle, *Stachys bullata*

Henderson's shooting star, *Dodecatheon hendersonii*

hollyleaf coffeeberry, *Rhamnus crocea ssp. ilicifolia*

honeysuckle, *Lonicera spp.*

horsetail, *Equisetum spp.*

hound's tongue, *Cynoglossum grande*

houndstongue hawkweed, *Hieracium cynoglossoides*

huckleberry, *Vaccinium spp.*

huckleberry oak, *Quercus vaccinifolia*

incense cedar, *Calocedrus decurrens*

Indian lovevine (Howell's dodder), *Cuscuta howelliana*

Indian pink, *Silene californica*

Indian warrior, *Pedicularis densiflora*

inside-out flower, *Vancouveria planipetala*

interior live oak, *Quercus wislizenii*

Ithuriel's spear, *Triteleia laxa*

Jeffrey pine, *Pinus jeffreyii*

Jeffrey's shooting star, *Dodecatheon jeffreyii*

Jessica's stickseed, *Hackelia jessicae*

juniper, *Juniperus spp.*

Klamath plum, *Prunus subcordata*

Kellogg's monkeyflower, *Mimulus kelloggii*

knobcone pine, *Pinus attenuata*

lace fern, *Cheilanthes gracillima*

lace pod, *Thysanocarpus curvipes var. elegans*

lady fern, *Athyrium filix-femina*

large-leaved lupine, *Lupinus polyphyllus ssp. superbus*

leather fern, *Polypodium scouleri*

leopard lily, *Lilium pardalinum*

little prince's pine, *Chimaphila menziesii*

lodgepole pine, *Pinus contorta*

lomatium, *Lomatium spp.*

lovely Clarkia, *Clarkia concinna*

lupine, *Lupinus spp.*

Macloskey's violet, *Viola macloskeyi*

madrone, *Arbutus menziesii*

maidenhair fern, *Adiantum jordani*

manzanita, *Arctostaphylos spp.*

mariposa lily, *Calochortus superbus*

meadow larkspur, *Delphinium pratense*

meadow lotus, *Lotus oblongifolius*

milkmaids, *Dentaria californica vars.*

milkweed, *Asclepias spp.*

mimulus, *Mimulus spp.*

miners lettuce, *Montia perfoliata*

mission bells, *Fritillaria lanceolata*

monkshood, *Aconitum columbianum*

morning glory, *Convolvulus spp.*

mountain aster, *Aster occidentalis and vars.*

mountain hemlock, *Tsuga mertensiana*

mountain pennyroyal, *Monardella odoratissima ssp. glauca*

mountain pride, *Penstemon newberryi*

mountain shieldleaf, *Streptanthus tortuosus*

mountain spiraea, *Spiraea densiflora*

mountain violet, *Viola purpurea*

mugwort, *Artemisia spp.*

mule ears, *Wyethia mollis*

mullein, *Verbascum thapsus*

naked stem buckwheat, *Eriogonum latifolium ssp. nudum*

narrow-leaved collomia, *Collomia linearis*

narrow-leaved mule ears, *Wyethia angustifolia*

narrow-petalled sedum, *Sedum stenopetalum*

nettle, *Urtica spp.*

northern buckwheat, *Eriogonum compositum*

ookow, *Dichelostoma spp.*

Oregon ash, *Fraxinus latifolia*

Oregon grape, *Berberis aquifolium*

Oregon white oak, *Quercus garryana*

Pacific dogwood, *Cornus nuttallii*

paintbrush, *Castilleja spp.*

pale pennyroyal, *Monardella odoratissima ssp. pallida*

pearly everlasting, *Anaphalis margaritacia*

penstemon, *Penstemon spp.*

phacelia, *Phacelia spp.*

pinedrops, *Pterospora andromedia*

pinemat manzanita, *Arctostaphylos nevadensis*

pink stickseed, *Hackelia mundula*

Piper's lomatium, *Lomatium piperi*

pipsissewa (prince's pine), *Chimaphila umbellata var. occidentalis*

poison oak, *Toxicodendron diversiloba*

ponderosa pine, *Pinus ponderosa*

popcorn flower, *Plagiobothrys nothofulvus*

prickly currant, *Ribes montigenum*

prickly poppy, *Argemone munita ssp. rotundata*

primrose monkeyflower, *Mimulus primuloides*

Purdy's sedum, *Sedum purdyi*

purple milkweed, *Asclepias cordifolia*

pussy ears (beavertail grass), *Calochortus coeruleus*

pussy paws, *Calyptridium umbellatum*

rabbitbrush, *Chrysothamnus nauseosus*

ranger's buttons, *Sphenosciadium capitellatum*

raspberry, *Rubus leucodermis*

rattlesnake plantain, *Goodyera oblongifolia*

redbud, *Cercis occidentalis*

red elderberry, *Sambucus microbotrys*

red fir, *Abies magnifica*

red larkspur, *Delphinium nudicaule*

red penstemon, *Penstemon corymbosus*

redwood, *Sequoia sempervirens*

redwood sorrel, *Oxalis oregana*

roundtooth ookow, *Dichelostemma multiflorum*

rosy sedum, *Sedum rosea*

rush, *Juncus spp.*

* salsify, *Tragopogon dubius*

Sargent's cypress, *Cupressus sargentii*

saxifrage, *Saxifraga spp.*

scarlet fritillary, *Fritillaria recurva*

scarlet gilia, *Ipomopsis aggregata*

scarlet monkeyflower, *Mimulus cardinalis*

scouring rush, *Equisetum hyemale*

sedge, *Carex spp.*

seep-spring monkeyflower, *Mimulus guttatus*

serviceberry, *Amelanchier alnifolia ssp.*

Sequoia gooseberry, *Ribes tularense*

Shasta red fir, *Abies magnifica var. shastensis*

* sheep sorrel, *Rumex acetosella*

Shelton's violet, *Viola sheltonii*

shooting star, *Dodecatheon spp.*

showy phlox, *Phlox speciosa var. occidentalis*

Siberian miner's lettuce, *Montia sibirica*

Sierra cliff brake, *Pellaea brachyptera*

Sierra gooseberry, *Ribes roezlii*

Sierra rein orchid, *Habenaria dilatata*

silver lupine, *Lupinus albifrons*

slender Orcutt grass, *Orcuttia tenuis*

slim Solomon's seal, *Smilacina stellata*

slink pod (fetid adder's tongue), *Scoliopus bigelovii*

small flowered flax, *Hesperolinon micranthum*

snapdragon skullcap, *Scutellaria antirrhinoides*

sneezeweed, *Helenium bigelovii*

snowberry, *Symphoricarpos vaccinoides*

soap plant (soaproot), *Chlorogalum pomeridianum*

spotted coral root orchid, *Corallorhiza maculata*

spotted mountain bells, *Fritillaria atropurpurea*

spreading larkspur, *Delphinium patens ssp. greenei*

spreading phlox, *Phlox diffusa*

squaw bush, *Rhus trilobata*

squaw carpet, *Ceanothus prostratus*

starflower, *Trientalis latifolia*

* star thistle, *Centaurea spp.*

star zygadene, *Zigadenus fremontii*

steer's head, *Dicentra uniflora*

stickseed, *Hackelia spp.*

sticky currant, *Ribes viscosissimum*

sticky monkeyflower, *Diplacus aurantiacus*

stonecrop, *Sedum spp.*

stream violet, *Viola glabella*

striped coral root orchid, *Corallorhiza striata*

sugar pine, *Pinus lambertiana*

sugarstick, *Allotropa virgata*

sulphur flower, *Eriogonum umbellatum*

swamp onion, *Allium vallidum*

sword fern, *Polystichum californicum*

tanoak, *Lithocarpus densiflorus*

tarweed, *Madia spp.*

thimbleberry, *Rubus parviflorus*

* thistle, *Cirsium spp.*

tobacco bush, *Ceanothus velutinus*

toyon, *Heteromeles arbutifolia*

three-bracted onion, *Allium tribracteatum*

tongue Clarkia, *Clarkia rhomboidea*

Torrey's blue-eyed Mary, *Collinsia torreyi var. latifolia*

trail plant, *Adenocaulon bicolor*

trillium, *Trillium ovatum*

tule, *Scirpus acutus*

turkey mullein, *Eremocarpus setigerus*

twinberry, *Lonicera involucrata*

twisted stalk, *Streptopus amplexifolius var. denticulatus*

two-eyed violet, *Viola ocellata*

umbrella plant, *Peltiphyllum peltatum*

valley oak, *Quercus lobata*

vanilla grass, *Hierochloe occidentalis*

vanilla leaf, *Achlys triphylla*

vari-leaf nemophila, *Nemophila heterophylla*

verbena, *Verbena lasiostachys*

vetch, *Vicia spp.*

warty-leaved ceanothus, *Ceanothus papillosus*

waterleaf, *Hydrophyllum spp.*

watershield, *Brasenia schreberi*

western bladder pod, *Lesquerella occidentalis*

western coltsfoot, *Petasites palmatus*

western dog violet, *Viola adunca*

western juniper, *Juniperus occidentalis*

western mugwort, *Artemisia ludoviciana*

western wallflower, *Erysimum asperum*

western white pine, *Pinus monticola*

white alder, *Alnus rhombifolia*

white brodiaea, *Brodiaea hyacynthina*

white fir, *Abies concolor*

white-flowered hawkweed, *Hieracium albiflorum*

white oak, *Quercus garryana*

whitethorn, *Ceanothus leucodermis*

white-veined shinleaf, *Pyrola picta*

wild celery, *Apium graveolens*

wild cucumber, *Marah fabaceus*

wild ginger, *Asarum caudatum*

wild grape, *Vitis californica*

wild onion, *Allium spp.*

willow, *Salix spp.*

windflower, *Anemone deltoida*

woodland star, *Lithophragma parviflorum*

wood rose, *Rosa gymnocarpa*

wood strawberry, *Fragaria californica*

woodwardia fern, *Woodwardia fimbriata*

yampa, *Perideridia spp.*

yarrow, *Achillea lanulosa*

yerba de selva, *Whipplea modesta*

yerba santa, *Eriodictyon californicum*

* Introduced species

BIBLIOGRAPHY

Aginsky, Burt W. and Ethel G., *Deep Valley*, Stein and Day Publishers, New York, 1967.

Alt, David D. and Donald Hyndman, *Roadside Geology of Northern California*, Mountain Press Publishing Co., Missoula, Montana, 1975.

Brown, Vinson and Douglas Andrews, *The Pomo Indians of California and their Neighbors*, Naturegraph Publishers, Happy Camp, California, 1969.

Grillos, Steve J., *Ferns and Fern Allies of California*, University of California Press, Berkeley, 1987.

Jepson, Willis L., *Manual of the Flowering Plants of California*, Sather Gate Bookshop, Berkeley, 1923.

Jones, Alice Goen, *Flowers and Trees of the Trinity Alps*, Trinity County Historical Society, Weaverville, California, 1986.

Klages, Ellen, *Harbin Hot Springs: Healing Waters, Sacred Land*, Harbin Springs Publishing, Middletown, California, 1991.

Knudtson, Peter M., *The Wintun Indians of California and their Neighbors*, Naturegraph Publishers, Happy Camp, California, 1977.

Keator, Glenn and Ruth Heady, *Pacific Coast Fern Finder*, Nature Study Guild, Berkeley, 1978.

Keter, Thomas, *Settlement and Conflict: The Refuge Period and Historic Settlement in the North Fork Eel River Basin, 1854-1864*, unpublished paper, 1990.

Kroeber, A. L., *Handbook of the Indians of California*, Dover Publications, New York, 1976.

Lyons, Kathleen and Mary Beth Cuneo-Lazaneo, *Plants of the Coast Redwood Region*, Looking Press, Los Altos, California, 1988.

MacPherson, Glenn Joseph, *Geology and Petrology of the Mesozoic Submarine Volcanic Complex at Snow Mountain, Northern Coast Ranges, California: An On-land Seamount*, dissertation. 1981.

Niehaus, Theodore F. and Charles L. Ripper, *A Field Guide to the Pacific States Wildflowers*, (Peterson Field Guide Series), Houghton Mifflin, Boston, 1976.

Petrides, George A. and Olivia, *A Field Guide to Western Trees*, (Peterson Field Guide Series), Houghton Mifflin, Boston, 1992.

Thomas, John Hunter and Dennis R. Parnell, *Native Shrubs of the Sierra Nevada*, University of California Press, Berkeley, 1974.

Wallace, David Rains, *The Dark Range: A Naturalist's Night Notebook*, Sierra Club Books, San Francisco, 1978.

Wallace, David Rains, *The Klamath Knot: Explorations of Myth and Evolution*, Sierra Club Books, San Francisco, 1983.

Weeden, Norman F., *A Sierra Nevada Flora*, Wilderness Press, Berkeley, 1986.

Young, Dorothy King, *Redwood Empire Wildflowers*, Third Edition, Naturegraph Publishers, Happy Camp, California, 1976.

INDEX

239

ABOUT BORED FEET

We began Bored Feet Publications in 1986 to publish and distribute *The Hiker's hip pocket Guides*. If you would like to receive updates on trails included in our publications, send us your name and address, specifying your counties of interest.

We provide a retail mail order service specializing in books and maps about Northern California. Your purchases directly from Bored Feet support our independent publishing efforts to bring you more information about Northern California's spectacular natural beauty. Thanks for your support!

BORED FEET
P.O. BOX 1832
MENDOCINO, CA 95460
(707) 964-6629